ASHRAE
GreenGuide

This publication was developed under the auspices of the GreenGuide Subcommittee of TC 1.10, Energy Resources, and TC 2.8, Building Environmental Impacts and Sustainability. TC 1.10 and TG 2 BIE, Buildings' Impacts on the Environment, were merged in October 2002 to form TC 2.8.

ABOUT THE EDITOR

David L. Grumman, P.E., started his own energy consulting firm in 1973. His technical specialties have included energy conservation, conceptual design, indoor air quality, chilled water distribution, thermal storage, and controls. Grumman/Butkus Associates is now a well-established consultancy for energy-effective design and retrofit for hotels, health care facilities, educational institutions, and laboratories. Retired from active employment and ownership in 1996, he continues his association with the firm as chairman of the board.

An ASHRAE Fellow, he has been active in the Society since the early 1960s and has served on numerous standing committees. He was founding chair of the predecessor TG for TC 1.10, Energy Resources (now merged into TC 2.8), which initiated creation of the *ASHRAE GreenGuide*.

LIST OF CONTRIBUTORS

James Benya
Benya Lighting Design, West Linn, OR

Stephen Carpenter
Enermodal Engineering, Ltd., Kitchener, ON CAN

Michael Deru
National Renewable Energy Laboratory, Golden, CO

Kevin Dickens
Jacobs Facilities, Inc., St. Louis, MO

H. Jay Enck
Commissioning + Green Building Services, Atlanta, GA

David L. Grumman
Grumman/Butkus Associates, Evanston, IL

Michael Haggans and Garrick Maine
Flad & Associates, Madison, WI

Jordan L. Heiman
St. Louis, MO

Mark Hydemann
Taylor Engineering, Alameda, CA

James Keller
Gausman & Moore, St. Paul, MN

John Kokko
Enermodal Engineering, Ltd., Kitchener, ON CAN

Nils L. Larsson
CETC, National Resources Canada, Ottawa, Ontairo, Canada

Thomas Lawrence
Purdue University, West Lafayette, IN

Malcolm Lewis
Constructive Technologies Group, Inc., Irvine, CA

Blair McCarry
Keen Engineering Co., Ltd., North Vancouver, BC, CAN

Ron Perkins
Supersymmetry USA, Navasota, TX

Douglas T. Reindl
University of Wisconsin-Madison, Madison, WI

Wayne Robertson
Energy Ace, Inc., Decatur, GA

Marc Rosenbaum
Energysmiths, Meriden, NH

Mick Schwedler
Trane, La Crosse, WI

Eugene Stamper
New Jersey Institute of Technology (retired), Newark, NJ

Paul Torcellini
National Renewable Energy Laboratory, Golden, CO

Stephen Turner
Brown University, Providence, RI

Charles Wilkin
Hanson Professional Services, Inc., Springfield, IL

ASHRAE
GreenGuide

An ASHRAE Publication Addressing Matters of Interest
to Those Involved in Green or Sustainable Design of Buildings

David L. Grumman, Editor

 American Society of Heating, Refrigerating and Air-Conditioning Engineers, Inc.

ISBN 1-931862-41-9

©2003 American Society of Heating, Refrigerating
and Air-Conditioning Engineers, Inc.
1791 Tullie Circle, N.E.
Atlanta, GA 30329
www.ashrae.org

Cover design by Tracy Becker. **Note:** Image of the Solaire building was provided by the National Renewable Energy Laboratory. The Solaire building in New York is the first Green residential high-rise building in the United States. Visit: www.thesolaire.com.

ASHRAE STAFF

SPECIAL PUBLICATIONS

Mildred Geshwiler
Editor

Erin S. Howard
Assistant Editor

Christina Helms
Assistant Editor

Michshell Phillips
Secretary

PUBLISHING SERVICES

Barry Kurian
Manager

Jayne Jackson
Production Assistant

PUBLISHER

W. Stephen Comstock

Tomorrow's Child

Without a name, an unseen face,
And knowing not the time or place,
Tomorrow's Child, though yet unborn,
I saw you first last Tuesday morn.
A wise friend introduced us two,
And through his shining point of view
I saw a day, which you would see,
A day for you, and not for me.
Knowing you has changed my thinking,
Never having had an inkling
That perhaps the things I do
Might someday threaten you.
Tomorrow's Child, my daughter-son,
I'm afraid I've just begun
To think of you and of your good,
Though always having known I should.
Begin I will to weigh the cost
Of what I squander, what is lost,
If ever I forget that you
Will someday come to live here too.

by Glenn Thomas, ©1996

Reprinted from *Mid-Course Correction: Toward a Sustainable Enterprise: The Interface Model* by Ray Anderson. Chelsea Green Publishing Company, 1999.

Contents

GREENTIPS

SIDEBARS

FIGURES

TABLES

Foreword

by
William Coad

Mechanical engineering has been defined as "the applied science of energy conversion." ASHRAE is the preeminent technical society representing the engineers practicing in the fields of heating, refrigeration, and air conditioning, the technology that utilizes approximately one-third of the global nonrenewable energy consumed annually.

ASHRAE membership has been actively pursuing more effective means of utilizing these precious nonrenewable resources for many decades, from the standpoints of source availability, efficiency of utilization, and technology of substituting with renewable sources. One significant publication in *ASHRAE Transactions* is a paper authored in 1951 by G.W. Gleason, dean of engineering at Oregon State University, titled "Energy—Choose it Wisely Today for Safety Tomorrow." The flip side of the energy coin is the environment, and again ASHRAE has historically dealt with the impact that the practice of the HVAC&R sciences have had upon both the indoor and the global environment.

However, the engineering community, to a great extent, serves the needs and desires of accepted economic norms and the consuming public, a large majority of whom have not embraced the energy/environmental ethic. As a result, much of the technology in energy effectiveness and environmental sensitivity that ASHRAE members have been developing over this past century has had limited impact upon society.

In 1975, when ASHRAE published Standard 90-75, that standard served as our initial outreach effort to develop an awareness of the energy ethic and to extend our capabilities throughout society as a whole. Since that time updated revisions of Standard 90 have moved the science ahead. In 1993, the chapter on "Energy Resources" was added to the *ASHRAE Handbook—Fundamentals*. In 2002 ASHRAE entered into a Partnering Agreement with the U.S. Green Building Council, and it is intended that this design guide will assist that organization in their efforts at promoting sustainable design.

Recently, the consuming public and other representative groups of building professionals have discovered the societal need to provide buildings that are more energy resource effective and environmentally compatible. This publication, authored by ASHRAE volunteers, is intended to complement those efforts. The reader is cautioned that a successful green design, like any other successful design, must achieve a high level of environmental comfort and air quality.

Preface

by
David L. Grumman, P.E.

BACKGROUND ON THE ASHRAE GREENGUIDE'S DEVELOPMENT

Comments heard by 1999/2000 ASHRAE President Jim Wolf, as he traveled around to chapters talking to grassroots members during his term were that ASHRAE was "missing the boat" in the "green" building design area. Many sister organizations had already published documents addressing this issue for their members. President-elect Bill Coad was assigned to follow up, and he requested TC 1.10 (Energy Resources) to form a subcommittee to develop a handbook or guide on green or sustainable building design, specifically for ASHRAE members.

The effort was kicked off with a conference call of interested TC 1.10 members on November 20, 2000, organized by then-TC Chair Sheila Hayter. During that call, numerous ideas were expressed about what the publication should and should not be and what it should contain. A green guide subcommittee was set up under the chairmanship of TC 1.10 member David L. Grumman, with Sheila Hayter and Jordan Heiman being the other members. The subcommittee then set up several meetings at the January 2001 Atlanta Winter Meeting to discuss the direction such a green guide should take. As many interested ASHRAE members coming to Atlanta as could be identified in a short time frame were invited to attend the first meeting, held just prior to the regular TC meeting. As a result of that meeting and subsequent actions, a direction was established, a content outline prepared, and interested and qualified authors sought.

As the authors' contributions came in, they were placed into the outline format and the result edited by the subcommittee members. Difficulties were experienced in achieving consistency in the pieces submitted and in obtaining authors for areas initially not covered, which slowed the process. In addition, work by the authors and editors was all voluntary.

WHAT THE ASHRAE GREENGUIDE IS AND IS NOT

When the subcommittee started its work, it set forth some characteristics of what the guide was to be. One was that it have a well-defined purpose. That purpose, unlike many treatises written on this subject, was to provide guidance on how to apply green design techniques, not necessarily to motivate the use of them. Much has been written on the need for green building design, and this aspect is covered briefly herein. The reader should assume that when the HVAC&R designer finds himself or herself in a situation where a green design is to be done, this guide will help answer the question: "What do I do now?"

Other characteristics sought were that it be relevant to the target audience, useful and practical, concise and succinct, well organized and logical. Further, we wanted it to encourage team effort and to stimulate innovative ideas and independent thought.

Finally, we wanted the reader to be able to find information easily (a good reference) and find the guide graphically pleasing to the eye.

This guide should be regarded as the collected views and opinions of experts in the respective technical fields they are addressing. It is not a consensus document. It has not been widely reviewed and commented on, except by a limited group (primarily the authors and a review panel) and all members of the developing subcommittee and its technical committee and/or meeting attendees. One does not have to agree with everything written here for this guide to be helpful.

WHO SHOULD USE THE ASHRAE GREENGUIDE

The *ASHRAE GreenGuide* is primarily for HVAC&R designers. Architects, owners, building managers, operators, contractors, and others in the building industry, while perhaps finding certain areas of interest, are likely to find the guide less useful. Writing it for a specific audience keeps the document concise and focused. Nevertheless, from the design standpoint, the reader will see that considerable emphasis is placed on close coordination between parties and on teamwork.

The guide is not intended to be "the last word" or "the complete reference" on green design for engineers—nor, for that matter, a design guide proper. Liberal use of references to other sources is included, especially for details. For instance, throughout the guide, numerous techniques, processes, measures, or special systems are described succinctly in a modified outline or bullet form—but always in the same format. These are called **ASHRAE GreenTips**. The purpose of these is to give the designer enough familiarity with the subject to enable him or her to determine whether it might be suitable for the project being worked on. Each GreenTip concludes with a listing of other sources that may be referenced for greater detail. That source could be another book, a magazine article, a research paper, an organization, a Web site, or some other resource to which the designer could turn to seek more information on a subject that has promise of being applicable to the particular project at hand. Thus, there is a substantial bibliography included in this guide.

Even though this guide is intended for HVAC&R designers, related engineering disciplines are not omitted. The areas of plumbing and water management are definitely included (many HVAC&R types do plumbing design too). Also, because lighting systems have such a big impact on energy use, this subject is covered to the extent of lighting's impact on energy use and the building's HVAC&R system. (The aesthetic aspects of lighting design would not be appropriate here, however, and are thus excluded.) Likewise, there are many architectural features that have a large impact on energy use, and the engineer—even though not usually the designer of those features—should be generally familiar with these impacts. A brief chapter on architectural impacts is thus included.

This was intended to be a document that a design engineer, about to embark on a green building design project as part of a team, could pick up and *immediately get ideas and guidance* of what to do, where to turn, what to advise, and how to interact with other team members in a productive way. We want that engineer to be able to find information with ease on a subject of green-design relevance that may arise. (There is included a comprehensive index to seek out info on a given subject rapidly.)

Finally, although this guide has many specific and practical suggestions and tips on achieving green design, a designer who just tries to incorporate as many of these as possible and does little else is *not* assured of success. Considerable stress is placed on *coordinating efforts* with other members of the project team and seeking mutually acceptable solutions to the green design challenge. It will take innovative and synergistic designs that cut across design disciplines to achieve true success.

HOW TO USE THIS ASHRAE GREENGUIDE

This document is intended to be used more as a *reference* than as something one would read in sequence from beginning to end. Depending on the needs and experience level of the reader, there are portions that may warrant more attention than others; indeed, there may well be portions that certain readers might skip altogether. The following is intended to provide some helpful guidelines for using this document effectively.

First, the table of contents is the best place for any reader to get an overall view of what is covered in this document. Next, all readers should take the time to read this preface and chapter 1, "Green Design, Sustainability and 'Good' Design," because they cover the background and philosophy behind this effort and provide some essential definitions and meanings of key terms.

Chapters 2 and 3, "Motivation" and "Background and Fundamentals," respectively, might well be skipped by the more experienced designer/readers. The former covers the "why" of green design—those factors that drive owners to undertake such a project. The latter covers the background of the green design movement and what other organizations have done. The second part of chapter 3 then reviews some engineering fundamentals that govern the technical engineering aspects of green design. The reader may find this part intimidating—perhaps offering more than he or she wants to know. Thus, only the engineering designer who feels a need for a review of such technical fundamentals should undertake to read through it. (Of course, it is always there for later reference, as the need may dictate.)

The reader who is interested in how the green design process works, however, should read chapter 4, "The Design Process—Early Stages." It covers such topics as creating a green design team, identifying the "players," defining each of their roles, and outlining some green design processes that others have found to work. It is not until after this chapter that the reader gets into the components of what makes up green building design proper.

The reader who wants to go directly to the practical things that can be done to implement a green design should start at chapter 5, "Architectural Design Impacts," which covers how architectural features impact green design. The nitty-gritty engineering aspects, however, start at chapter 6 and run through chapter 13. *This is where the reader will find*

virtually all the practical suggestions for possible incorporation in a green design, The ASHRAE GreenTips. (A listing of all GreenTips and their page numbers, for quick and easy reference, can be found in the table of contents.)

Chapters 14 and 15 cover more aspects of the design process—including some of the analysis tools available. Again, these sections are probably better suited for occasional reference rather than "must" reading first time through.

The remainder of the *GreenGuide*, Chapters 16–19, covers what happens after the project's design is done—that is, during construction and after. There are some sound advice and helpful tips in that section, and the designer would be well served to be aware of the information contained therein early on in design. Thus, even though it covers a post-design time frame, *reading that section should not be put off until construction begins*.

For quick and ready reference, the *GreenGuide* includes up front not only a listing (with page numbers) of GreenTips but also all figures, charts and sidebars—and then at the back end a comprehensive bibliography, which compiles all the sources mentioned throughout the guide (and then some)—and an index for rapid location of a particular subject of interest.

Acknowledgments

The following individuals contributed written materials on various topics for the ASHRAE GreenGuide. All or portions of these contributions have been incorporated, with editing.

James Benya
Benya Lighting Design, West Linn, OR

James Keller
Gausman & Moore, St. Paul, MN

Stephen Carpenter
Enermodal Engineering, Ltd., Kitchener, ON CAN

John Kokko
Enermodal Engineering, Ltd., Kitchener, ON CAN

Michael Deru
National Renewable Energy Laboratory, Golden, CO

Nils L. Larsson
CETC, National Resources Canada, Ottawa, ON CAN

Kevin Dickens
Jacobs Facilities, Inc., St. Louis, MO

Thomas Lawrence
Purdue University, West Lafayette, IN

H. Jay Enck
Commissioning + Green Building Services, Atlanta, GA

Malcolm Lewis
Constructive Technologies Group, Inc., Irvine, CA

David L. Grumman
Grumman/Butkus Associates, Evanston, IL

Blair McCarry
Keen Engineering Co., Ltd., North Vancouver, BC CAN

Michael Haggans and Garrick Maine
Flad & Associates, Madison, WI

Ron Perkins
Supersymmetry USA, Navasota, TX

Jordan L. Heiman
St. Louis, MO

Douglas T. Reindl
University of Wisconsin-Madison, Madison, WI

Mark Hydemann
Taylor Engineering, Alameda, CA

Wayne Robertson
Energy Ace, Inc., Decatur, GA

Marc Rosenbaum
Energysmiths, Meriden, NH

Mick Schwedler
Trane, La Crosse, WI

Eugene Stamper
New Jersey Institute of Technology (retired), Newark, NJ

Paul Torcellini
National Renewable Energy Laboratory, Golden, CO

Stephen Turner
Brown University, Providence, RI

Charles Wilkin
Hanson Professional Services, Inc., Springfield, IL

The Green Guide Subcommittee of ASHRAE Technical Committee (TC) 1.10, Energy Resources, was responsible for creating this guide. (Just prior to its completion, TC 1.10 merged with Task Group (TG) BIE, Buildings' Impact on the Environment, to form TC 2.8, Building Environmental Impact and Sustainability.) Members of that subcommittee were David L. Grumman, Fellow ASHRAE, chair; Jordan L. Heiman, Fellow ASHRAE; and Sheila Hayter, chair of TC 1.10. Sheila Hayter created the subcommittee and initiated the initial discussions and meetings. Jordan Heiman was responsible for identifying authors, carrying on most communications with them, and creating the Bibliography. David Grumman was responsible for creating the topic format, assembling the various chapters, and editing the document.

Prior to approval by TC 2.8, the document was reviewed by a three-person review panel consisting of Theodore Pannkoke, P.E.; William Coad, P.E., Fellow ASHRAE, and Presidential Member; and Thomas Cappellin, P.E.—all members of TC 2.8.

The idea for this publication was initiated by 1999-2000 ASHRAE President Jim Wolf and carried forward by then President Elect (and subsequently President) William J. Coad.

All work performed—by the authors, editors, developing subcommittee, review panel, and TC participants—was voluntary.

Section 1: Basics

Chapter 1
Green Design, Sustainability, and "Good" Design

WHAT "GREEN" MEANS

In recent years, much information has been put forth about the impact of the built environment (e.g., buildings) on the natural environment. This information has been both written and spoken, and there have been conferences and seminars on the subject and organizations have sprung up devoted specifically to this issue. Not only have the messages contained in this outpouring of information attempted simply to explain what this issue is, but they have variously promoted the concept of "green" design, exhorted to action, strived to motivate, warned of consequences from ignoring it, and instructed how to do it.

While this vast amount of promotion has often been helpful, much has been either largely irrelevant or simply not useful to the practicing designer of HVAC&R systems and equipment for buildings (i.e., to the ASHRAE member involved on a day-to-day basis in the mechanical/electrical building system design process). Based on input received from grassroots ASHRAE members, a need was felt for guidance on the green building concept *specifically directed toward such practitioners*. A desire was also expressed that it contain information of *direct practical use*. This guide is an attempt to meet that need.

Authors contributing to this chapter are David Grumman, Jordan Heiman, and Nils Larsson.

"Green" is one of those words that can have more than a half-dozen meanings, depending on circumstances. One of these is the greenery of nature (grass, trees, leaves). It is this reference to nature—symbolic, if you will—that is the meaning this term denotes in this publication. While not *all* things in nature are green, we believe that the term "green" serves as a fitting verbal symbol of the concept and practices this guide strives to promote.

So how do we define the concept of green, particularly as applied to the portions of building systems ASHRAE is concerned with? A design that is green is one that is aware of and respects nature and the natural order of things; it is a design that minimizes the negative human impacts on the natural surroundings, materials, resources, and processes that prevail in nature. It is not necessarily a concept that denies the need for any human impact, for human existence is part of nature too. Rather, it endorses the belief that humankind can exist, multiply, build, and prosper in accord with nature and the earth's natural processes *without* inflicting irreversible damage to those processes and the long-term habitability of the planet.

Our definition of green buildings inevitably extends beyond the concerns of HVAC&R designers alone since the very concept places an emphasis on the integration of mechanical, electrical, architectural, and other systems.

Specifically, although there are somewhat differ-

3

ent interpretations from different sources, the view of this chapter's authors is that *a green building is one that achieves high performance, over the full life-cycle, in the following areas*:

- Minimal consumption—due to reduction of need and more efficient utilization—of non-renewable natural resources, depletable energy resources, land, water, and other materials as well. (Corollary to this is maximization of the effective use of renewable resources to meet building needs.)
- Minimal atmospheric emissions having negative environmental impacts, especially those related to greenhouse gases, global warming, particulates, or acid rain.
- Minimal discharge of harmful liquid effluents and solid wastes, including those resulting from the ultimate demolition of the building itself at the end of its useful life.
- Minimal negative impacts on site ecosystems.
- Maximum quality of indoor environment, including air quality, thermal regime, illumination, acoustics/noise, and visual aspects.

It should be noted that the last of the above five bullets is included here with reservations. The main reason it *has* been included is so that this guide's definition of a green building is compatible with the definitions of other organizations. The main issue is *not* whether a superior indoor environment is a worthwhile goal of building design, but rather whether this particular characteristic should be included as a goal of *green* design—especially in light of the definition of the green concept put forth in the first section of this chapter. (Please see the later section in this chapter on "good" design for a discussion of how the elements of this bullet relate to green design.)

RELATIONSHIP TO SUSTAINABILITY

And this leads into the concept of sustainability, another green-related term. "Sustainable design" has become very commonly used, almost to the point of losing any consistent meaning. While there have been some rather varied and complex definitions put forth (see sidebar below), we prefer a simple one (very similar to the third one in the sidebar). **Sustainability is "providing for the needs of the present without detracting from the ability to fulfill the needs of the future."**

While this is a simple and good general definition when applied to planet Earth as a whole, it is difficult to apply it in a meaningful way, without being arbitrary, to an individual earthly component (building, automobile, industrial plant, oil field) on the planet. Ultimately, sustainability of the planet depends on the *collective contribution to sustainability* of the various elements of the planet; but who is to say just how much each element should contribute?

As is well known, there are many natural events (volcanic eruptions, forest fires, earthquakes, floods) that impact the sustainability of life as we know it; likewise, recent history has seen deliberately evil acts of mankind that have had a substantial negative impact as well. (The terrorist events of September 11, 2001, and former Iraqi premier Saddam Hus-

SOME DEFINITIONS AND VIEWS OF SUSTAINABILITY FROM OTHER SOURCES

- "Everyone talks about sustainability, but no one knows what it is." *(Dr. Karl-Henrik Robert, founder of the organization, The Natural Step)*
- "Humanity must rediscover its ancient ability to recognize and live within the cycles of the natural world." *(The Natural Step for Business)*
- Development is sustainable "if it meets the needs of the present without compromising the ability of future generations to meet their own needs." *(Brundtland Commission of the United Nations)*
- To be sustainable, "a society needs to meet three conditions: Its rates of use of renewable resources should not exceed their rates of regeneration; its rates of use of non-renewable resources should not exceed the rate at which sustainable renewable substitutes are developed;

and its rates of pollution emissions should not exceed the assimilative capacity of the environment." *(Herman Daly)*

- "Sustainability is a state or process that can be maintained indefinitely. The principles of sustainability integrate three closely intertwined elements – the environment, the economy, and the social system – into a system that can be maintained in a healthy state indefinitely." *(Design Ecology Project)*
- "In this disorganized, fast-paced world, we have reached a critical point. Now is the time to re-think the way we work, to balance our most important assets." *(Paola Antonelli, Curator, Department of Architecture and Design, New York City Museum of Modern Art.)*

sein's igniting of the Kuwaiti oilfields during the 1991 Gulf War are prime examples.) Should there be a global "accounting system" to tabulate all the positive and negative impacts to determine if earth will remain sustainable over the long term? Ideally, yes—but that is impractical in reality.

The above discussion suggests that the concepts of "green design" and "sustainability" have no absolutes: that is, they cannot be defined in black and white terms. These terms are more useful when thought of as a mindset—a goal to be sought, a process to follow. Inducing designers of buildings, building systems, and equipment to achieve green building design or sustainable design is something that cannot be dictated. What *can* be done is to make people aware of these concepts and why they are important and—as this guide strives to do—to set forth some practical techniques to help practitioners achieve the goal of green design and thus make a significant contribution to earth's sustainability.

"GOOD" DESIGN

"Good design" might be said to be the process that results in a well-designed building.

Does good design intrinsically mean that green design has been achieved as well? More significantly, does green design automatically incorporate the characteristics of good design? It is important to clarify this question for users of this guide because many definitions of green design *do* assume that it includes at least some, if not all, the characteristics of good design (Grondzik 2001).

The broad characteristics of good building design, encompassing both the engineering and non-engineering disciplines, might be briefly outlined as follows:

- Meets the purpose and needs of the building's owners/managers and occupants

- Meets the requirements of health, safety, and environmental impact as prescribed by codes and recommended by consensus standards
- Achieves good indoor environmental quality (IEQ), which in turn encompasses high quality in the following dimensions:
  - Thermal comfort
  - Indoor air quality (IAQ)
  - Acoustical comfort
  - Visual comfort
- Is compatible with and respectful of the characteristics, history, and culture of the immediate surroundings
- Creates the intended emotional impact on the building's occupants and beholders

A green design proponent might be inclined to add to the above list one or more items concerning energy conservation, environmental impact, low impact emissions, and waste disposal—those very characteristics that are incorporated in the foregoing definition of green design. While this may be true someday, we are not there yet. There are still plenty of designs being built today that exhibit few or no green design characteristics. Many of these are still characterized as well-designed buildings—largely because the generally accepted characteristics of good design do not (at least, not yet) incorporate those of green design. (This is *not* to say that this is as it should be.)

Thus, the authors choose to make the distinction between the characteristics of good design and green design—but at the same time **strongly advocate that buildings should strive to achieve both.** In summary, green design does not necessarily incorporate many important characteristics of good design; but good design, on the other hand, does not yet include those green design characteristics that this guide strives to promote—though many would say it should.

Chapter 2
Motivation

If green building design is going to take place, there must be strong motivation behind it. This chapter explores briefly what causes green design to take place.

WHAT DRIVES GREEN DESIGN

Green design advocates can cite plenty of reasons why buildings *should* be designed "greenly." (See "Justifications for Green Design" on page 8.) The fact that these reasons exist does *not* make it happen; nor does the existence of designers—or design firms—with green design experience. *The main driver of green building design is the motivation of the owner*—the one who initiates the creation of a building, the one who pays for it (or who carries the burden of its financing), the one who has (or has identified) the need to be met by the building in question. If the owner does not believe that green design is needed, thinks it is unimportant, or thinks it is of secondary importance to other needs, then it will not happen.

It is possible that owners commissioning a new building without any intent to have it be a green design can be convinced that it would be in their interest to do so. In the very early stages of a building's development—perhaps during the designer interview process or before a designer has even been

Authors contributing to this chapter are Jay Enck and Steve Turner.

engaged—an owner may become informed on the latest trends in building design. This may occur through an owner doing research, conferring with others in the field, or discussing the merits of green design with the designer/design firm the owner intends to hire.

This initial interaction between the owner and the design professional is where the design firm with green design experience can be very effective in turning a project not initially so destined into one that's a candidate for green design. When an owner engages a designer, it is because the owner has faith in the professional ability of that designer and is inclined to listen to that designer's ideas on what the building's design direction and themes should be. Thus, *designers should regard the very early contacts with a potential owner as a golden opportunity to steer the project in a green direction.*

INGREDIENTS OF A SUCCESSFUL GREEN DESIGN ENDEAVOR

The following ingredients are essential in delivering a successful green design:

- **Commitment** from the entire project team, starting with the owner
- **Establishing green design goals early** in the design process
- **Integration of team ideas**
- **Effective execution** throughout project.

7

JUSTIFICATIONS FOR GREEN DESIGN

Doing the Right Thing

The motivations and reasons for implementing green buildings are diverse but can be condensed into essentially wanting to do the right thing to protect the earth's resources. For some, a wakeup call occurred in 1973 with the oil embargo – and with it a realization that there may be a need to manage our planet's finite resources.

Regulations

Society has recognized that previous industrial and developmental actions caused long-term damage to our environment, resulting in loss of food sources and plant and animal species, and changes to the earth's climate. As a result of learning from past mistakes and studying the environment, the international community identified certain actions that threaten our ecosystem's bio-diversity—and consequently it developed several governmental regulations designed to protect our environment. Thus, in this sense, the green design initiative began with the implementation of building regulations. An example is the regulated phasing out of chlorofluorocarbons (CFCs).

Lowering Ownership Costs

A third driver for green design is lowering the total cost of ownership in terms of resource management and energy efficiency. Examples include controlling site storm water for use in irrigation, incorporating energy efficiency measures in HVAC design, or developing maintenance strategies to ensure continued high-level building performance.

A recent study by an international engineering firm indicated that treating storm water on site cost one-third as much as having the state or local government treat stormwater at a central facility—significantly lowering the burden to the tax base. A 123,000 ft^2 higher education building constructed in 1997 in Atlanta, Georgia – a building that already had many sustainable principles applied during its design—provides an example of how commissioning, measurement, and verification plays a critical role in ensuring that the sustainable attributes designed into the building are actually realized to lower total cost of ownership. Although this facility was already believed to be one of the best buildings on campus, the owner, wanting to move the campus to an even greater degree of sustainability, decided that this building would be a good starting point for incorporating sustainability principles into daily operation.

The result was identifying several seemingly inconspicuous operational practices that were causing higher-than-needed consumption in the following areas: chilled water cooling, by 40%; steam, by 59%; and electricity, by 15%. Recommissioning the facility reduced operating costs approximately $88,000 per year. Implementing continuing measurement and verification ensures that the building will continue to perform as designed, again lowering the total cost of ownership.

Increased Productivity

Another driver for green design is the recognition of increased productivity from a building that is comfortable and enjoyable and provides healthy conditions.

Comfortable occupants are less distracted, able to focus better on their tasks/activities, and appreciate the physiological benefits good green design provides. A case study conducted by Pacific Northwest Laboratory points out many interesting observations about human response to daylighting, outside views, and thermal comfort. The study, which compares worker productivity in two buildings owned by the same manufacturer, illustrates both the positive and negative impact application of green design principles can have on human productivity. (Heerwagen, Judith H., Pacific Northwest Laboratory. *Assessing the Human and Organizational Impacts of Green Buildings*.)

The first building is an older, smaller industrial facility divided into offices and a manufacturing area. It has high ribbon windows around the perimeter walls in both office and manufacturing areas, providing only limited daylighting. It has an employee lounge, a small outdoor seating area with picnic tables, and conference rooms.

The newer facility is 50% larger with energy-efficient features such as large-scale use of daylighting, energy-efficient florescent lamps, daylighting controls, DDC HVAC controls, environmentally sensitive building materials, and a fitness center at each end of the manufacturing area.

The study focuses on individual quality-of-work issues and the manufacturer's own production performance parameters. The study provides a mixed review of green design and gives insight on what conditions need to be avoided. While occupants perceived satisfaction and comfort stemming from daylighting and outside views, they also expressed complaints about glare and lack of thermal comfort. The green building studied did not appear to have controlled the quality of daylight through proper glazing selection, which may be the cause of the complaints about glare and thermal comfort.

Subsequent chapters discuss specific design parameters relative to building envelope design including daylighting, energy efficiency, and thermal comfort.

See also chapter 16 for further data on the relationship between human labor costs and other costs of operating a business and for some further examples.

Filling A Design Need

There are increasing numbers of building owners and developers asking for green design services. As a result, there is considerable business for design professionals who can master the principles of green design and provide leadership in this arena

Some publications that demonstrate the drivers of green design include *Economic Renewal Guide* (Kinsley 1997); *Natural Capitalism* (Hawken, Lovins, and Lovins 1999); and *Earth From Above* (Yann).

Commitment

Green design requires more than a project team with good intentions; it requires commitment from the owner. The most successful projects incorporating green design are ones with dedicated, proactive owners who are willing to examine the entire spectrum of ownership—from design to construction to long-term operation of their facilities. These owners understand that green buildings require more planning, better execution, and commitment to finding solutions that reduce the total cost of ownership and long-term environmental impacts.

Implementing green design does raise the initial "soft" costs associated with a project. Additional design services, commissioning, and certain green features may add as much as one percent of total project cost to the front end. However, experienced practitioners of green design have found that this investment, more often than not, has led to lower total project costs before construction is done, resulting in a net savings that may equal cost of the construction contingency. In addition, significant savings can be realized for the life of the building through lower total cost of ownership

Establishing Green Design Goals Early

Establishing goals early in the project planning stages is key to developing a successful green design. It is easy to say that goals need to be established, but many designers and owners struggle with what green design is and what goals should be established. Some typical questions are: What does it cost to design and construct a green project? Where do you get the best return for the investment? How far should the team go to accomplish a green design?

Chapter 3 presents several rating systems and references on environmental performance improvement. The essence of these documents is guidance on how to reduce the impact growth will have on the environment. While the approaches and goals contained in each differ, all suggest common principles that designers may find helpful to apply on their particular projects.

Integration of Team Ideas

No green design effort will be successful if the various design disciplines do not work in close coordination from the earliest stages. No longer can the engineer become involved only after the building's form and space arrangements are set (i.e., end of Schematic Design); that is far too late for the necessary cross-pollenization of ideas between engineering and architectural disciplines that must occur for green design to be effective.

Effective Execution

Still, all the good intentions an owner and project team may have at the early stages are meaningless without follow-through, not only during the construction process, but thereafter over the entire life of the facility by those responsible for operation and maintenance. Thus, ideally, success requires a committed owner, sustainable project goals established in predesign, knowledgeable design practitioners working in concert to develop a green design, a third-party commissioning authority, competent contractors who buy into the green concept, and, finally, operators properly trained and dedicated to keeping the facility operating at peak performance for its life.

THE ENGINEERING/ENERGY CONSERVATION ETHIC

Since the 1973 oil embargo, the HVAC&R industry has continued to improve the efficiency of air-conditioning systems and equipment, promulgated energy conservation standards, developed energy-efficient designs, experimented with a wide variety of design approaches, strived for good indoor air quality, and shared the lessons learned with industry colleagues. As in the past, efforts must be continued to find new and better solutions to improve energy efficiency, further reduce our dependence on nonrenewable energy sources, and increase the comfort of people in the buildings they occupy.

Most designers have guided owners through life-cycle analyses of various options, identified approaches to improve building efficiency, and developed strategies to meet the stated goals of owners. They have also had owners reject their ideas because of too-long payback periods due to project budget constraints. Despite those setbacks, movement toward sustainable design is becoming more prevalent. It is thus incumbent on our industry to recognize the impact its work has on the environment, which goes beyond matters of first cost, recurring cost, and even life-cycle cost. The ethic of the industry requires its practitioners to strive to identify these environmental costs and assign values to them, values that represent the total cost to society rather than just conventional measurements of capital.

The building industry must strive to inform both itself and its clients about the value of natural capital, and it must begin to base decisions on other than just the traditional metrics of financial, manufactured, and human capital. It took nature a very long time—3.8 billion years—to generate the earth's natural capital. The amazing fact is that, in the last 200 years, humans have consumed most of this natural capital while at the same time earth's population has grown exponentially (Hawken et al. 1999).

INCENTIVES

For both individuals and firms in the HVAC engineering profession, many incentives exist to perform sustainable design. As with any aspect of engineering practice that adds value to a project, fees and client expectations must be carefully managed. While a client may balk at added fees charged for better work that is still part of a traditional engineering scope, some clients welcome additional services of the right type. First, the appetite of the project client and full design team for sustainable design must be gauged; then the commensurate level of engineering services can be provided. The earlier such understandings are reached and reduced to writing, the better—ideally upon initial fee proposal and acceptance.

Green engineering design capabilities can positively impact engineers' careers and the firms that employ them. Firms can enhance these capabilities by providing leadership on green issues, building individual competencies, providing ongoing support for professional development in relevant areas, rewarding accomplishments, marketing or promoting green success stories, and building their clientele's interest in green engineering design.

When properly delivered, green engineering capabilities can enhance service to clients, build repeat business, obtain public relations and marketing value, and increase demand for engineering services, especially among the architects or owners that represent a substantial proportion of many firms' billings. In addition, many engineering firms can better retain employees and raise their satisfaction level. Finally, green engineering competency can reduce risks in practice: knowledge of green issues is necessary to manage risk when participating in aggressively green projects.

Some projects may lend themselves to the incorporation of green engineering design concepts without incurring additional engineering costs beyond the designer's own investment in the knowledge of and experience with green design. Other sustainable design projects may require additional services for a greater number of design considerations not customarily included in ordinary engineering fees, such as extended energy analysis, daylighting/solar load analysis or extended review (of materials and components, environmental impacts, such as embodied energy, transportation and construction impacts, composition, and IAQ performance). Other categories of additional services may include project-specific research or training of the engineering team where required and client education and communication.

If the engineer can demonstrate how these additional services can benefit the project in terms of specific positive results, then these services can be proposed, and hopefully accepted, at the outset of the project. The desired level of service can also be provided to the project. As has been demonstrated on many projects where case studies are available, sustainable design has resulted in lower long-term operating and ownership costs. The owner who understands these savings is more likely to accept the short-term costs of additional engineering design services in pursuit of the long-term benefits of optimized life-cycle cost. If, due to a designer's enhanced engineering capabilities, the need to include one or more ancillary consultants on a design team is eliminated or reduced, then the short-term benefit to the client may be quite clear. Even when a sustainability or environmental consultant is added to the project team, there remain opportunities to extend engineering scope within the limits of the competency and experience of the engineers on the design team.

Many forms of incentives can be conferred on a project through judicious selection and pursuit of sustainable design goals. Today's HVAC&R professionals can add value to their offerings and distinguish themselves in the marketplace by leveraging external incentives to reduce clients' project costs. Sustainable engineering design also provides opportunities to develop internal incentives to reinforce green goals; such incentives can help the design team make green choices throughout the design and construction process. These two broad categories of incentives, external and internal, can each encompass both direct and indirect financial benefits and nonfinancial advantages.

The familiar range of energy incentives offered by many utility-administered, state-mandated, demand-side management programs represent one obvious form of external financial incentive—the rebate check available to owners or utility ratepayers who pursue energy conservation measures in buildings and mechanical/electrical systems. Of course, availability of these and other financial incentive offerings varies from place to place and project to project. But many other external financial incentives can reduce project costs where applicable, such as:

- sustainable design tax credits (now offered by New York)
- marketable emissions credits
- tax rebates
- brownfield funds
- historic preservation funds

- community redevelopment funds
- economic development funds
- charitable foundation funds.

Incentives internal to a project itself can be created through contractual arrangements. The simplest example is added fee for added scope, as discussed above. At the other end of the spectrum, some proactive firms offer design review and commissioning services on a performance basis. Construction project insurance offerings have offered "rebates" if no IAQ claims are made a predetermined number of years after construction is completed. If both client and firm are willing, there are many ways to create internal incentives for green engineering design on a project-specific basis. (See further discussion on incentive fees in chapter 16.)

Many individuals and groups have done valuable work in exploring various incentives for green design. The *ASHRAE Journal* and many other industry periodicals carry case studies with green engineering elements. Assembling and familiarizing oneself with the many successfully completed green projects provides useful tools for selling and delivering green engineering services.

BUILDING TEAM SPIRIT

The essence of building team spirit is acknowledging that everyone on the team is important to the success of a project, from the visionaries on the design team to the laborers at the construction site. Each contributor must have pride in his or her efforts and need to feel the efforts put forth are valued and appreciated. Sustainable development requires buy-in by all parties, from the owner initiating the project, to the CADD operator in the design office, to the contractor supervising construction, to the maintenance person keeping the facility functioning, each playing an indispensable role.

Chapter 3
Background and Fundamentals

The use of green engineering concepts has evolved quite rapidly in recent years and is today a legitimate and spreading movement in the HVAC&R and related engineering professions. Much of this recent work has been driven by the emergence of green architecture, also commonly referred to as *sustainable* or *environmentally conscious* architecture; this, in turn, is being encouraged by increased client demand for more sustainable buildings.

The emergence of green building engineering is best understood in the context of the movement in architecture toward sustainable buildings and communities. Detailed reviews of this movement appear elsewhere and fall outside the scope of this document. A brief review of the history and background of the green design movement is provided, followed by a discussion of its applicability. Several leading methodologies for performing and evaluating green building design efforts are reviewed.

SUSTAINABILITY IN ARCHITECTURE

Prior to the industrial revolution, building efforts were often directed throughout design and construction by a single architect—the so-called "master builder" model. The master builder alone bore full responsibility for the design and construction of the

Authors contributing to this chapter are Kevin Dickens, David Grumman, Nils Larsson, Tom Lawrence, Eugene Stamper, and Steve Turner.

building, including any "engineering" required. This model lent itself to a building designed as one system, with the means of providing heat, light, water, and other building services often closely integrated into the architectural elements. Sustainability, semantically if not conceptually, predates these eras, and some modern unsustainable practices had yet to arise. Sustainability in itself was not the goal of yesteryear's master builders. Yet, some of the resulting structures appear to have achieved an admirable combination of great longevity and sustainability in construction, operation, and maintenance. It would be interesting to compare the ecological footprint (a concept discussed later in this document) of, say, Roman structures from two millennia ago heated by radiant floors to a 20th century structure of comparable size, site, and use.

In the 19th century, as ever more complicated technologies and the scientific method developed, the discipline of engineering emerged separate from architecture. This change was not arbitrary or willful but rather was due to the increasing complexity of design tools and construction technologies and a burgeoning range of available materials and techniques. This complexity continued to grow throughout the 20th century and continues today. With the architect transformed from master builder to lead design consultant, most HVAC&R engineering practices performed work predominantly as a sub-consultant to the architect, whose firm, in turn, was retained by the client. Hand-in-hand with these trends emerged the 20th century doctrine of "buildings-over-nature," an approach still widely demanded by clients and supplied by architectural and engineering firms.

Under this approach—buildings designed under the architect as prime consultant following the "buildings-over-nature" paradigm—the architect conceives the shell and interior design concepts first. Only then does the architect turn to structural engineers, then HVAC&R engineers, then electrical engineers, etc. (Not coincidentally, this hierarchy and sequence of engineering involvement mirrors the relative expense of the subsystems being designed.)

With notable exceptions, this sequence has reinforced the trend toward "buildings-over-nature": relying on the brute force of sizable HVAC&R systems that are resource-intensive to build and maintain—and energy-intensive to operate—to achieve conditions acceptable for human occupancy. In this approach to the design process, many opportunities to integrate architectural elements with engineered systems are missed—often because it's too late. Even with an integrated design team to "bridge back" over the gaps in the traditional design process, sustainably designed buildings with optimally engineered subsystems do not result if not provided by professionals with appropriate knowledge and insight.

When Green Design Is Applicable

One leading trend in architecture, especially in the design of smaller buildings, is to "invite nature in" as an alternative to walling it off with a shell and then providing sufficiently powerful mechanical/electrical systems to perpetuate this isolation. This situation presents a significant opportunity for engineers today. Architects and clients who take this approach require fresh and complementary engineering approaches, not tradition-bound engineering that incorporates extra capacity to "overcome" the natural forces a design team may have "invited" into a building. Natural ventilation and hybrid mechanical/natural ventilation, radiant heating and radiant cooling are examples of the tools with which today's engineers are increasingly required to acquire fluency. (See chapter 7 for some GreenTips relating to alternative ventilation techniques and see Watson and Chapman [2002] for radiant heating/cooling design guidance.)

Fortunately, many information sources are available, and many projects have been accomplished and documented to inform engineers. Further, new tools for understanding and defending engineering decisions in such projects are merging, including a revised ASHRAE thermal comfort standard, Standard 55 (latest approved edition), that provides an adaptive design method more applicable to buildings that interact more freely with the outdoor environment.

Another more widely demanded approach to green HVAC&R engineering presents another significant opportunity for engineers. This approach applies to projects ranging from flagship green building projects to more conventional ones where the client has only some "appetite" for green. The demand for environmentally conscious engineering is evidenced by the expansion of engineering groups, either within or outside architectural practices, that have built a reputation for a green approach to building design.

Work done by others on such projects can inform engineers' building design. In addition, many informative resources are available to help engineers to better understand the principles, techniques, and details of green building design and to raise environmental consciousness in their engineering practices. By learning and acquiring appropriate resources, obtaining project-based experience, and finding like-minded professionals, engineers can reorient their thinking to deliver better services to their clients.

Green HVAC engineering can be provided for its own sake, independent of any client or architect demand. The appetite for environmentally conscious engineering must be carefully gauged and opportunities to educate the design team carefully seized. In this way, engineers can bring greater value to their projects and distinguish themselves from competing individuals and firms.

Green Building Rating Systems/Environmental Performance Improvement Programs

There are two general types of programs that exist to encourage green building design. One type might be termed a rating system per se and the other a guide or program to encourage and assist designers in achieving green building design. (This document is in the latter category.)

Green Building Rating Systems. There are two major rating systems developed by reputable organizations (one United States based, the other international) that purport to provide a rating to indicate how well a building meets prescribed requirements and to determine whether a building design is green or not or the degree of "greenness" it has. Each can provide some useful tools to identify and prioritize key environmental issues. These tools incorporate a coordinated method for accomplishing, validating, and benchmarking sustainably designed projects.

As with any generalized method, each has its own limitations and may not apply directly to every project's regional and other specific aspects. As Walter Grondzik notes in his paper addressing how extensively the rating systems address *all* elements of indoor environmental quality (IEQ) (see chapter 1), some of those elements are overlooked (Grondzik 2001).

It should not be implied that this guide advocates exclusion of these elements. By advocating both *green* as well as *good* design in any building design endeavor (as discussed in chapter 1), this is avoided. Yet, at the same time this guide does not intend to *discourage* use of the mentioned rating systems or other programs by ASHRAE members or by the design teams in which its members participate. Thus, while this guide does not endorse or recommend use of any one rating system or program, it is also not opposed to the use of one if it is perceived that such will be of help in achieving a green design. Each method may play a valuable role in increasing an engineer's ability to help deliver sustainably designed projects.

The leading *rating* methods are:

1. *LEED^R*, the *Leadership in Energy & Design Green Building Rating System*

The U.S. Green Building Council (USGBC) started offering this system in 1998 and describes it as a "voluntary, consensus-based, market-driven building rating system based on existing proven technology. It evaluates environmental performance from a 'whole building' perspective over a building's life-cycle, providing a definitive standard for what constitutes a 'green building'." LEED has been applied to numerous projects and offers a range of project certification levels. LEED also qualifies individuals as LEED consultants, although it does not require such consultants on projects seeking LEED ratings.

2. *BREEAM^R*, the *Building Research Establishment Environmental Assessment Method*

The Building Research Establishment in England launched this voluntary, consensus-based, market-oriented assessment program in 1990. With one mandatory and two optional assessment areas, BREEAM encourages and benchmarks sustainably designed office buildings. The mandatory assessment area is the potential environmental impact of the building; the two optional areas are design process and operation/ maintenance. Several other countries and regions have developed or are developing related spin-offs inspired by BREEAM.

Environmental Performance Improvement Programs. Several other programs exist with the purpose of guiding or encouraging green building design but without assigning a specific rating. They are:

1. *GBC, the Green Building Challenge*

Canada is currently leading a process called the Green Building Challenge involving about 20 countries developing and testing a second-generation environmental performance assessment system. That system is designed to reflect the very different priorities, technologies, building traditions, and even cultural values that exist in various regions and countries.

The GBC offers criteria for the following general categories: context factors, transportation, resource consumption, environmental loadings, indoor environmental quality (IEQ), service quality, economics, and management.

2. *C-2000, Integrated Design Process*

Natural Resources Canada initiated the C-2000 program in 1993 as a small demonstration of achieving very high levels of building performance. It was assumed that some level of financial incentive would be required at various stages of the building process to make the program a success. Its technical requirements cover energy performance, environmental impacts, indoor environment, functionality, and a range of other parameters.

Experience with the program in the first group of projects to which it was applied yielded the fact that the program's guidance in producing integrated design was the main reason high performance levels were achieved. The program was then called the Integrated Design Process, and it now focuses its project interventions on design advice in the very early stages.

3. *CBIP, Commercial Buildings Incentive Program*

An offshoot of the C-2000 Program, CBIP was an effort to create a larger national program to move the Canadian building industry toward energy efficiency. Its financial incentives provide incremental costs for the design process. Because it attempts to address a larger audience, it is simpler than the C-2000 program in that it does not need to provide customized support and that it concentrates on energy performance.

4. Other Programs

Other guides and methods include:

- The Whole Building Design Guide
- Green Building Advisor

- California Collaborative for High Performance Schools
- Minnesota Public Schools
- New York Guidelines for Sustainable Buildings

Work referred to by architects includes:

- AIA *Environmental Resource Guide*
- The Hannover Principles
- GreenSpec
- The Natural Step

These and additional works by such entities as the National Renewable Energy Laboratory (NREL) and the Rocky Mountain Institute (RMI) are listed in the references or at the end of this chapter.

LAWS OF THERMODYNAMICS

Understanding the basic tenets that define the engineer's profession is imperative for thoughtful design. While this guide is not intended to serve as an engineering textbook, it is helpful to review the first and second laws of thermodynamics as well as other engineering relationships. This will provide the reader with insights into the opportunities available for energy conservation as well as other green building design opportunities.

Overview

The first law in its basic form is:

$$Q = \Delta U + \Delta E_{potential} + \Delta E_{kinetic} + W_{flow} + W_{shaft}$$

For a system in steady state and substituting in for the internal, potential, and kinetic energy terms leads to the following.

$$\dot{Q} - \dot{W} =$$
$$\dot{m}[(u_2 - u_1) + (p_2 v_2 - p_1 v_1) + (V_2^2 - V_1^2)/2 + g(z_2 - z_1)]$$

where
Q = heat transferred to or from the system; the dotted symbol refers to the *rate* of heat being transferred

E = energy contained in the system (potential or kinetic)

W = work produced or required by the system; the dotted symbol refers to the *rate* of heat being transferred

u = internal energy of the fluid (i.e., water, steam, air, refrigerant) per unit mass

m = mass of fluid

pv = product of the pressure and specific

volume of the fluid

V = velocity of the fluid in the system

h = enthalpy of the fluid per unit mass, expressed as (u + pv)

z = height or potential energy of the fluid

1 and 2 = subscripts denoting *before* and *after* states of the parameter

The internal energy (u) and flow energy (pv) terms can be combined into the fluid enthalpy, given by

$$h = u + pv.$$

The second law is represented by several equations involving the change in entropy of the fluid, but for the purposes of making decisions on energy and green design, studying the Carnot cycle, as represented on temperature-entropy coordinates, is particularly useful.

One common application of the first law equation to a building HVAC system is the combustion processes generating heat to raise the temperature of a fluid for providing heat to a building. When looking at the heating means, be it a boiler, hot water generator, or warm air furnace, the terms for work (W), changes in kinetic energy ($V_2^2 - V_1^2)/2$ and potential energy ($z_2 - z_1$) are small in comparison to enthalpy difference so the first law becomes

$$\dot{Q} \cong \dot{m}(h_2 - h_1).$$

Green Design Implications

There are two types of energy: stored, or potential, energy and the energy of motion, called kinetic energy. Regardless of its form, however, the first law of thermodynamics always applies. For a closed system, in essence, it says:

Energy cannot be created or destroyed

A closed system is one in which energy and material do not flow across the system boundary. The first law is why energy efficiency and green design are a necessity. If we could create energy, there would be no reason to conserve it. We must be aware that we are largely dependent on sources of energy that are in finite supply. Therefore, it is logical to use less energy of this type as a rule and to move toward renewable, more efficient energy sources in general.

If energy is the ability to do work, then what happens when we tap that potential? The result is threefold: work, heat, and entropy. Work is the transfer of energy by mechanical means, such as a fan or pump. Heat refers to a transfer of energy from one object to another because of a temperature difference. And entropy, simply stated, is an indicator of the state of disorder of a system.

The second law of thermodynamics helps us to appreciate the relevance of sustainable design even more:

All processes irreversibly increase the entropy of a system and its environment

If you understand that the Earth is our system, then you realize that the limited amount of usable energy we have been granted (first law) will eventually and irreversibly be converted into unusable energy (second law), which brings us full circle. Of course, the earth is not a completely closed system in that energy is entering (via solar radiation) and leaving (such as earth radiating energy out into space). Regardless, our dependency on energy in a useful form, and the immutable laws of nature, set the tone for proper (green) design: *use energy judiciously and effectively.*

Application to HVAC&R Systems and Processes

Power Generation. For steam boilers, with the water undergoing phase change, the enthalpy difference is much larger than it is for either the water in hot water generators or the air in warm air furnaces, where the enthalpy change is proportional to the temperature rise of the fluid.

Combustion of the fuel/air mixture results in a high temperature of the flue gases being discharged to the chimney or vent. *Green design requires examining the recovery of the energy in the flue gases for possible reuse—as in preheating outside air, heating hot water for domestic use, or serving as a heat source for snow-melting systems or other building heating purposes.*

When looking at the generation of power for onsite power production (as, for example, with cogeneration systems) or at vapor compression refrigeration systems in building air conditioning (where the work produced or required is a major energy concern), looking at the first and second laws together is necessary.

The Carnot cycle is a rectangle on temperature-entropy coordinates (see Figure 3-1). The area of the rectangle represents the total energy (both work and thermal) involved in the case of a power plant generating power or of vapor compression refrigeration air conditioning or heat pump systems. For example, in Figure 3-1, the shaded area represents the heat load transported by a vapor compression refrigeration

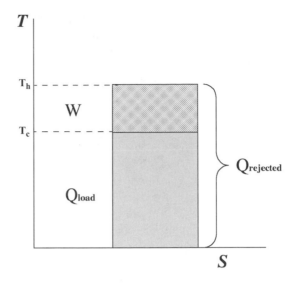

Figure 3-1 Carnot cycle for refrigeration.

cycle (Q_{load}) and the cross-hatched area the amount of work output necessary by the compressor to move the heat (W). The total of the two represents the heat rejected to the environment at the condenser ($Q_{rejected}$).

For power generation, the upper temperature, representing the high temperature in the Carnot cycle, T_h, should be as high as possible to maximize work output. Similarly, the lower temperature in the Carnot cycle, T_c, should be as low as possible. While real power generation systems do not operate precisely on the Carnot cycle, the principle is still valid.

Similarly, for refrigeration, where one wants to minimize the work input (power required), T_h should be as low as possible and T_c as high as possible.

Power Production. Many buildings or building groups use on-site electric power generation plants that, when combined with some sort of heat recovery, are termed *cogeneration plants.*

A common modern generation plant may employ a gas turbine, which requires compressing air before combustion of fuel in a combustion chamber; this, in turn, yields high-temperature combustion gases at high pressure, which expand through the turbine, generating power. The work required to compress a fluid is a function of the fluid density, with low-density fluids (such as air) requiring more work to achieve a given pressure than higher-density fluids (such as liquids like water). This results in relatively low-pressure gases entering the turbine and high-temperature exhaust from the turbine at the lower atmospheric pressure obtained after expansion through the turbine.

Modern combined cycle power plants use high-temperature turbine exhaust as the heating medium for heat recovery steam generators. These steam generators operate at much higher pressures than gas turbines since water is pumped to the high pressures entering the steam generators, and this high-density fluid requires much less energy to achieve the high pressure than the air in the gas turbine cycle. The steam expands through a steam turbine to low condensing temperatures, T_c, for heat rejection in a condenser. For on-site power generation without combined cycles, the gas turbine exhaust is used as a heat source for other building energy needs, achieving the lower T_c in that manner.

Air-Conditioning. In a refrigeration plant, where the end-purpose is the cooling of air for building cooling purposes, the chiller or direct expansion refrigerant should have the cooling fluid at as high a temperature (T_c) as possible to minimize work input. Of course, this temperature is limited by the temperature to which the air must be cooled. The closer T_c is to that air temperature, however, the more heat transfer surface will be required in the heat exchanger used to cool the air, in both the cooling coils in a DX systems or in chilled water coils.

The high temperature (T_h) at which heat is rejected is limited by the temperature of the air used in the air-cooled condenser or by the approach to the air wet-bulb temperature with water-cooled condensers used in conjunction with cooling towers. Again, the closer the refrigerant T_h is to the coolant temperature, the larger and more expensive will be the heat exchanger (condenser) required.

In real cycles, the work produced by the turbines (gas or steam) is the enthalpy difference across the turbine multiplied by the mass flow rate. The net power generated is the difference between this enthalpy difference and that required for the compression of combustion air plus the work to pump the water in the steam part of the cycle.

For the refrigeration cycle using expansion valves, the work input is the enthalpy difference across the compressor.

Hydraulic Machine (Pumps, Fans) Similarity Analysis. The performance of a pump or fan at one operating point can used be to predict the performance of the same (or similar) equipment at a different operating condition. This is done using similarity relations. Since the energy required in pumping water needed in chilled water systems—and that needed to power the fans used in air distribution systems—can be quite substantial, a closer look at these relations can be useful in analyzing possibilities for saving energy. Similarity relations, at the point of maximum efficiency, yield

$$\frac{Pv}{N^3 D^5}\bigg|_{Maximum\ Efficiency} = Constant$$

and

$$\frac{Q}{ND^3}\bigg|_{Maximum\ Efficiency} = Constant$$

where

Q = volumetric flow rate,
N = impeller rotative speed,
D = impeller diameter,
P = power input to the pump or fan, and
v = specific volume of the fluid.

When considering performance of the same pump or fan at different operating conditions, the impeller diameter is the same. The first similarity relation listed reduces to

$$\frac{Pv}{N^3}\bigg|_{Maximum\ Efficiency} = Constant.$$

Thus, the power input needed to run the pump or fan is proportional to N^3—or to the *cube of the rotative speed*. This gives rise to the use of variable speed drives, where part loads on the system result in decreased flow requirements that, in turn, can be accomplished by lowering the pump or fan rotating speed, N. Power needed will then decrease as the cube of N.

The use of variable speed (or variable frequency) drives does involve additional controls and engineering design analysis of operating conditions to ensure that the system will perform. This does add to the initial cost of the system, but the cost of equipment and controls needed has been decreasing.

KEY RELATIONSHIPS/DEPENDENCIES

The purpose of this section is to identify key relationships and dependencies using the language of the engineer: the formula. It is assumed that the reader is a practicing engineer with some experience rather than a neophyte, so this section is not meant to be a primer on the science behind HVAC&R. However, the author has attempted to remind the reader of the basics before delving into the greener aspects of the topic.

Webster defines a formula as "a general fact,

rule or principle expressed in mathematical symbols." In HVAC, the facts, rules, or principles we are most concerned with are the laws of thermodynamics (see previous section). It has been said that if you can write an equation for a problem, you have the solution. But we must not confuse a "plug-and-chug" approach using formulae with engineering: The successful engineer must be able to both write the formula and understand its underlying principles.

A formula is composed simply of constants and variables. Constants are defined (given) and cannot be influenced. Therefore, we can only resolve a problem (influence an outcome) by manipulating its variables. When this simple premise is understood, key relationships and dependencies manifest themselves and the solution becomes obvious.

Heat Transfer

Heat travels in three ways: conduction, convection, and radiation. Note the following general correlations:

Conduction $\approx$ Heat transfer by molecular motion in a material in direct contact

Convection $\approx$ Contact between a fluid in motion and a solid

Radiation $\approx$ No contact required; heat transfer by electromagnetic waves

In most heat transfer problems, more than one mode of transfer is involved at any given moment. But to keep things simple, we will look at each type of heat transfer separately.

Conduction. The amount of heat transferred by conduction can be quantified by calculating an overall heat transfer coefficient U:

$$U = 1/R$$

where R is the overall thermal resistance for the material or system in question, which may include a convective heat transfer resistance effect. Consider heat transfer through a wall. The process can be expressed as follows:

$$Q = U A \Delta t$$

where Q is the amount of heat transferred, A is the exposed surface area, and the temperature delta is the difference between the warm outdoor air and cooler indoor air. In this equation there are no fixed variables, although in our example the outdoor air temperature is dictated by the project's location. The design team has the ability to minimize Q by minimizing the U-factor, area, and temperature difference. Therefore, steps that can be taken include:

- Limit conductance by providing an envelope with a low overall U-factor. This can be accomplished through the use of insulating materials, air spaces in glass and walls, thermal breaks in construction, etc.
- Create an indoor environment wherein the space dry bulb can be higher or lower than traditional design norms in the summer and winter, respectively. This can be done using dehumidification and/or humidification as long as you stay within acceptable ranges (see ASHRAE Standard 55).
- Limit the surface area exposed to large temperature differentials by increasing shading, both on the building and occurring naturally through the use of landscaping. Considering low-profile, semi-buried buildings is another option.

Convection. There are numerous formulas describing energy transfer through convection. The ASHRAE Handbook—Fundamentals gives at least 12 factors used in determining convective heat transfer coefficients, and it lists no fewer than 25 equations for calculating heat transfer through forced convection. For the purpose of our discussion, we will limit ourselves to the comparison of natural versus forced convection.

Natural convection is often called free convection and is primarily due to differences in density and the action of gravity. To see convection in action, observe a LAVA® lamp. The "lava" gains heat from the light bulb and rises; as it cools, it falls again. Replace the light bulb with a hot water-filled finned tube and swap the "lava" for air, and you get a fair idea of how convection works in HVAC. The takeaway from this fairly obvious example is that natural convection is a simple law of nature that can be used to the designer's benefit in a number of ways:

- Supply cool air low and return high, often called displacement ventilation, and increase IAQ by naturally "lifting" pollutants out of the occupied space.
- Locate returns or exhaust directly over heat-generating equipment such as copiers and refrigerators, removing heat from the space at the source and thus lowering the imposed space sensible cooling load.
- Provide baseboard heat to warm the exterior envelope surfaces to reduce radiant heat loss from occupants to walls and windows. (Note: While this may increase comfort, it can increase heat loss through the surface by action of the

natural convective flow, reducing the surface heat transfer coefficient.)

- Alternatively, use perimeter radiant ceiling panels to counteract perimeter heating loss.
- Apply passive ventilation or hybrid ventilation, providing extreme outside conditions do not preclude its successful application.

By supplying low and returning high, you reduce the need for mixing that accompanies traditional overhead supply and return systems. By removing sensible load at the source, you reduce the sensible load in the space and, in turn, the supply air required to handle it. By allowing ventilation air to enter and exit a building naturally, the need for forced ventilation through air-handling systems and ductwork is eliminated. All of these steps decrease the amount of work required to address loads within a space, which leads to our next section.

Radiation. Heat transfer via radiation presents a unique challenge and opportunity for the designer. We have all stood next to a cold window and felt chilled even though the ambient temperature was at a comfortable level. The same holds true for sunny days when one can get too warm even though the thermostat says all is well. The simplified form of the equation describing radiant heat transfer is

$$Q = \varepsilon\sigma A(T_1^4 - T_2^4)$$

where ε is emissivity, σ is the Stefan-Boltzmann constant, A is surface area, and the T-term is the absolute temperature difference between the radiant object (subscript 1, with emissivity of ε) and its surroundings (subscript 2, a blackbody). Emissivity is primarily a function of a material's ability to re-emit absorbed energy. A dull black surface such as charcoal has an emissivity close to 1 (that of a blackbody), while shiny metallic surfaces have lower values, more in the range of 0.1 to 0.4. Surfaces with higher emissivity will absorb and emit more thermal energy. But notice the dramatic difference changing the temperature difference can make: The rate at which an object radiates or absorbs heat is proportional to the difference in the fourth powers of the absolute temperatures involved.

When the designer is faced with the challenge of minimizing the heat transferred by radiant means, the following steps can be taken for situations where cooling loads dominate:

- Explore the possibility of eliminating or drastically reducing the area (*A*) directly exposed to

the radiant source through shading or other means. For most building applications the radiant source is the sun, which can be treated as an object emitting energy at 5800 K, or 10,000°F.

- Recommend the use of low emissivity materials whenever possible, especially on roofs and in glazing.
- Avoid dark colors on the building exterior, which typically have a higher emissivity and absorb more heat.
- Limit east and west exposures, especially those with a large amount of glass.
- Offset the radiant load. For example, in a large atrium with a large glazing exposure and/or exterior walls, offsetting the radiant gains from the envelope with radiant cooling in the floor will produce a net effect that is significantly more comfortable for the occupant.

For situations where heating loads are significant and you are looking to maximize the heat gained, *Q*, as with solar collection or passive heating, do just the opposite of the above: Increase exposure, maximize surface area, and use dark colors and high-ε materials (ASHRAE 1996).

When heating or cooling with radiant panels, remember the power of the temperature difference to maximize thermal efficiency. You may be able to accommodate the architects' aesthetic sense by minimizing the need for excessive radiant surface area of high-ε materials. For example, refer to chapter 6, Figure 1, Radiation Heat Transfer from Heated Ceiling, Floor, or Wall Panel, in the ASHRAE Handbook—Systems and Equipment. Note that, assuming a 70°F room temperature and other factors being equal, raising the effective panel temperature from 100°F to 200°F would raise the radiant heat transfer by a factor to 5.7! In turn, significantly less panel surface area would be required to accomplish the same amount of heating. Standing under a higher temperature panel may result in a warmer head relative to the other body areas and, consequently, may cause discomfort.

Forced Convection and Mass Transfer

In HVAC, mass transfer by forced convection is used to facilitate a thermodynamic transfer of energy. Though all types of fluids and gases are moved in HVAC applications, the discussion here is limited to water and air. Note in the following the key relationship between mass flow rates, the fluid's thermal properties, and the load.

Water. The amount of energy required to address a sensible load *Q* within a system is found to be proportional to the fluid mass flow rate m into the system and to the temperature difference ΔT between the system and the fluid. This can be expressed as

$$Q_s = mcv\Delta T$$

where c is the specific heat at constant pressure p of the medium. For temperature changes that are not too great, c_p can be considered a constant. The sensible heat formula for water in IP is

$$Q_s = (gpm)(500)\Delta T.$$

The key relationships are clear. If Q is a given, then the only variables are flow and temperature difference: The greater the temperature delta, the less flow that will be required, and vice versa. If the load Q is variable, then one can react by varying flow, delta-T, or both. Recommended strategies include:

- Use high delta-T designs whenever feasible, barring any negative efficiency impacts that may result from a lowered chiller COP. The greater the temperature difference, the less flow that will be required.
- Maintain a constant delta-T and vary the flow in response to load. The value of this strategy becomes clearer when we discuss the affinity laws below.

Moist Air. When working with air, we are rarely dealing with a dry gas. Instead, air is usually a mixture of water and air. In turn, air-side energy calculations are as much about temperature difference as they are about changes of state. The sensible load in standard air is similar to that discussed above for water and can be quantified in IP as follows:

$$Q_s = (cfm)(1.08)\Delta T$$

The amount of energy required to address a latent load Q within a system is found to be proportional to the fluid mass flow rate m into the system and to the humidity ratio difference ΔW between the air in the system and the air entering the system, which can be expressed as

$$Q_L = ml\Delta W$$

where l is the latent heat of vaporization for water. For temperature changes that are not too great, l can be considered a constant. The latent heat equations in IP for standard air are:

$$Q_L = (cfm)(0.68)\Delta W_{Grains/(Lb)}$$

$$Q_L = (cfm)(4840)\Delta W_{Lb/Lb}$$

The key relationships again are obvious. If Q is a given, then the only variables are flow and moisture content of the air delivered. The greater the humidity ratio difference, i.e., the dryer the supply air, the less flow that will be required.

Last, addressing total heat in a space leads us to the following:

$$Q_T = Q_s + Q_L = m\Delta h$$

where Δh is the difference in enthalpy between the air/water vapor in the space and the supply air/water vapor. For standard air, the process (in IP) is

$$Q_T = (cfm)(4.45)\Delta h.$$

In all of the air formulas, the relationship remains. The only actions at our disposal are varying flow rates and altering thermal properties. To minimize the flow rate and energy required in air systems, consider the following possible steps:

- Move less air by supplying colder air and increasing the temperature difference, accounting for any negative chiller efficiency impacts due to lowered COP. High induction diffusers or fan terminal units can be used to temper the supply air at the point of distribution to avoid drafts and discomfort.
- Maintain a constant delta T and vary the airflow in response to load.
- Use energy recovery to pre-treat outside air to minimize mixed air differentials and, in turn, reduce the load associated with the dictated ventilation quantity.
- Consider passive pre-heating strategies, such as buried duct or solar walls, when introducing outdoor air in the winter, again to minimize the mixed air differentials and the associated load.
- Create an indoor environment wherein the space dry bulb can be higher than traditional design norms in the summer. Lowering relative humidity levels by means of passive dehumidification via return air bypass can allow a higher space temperature, which equates to a higher delta T in reference to the supply air.
- Create an indoor environment wherein the space dry bulb can be lower than traditional design

norms in the winter (see ASHRAE Standard 55). Utilize radiant task heating for comfort in lower ambient air temperatures (Chapman et al. 2001).

- Use hybrid radiant/convective systems where conditions, artifacts, or special needs of individuals conflict with comfort of viewers, visitors, or personnel.
- Capture sensible load at the source and remove it from the space. In turn, less supply air is then required to handle the space load.
- Use stratification strategies such as displacement ventilation and remove the ceiling load from the space comfort equation. Note that the central equipment still sees this load, but we don't have to move as much air in the space.

Work and Power

We know that it takes energy to change the thermal properties of our heating and cooling medium, i.e., temperature, enthalpy. We know that we want to take advantage of natural forces whenever possible, such as free convection and radiation. Further, we realize that we may have to help Mother Nature along with forced convection and mass transfer. So, to move all of that mass, we need to do work; work is quantified in terms of power, and we want to use as little power as possible.

Efficiencies

If moving a fluid, the efficiency E of the device and the motor/drive combination, combined with the specific gravity (sg) of the fluid, will determine the amount of power you will require. For a pump, the equation for motor horsepower (mhp) is

$$mhp = \frac{(gpm)(\Delta P\ ft\ hd)(sg)}{(3960)E_{Pump}E_{Motor/Drive}},$$

and for a fan

$$mhp = \frac{(cfm)(\Delta P\ in\ wg)(sg)}{(6356)E_{Fan}E_{Motor/Drive}}.$$

In most instances the specific gravity is fixed because the fluid is determined by the design (i.e., air at sea level, water, water with glycol, etc.). So the key actions that can be taken are to minimize flow and pressure drop and to maximize equipment and drive efficiencies. We have discussed flow already, but regarding pressure drop and efficiency, consider these steps:

- To the extent possible, minimize pressure drop by increasing conduit size (duct, pipe) and limiting the number of fittings. Obviously there is a "breakeven" point where increased size becomes unworkable, but that is a matter of judgment.
- Keep fluid specific gravity in check. For example, adding glycol not only decreases thermodynamic performance, but it also increases the amount of pumping energy required to move the fluid.
- Select equipment based on judicial review of the efficiency curves. Maximize efficiency, but avoid unsteady locations or fringe selections.
- Specify *premium* efficiency motors, not just high-efficiency motors. The difference is usually worth the added cost.
- Consider different pump speeds and types to maximize efficiency and performance (i.e., end suction-vertical in-line, 1750 rpm-3600 rpm).
- Evaluate the right fan for the right need, such as forward-curved vs. backward-inclined, prop versus centrifugal, plenum vs. housed.

The Affinity Laws

The affinity laws are often called the fan laws or the pump laws depending on which equipment you are using. The fact is that, regardless of the medium—be it air, water, or maple syrup—the affinity laws present a series of powerful relationships that can make or break a design.

$$\frac{rpm_2}{rpm_1} = \frac{Flow_2}{Flow_1}$$

$$\frac{\Delta P_2}{\Delta P_1} = \left(\frac{Flow_2}{Flow_1}\right)^2$$

$$\frac{mph_2}{mph_1} = \left(\frac{Flow_2}{Flow_1}\right)^3$$

The relationships are simple. Flow and speed are proportional. But, the static pressure in a system varies by the *square* of the flow, and the required motor horsepower varies by the *cube* of the flow! What does this mean in terms of energy required? See the following example.

Consider a typical office building at 10,000 ft² with a varying load. Peak load is 200 ft² per ton, or 600,000 Btuh. The original design utilized a constant flow, variable temperature multi-zone air-handling system. Design airflow is based on a 55°F supply temperature—or 20°F delta T. Fans were selected for 28,000 cfm at 4 in. total static. Fan efficiency is 75% and motor efficiency is 95%.

$$mhp = \frac{(cfm)(\Delta P\ in\ wg)(sg)}{(6356)\varepsilon_{Fan}\varepsilon_{Motor/Drive}}$$

$$= \frac{(28,000)(4\ in\ wg)(1)}{(6356)(0.75)(0.95)} \approx 25hp$$

The owner is considering replacing the aging system with a constant temperature, variable volume system. The average load diversity within the building is 75%, which means that the fan at any given time will have to deliver no more than 21,000 cfm. Based on fan energy alone, what kind of energy savings can we expect?

$$\frac{mhp_2}{mhp_1} = \left(\frac{Flow_2}{Flow_1}\right)^3$$

$$= \frac{mhp_2}{25hp} = \left(\frac{21000}{28000}\right)^3$$

$$mhp_2 = 10.5\ hp$$

$$\Delta mhp = 25 - 10.5 = 14.5\ hp$$

$$1\ hp = 2545\ btu/hr$$

$$(14.5\ hp)(2545\ btu/hr-hp) = 36,903\ btu/hr$$

Notice that a 25% decrease in flow equates to a *58%* decrease in required power, and these principles apply to variable flow water systems as well. Clearly there is an incentive to minimize flow and pressure drop whenever possible.

SUMMARY

* Understanding a formula's key relationships and dependencies will often make green-oriented measures obvious.
* Because we have a limited supply of energy and cannot create it, a good sustainable design will work to conserve energy.
* When designing building envelopes, heat transfer by conduction and solar radiation should be optimized for the energy transfer process (heating, cooling) involved.

* When designing heating and cooling systems, the use of heat transfer and ventilation through natural means, such as natural convection or radiation, should be considered from the beginning of the design process and utilized fully when possible.
* When forced convection and mass transfer are necessary, minimize flow and pressure drop, maximize the effect of thermal characteristic differences (delta-T, delta-h, delta-W), and specify equipment with the highest efficiencies.

REFERENCES

Published

AIA. 1996. *Environmental Resource Guide*. Edited by Joseph Demkin. New York: John Wiley & Sons.

Brand, Stewart. 1995. *How Buildings Learn: What Happens After They're Built*. New York: Viking Penguin USA.

McDonough, William. 1992. The Hannover Principles: Design for Sustainability. Presentation, Earth Summit, Brazil, 1992.

Online

American Institute of Architects
http://www.aia.org
BREEAM® Canada
http://www.breeamcanada.ca
BuildingGreen
http://www.greenbuildingadvisor.com
Center of Excellence for Sustainable Development (CESD)
http://www.sustainable.doe.gov
Energy Efficiency and Renewable Energy Network (EREN)
http://www.eren.doe.gov.
Green Building Challenge
http://www.greenbuilding.ca
High Performance Buildings Research Initiative
http://www.highperformancebuildings.gov
Lawrence Berkeley National Laboratories
http://www.arch.ced.berkeley.edu/vitalsigns
LEED®[see *U.S. Green Building Council below*]
Minnesota Sustainable Design Guide
http://www.sustainabledesignguide.umn.edu
National Renewable Energy Laboratory
http://www.nrel.gov
NAVFAC. "Design of Sustainable Facilities and Infrastructure."
http://www.efdlant.navfac.navy.mil/Lantops_15/sustainable_design.htm

Oikos: Green Building Source
http://www.oikos.com

Rocky Mountain Institute
http://www.rmi.org

Solstice/Center for Renewable Energy and Sustainable (CREST)
http://solstice.crest.org

Sustainable Communities Network (SCN)
http://www.sustainable.org

Sustainable Buildings Industry Council
http://www.sbicouncil.org

U.S. Green Building Council LEED^R Green Building Rating System
http://www.usgbc.org or http://www.wbdg.org

Section 2:
The Design Process

Chapter 4
The Design Process—
Early Stages

OVERVIEW

The design process is the first crucial element in producing a green building. Once designed, the building must be constructed, commissioned, and operated in a way that supports the green concept. If it is not designed with the intent to make it green, the desired results will never be achieved.

Figure 4-1 shows conceptually the impact of providing design input at succeeding stages of a project relative to the cost and effort required. The solid curve shows is that it is much easier to have a major impact on the performance (potential energy savings) of a building if you start at the very earliest stages of the design process; the available impacts diminish thereafter as you proceed through the subsequent design and construction phases. A corollary to this is that the cost of implementing changes to improve building performance rises at each successive stage of the project (cost is shown as the dotted curve of this graph).

Designers are often challenged and sometimes affronted by the idea of green design, for many feel they have been doing good designs for years. The experience of many is that they have been forced to design with low construction cost in mind, and when

Authors contributing to this chapter are Michael Deru, Jay Enck, David Grumman, Michael Haggans, Nils Larsson, Blair McCarry, Mark Rosenbaum, and Steve Turner.

they offer opportunities to improve a building's design, they are often blocked by the owner due to budget constraints. The typical experience is that owners will not accept cost increases that do not show a return in potential savings in five years or less, and many demand 18 months or less.

Achieving green or sustainable design goals requires a different approach than has been customarily applied. Some have expressed the view that significant reductions in energy usage and greenhouse

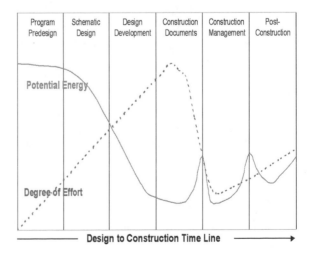

Figure 4-1 Impact of early design input on building performance.

gas emissions will never occur by simply tweaking current practice. In other words, simply installing high-efficiency systems or equipment will not reduce energy usage sufficiently.

Sustainable design requires designers to take a holistic approach and go beyond designing for just the owner and building occupants; they need to look at the long-term environmental impacts the development of a building will create. Engineers and other designers are asked to become advocates, not just objective designers. This may make many uncomfortable because it seemingly asks them to go beyond their area of expertise.

Starting in pre-design and carrying through to post-occupancy is essential for the success of green design. It starts with examining every aspect of the process—from the owner's site selection to building configuration, from architectural elements to efficient construction and operation—and can only occur with an integrated approach. Setting goals, even before site selection, if possible, is the suggested starting point.

At the very start of the project, green design goals have to be discussed, agreed to, and in fact embraced by the extended project team. This is often done in a charette format or simply a session spent discussing the issues.

Goals for a project traditionally include the functional program, leasable or usable area, capital cost, schedule, project image, and similar issues. The charette simply puts environmental goals on a plane with the capital cost and other traditional goals.

One of the goals may be to achieve the environmental goals at the same or similar capital cost. (As with any goals, the environmental goals should be measurable and verifiable.) Another of the goals may be a specific green building rating system target, with possibly an energy target as well or perhaps an energy target alone.

A typical set of goals for a green design project might be:

1. Achieve a level of energy use at least 50% lower than the DOE-compiled average levels for the same building type and region, both projected and in actual operation. (Actual energy numbers may be adjusted for actual-vs.-assumed climatic conditions and hours of usage.)

2. Achieve an actual peak aggregate electrical demand level not exceeding 4.5 kW per ft² of building gross area.

3. Provide at least 15% of the building's annual energy use (in operation) from renewable energy sources. (Such energy usage may be discounted from the aggregate energy use determined under goal 1 above.)

4. Taking into account the determinations of goals 1, 2 and 3 above, assess the impact of the lesser net energy use on raw energy resource use (including off-site) compared to that of a comparable but conventional building, including the changed environmental impacts from that resource use, and verify that the aggregate energy and environmental impacts are no greater.

5. Achieve a per capita (city) water usage 40% lower than the documented average for this building type and region.

6. Achieve an aggregate up-front capital cost for the project that does not exceed x dollars per ft² of building gross area, which has been deemed by the project team to be no higher than 105% of what a "conventional" building would cost.

7. Recycle (or arrange for the recycling of) at least 60% of the aggregate waste materials generated by the building.

8. By means of post-occupancy surveys of building users conducted periodically over a five-year period, achieve an aggregate satisfaction level of 85% or better. Survey shall solicit occupant satisfaction with the indoor environment as to the following dimensions: thermal comfort, air quality, acoustical quality, and visual/general comfort.

9. Obtain a gold-level USGBC LEED^R certification for the building.

(For an example of what one major firm has done, see "One Firm's Green Building Design Process Checklist" on page 37.)

THE OWNER'S ROLE

Of all of the participants, it is the owner who is the most crucial in making a green building happen. With the owner's commitment, the design, construction, and operating teams will receive the motivation and empowerment needed to create a green design.

Key design team members can—and should—attempt to persuade the owner to strive for a green design, particularly if the owner is unfamiliar with the concept. After all, experienced design team members are in the best position to sell the merits of green design. However, such a commitment on the part of the owner, to be effective, must be made early in the design process.

Specific roles that an owner can fill in making a green design effort successful include the following:

- Expressing commitment and enthusiasm for the green endeavor
- Establishing a basic value system (i.e., what is important, what is not)
- Participating in selection of design team members
- Setting schedules and budgets
- Participating in the design process, especially the early stages
- Maintaining interest, commitment, and enthusiasm throughout project.

Strictly speaking, the "owner" on a project could be a corporation or small business, hospital, university or college, office building developer, nonprofit organization, or even an individual. In any case, that owner will be represented in the building project by a designated person, presumably one who accurately reflects the real owner's views and philosophy and can speak for that owner with authority. It would be preferable to have the owner's representative on the design team be an individual in as high a position in the owner's organization as possible (president, CEO, or business manager, if their time is available) but, failing that, certainly someone who knows the mind of the owner and can speak for the owner with authority and reliability.

THE DESIGN TEAM

Setting It Up

One of the first tasks in a green design project is forming the design team. This is a task that should involve the design team leader (often the architect), the owner, and probably the engineer as well. Much of the design team's successful functioning depends, not just on having ideas about what should go into the project, but on being able to analyze the ideas quickly and accurately for their impact. A good part of this analysis will fall to one of the engineering disciplines to accomplish.

A project design team may include the following roles:

- Owner
- Traditional design team members:
  - Project manager
  - Architect
  - HVAC&R engineer
  - Plumbing/fire protection engineer
  - Electrical engineer
  - Lighting designer
  - Structural engineer
  - Landscaping/site specialist
  - Civil engineer

- Energy analyst
- Environmental design consultant
- Commissioning authority
- Construction manager/contractor
- Cost estimator
- Building operator
- Building users/occupants
- Code enforcement official

The above lists the *possible roles* that might need to be filled on a reasonably large design project. Some roles may not be applicable or even needed on certain types of projects (e.g., civil engineer or landscaping/site specialist), and other roles may not be feasible to have represented in the early stages of project (e.g., building operator, building users, code enforcement official). Further, the variety of roles does not mean that there needs to be an equal number of distinct individuals to fill them; one individual may fill several roles: e.g., the architect often serves as project manager, the HVAC&R engineer as plumbing engineer or energy analyst, the electrical engineer as lighting designer, and a contractor on the team as cost estimator. Likewise, depending on the type of project, there could be other specialists as well.

Certain nontraditional roles are particularly important in green design:

Energy Analyst. Although this role has existed for some time, it assumes a much more intense and timely function in green design, as there is a need to quickly evaluate various ideas (and interactions between them) in terms of impact on energy. These can range from different building forms and architectural features to different mechanical and electrical systems. The person in this role must be intimately familiar with energy analysis modeling tools and able to provide feedback on ideas expressed reasonably quickly. In short, he or she is a much more integral part of a green design team than in a traditional design effort. In this respect, for a sizable project, it might be difficult for a single person to fill this role plus another as well.

Environmental Design Consultant. As owners begin to request green buildings from the design professions, a new discipline has emerged: the environmental design consultant (EDC). The role of this person is to integrate the design process across disciplines, with the intent of creating an outcome with much lower environmental impact and higher user satisfaction. Leading projects show that this can often be accomplished without adding cost. The EDC has input in areas such as site, water, waste, materials, indoor environmental quality, energy, durability, envelope design, renewable energy, and transportation. Although this guide will focus primarily on those areas pertinent to the HVAC&R design professional, it is becoming evident that this profession must broaden its sphere of concern in order to contribute meaningfully to the creation of green buildings.

An EDC would work collaboratively with the HVAC&R team and others throughout the process and may raise the following types of questions:

- Is the building orientation optimized for minimum energy use?
- Is the combined system of building envelope, including glazing choices and the HVAC system, optimized for minimum energy use and lowest life-cycle cost?
- Are the loads, occupancy, and design conditions properly described?
- Are the proposed analytical tools adequate to the task of computing life-cycle costs and guiding design decisions?
- Is the proposed mechanical approach going to deliver excellent air quality to occupants under all conditions?
- Is the proposed mechanical approach going to deliver thermal comfort to occupants under all conditions?
- Is the proposed mechanical approach going to be easy to maintain? Is there enough space for mechanicals and adequate access to service and perhaps to eventually replace them?
- Is the proposed mechanical approach going to give appropriate control of the system to users?
- Is the proposed mechanical approach going to consume a minimum amount of parasitic energy to run pumps and fans?
- Are there site or other conditions likely to impact the mechanical system in unusual ways?
- Have all the impacts of the building on the site and surroundings been identified and taken into account?
- Are the proposed systems properly sized for the loads?

While it may seem that the role of the environmental design consultant (EDC) is very similar to that of the energy analyst, the roles differ in that the EDC is more of a question-asker or issue-raiser than one who necessarily provides the answers. The EDC's brief is broader and more comprehensive in scope; his or her role is to stand back somewhat from the project and ask the broader questions regarding the environmental impact of the project. On rela-

tively small projects, however, it is quite possible that the same person would fill both roles.

Commissioning Authority. (Please refer also to chapter 19, "Commissioning.") The commissioning authority (CA) has the very important role of documenting the owner's project requirements as early as possible, starting in the pre-design phase of the project. This function is beneficial to both the owner and project team in that it condenses the mass of information into a single, cogent document; it records the various changes in design direction, why they occurred, and the assumptions made by the design team. The document is updated as changes occur throughout the project and tracks why these changes were necessary.

Successful cost-effective application of green design principles must start early and be defined in pre-design; this allows the team to look for synergies that help control hard and soft costs by more accurately defining design direction. The commissioning authority helps the design team define what the owner is communicating and can help draw out how the owner expects the building to function and perform.

The commissioning authority incorporates the information into the Owner's Project Requirements (OPR), which is used during the project as a benchmark for judging how well the project team meets the project requirements; it also serves as a written reminder of the goals and decisions that resulted in the final deliverable to the owner. The final version of the OPR should be refined to approximately 20 to 30 pages in length and delivered along with the commissioning report as a reminder of the designer's original charge and the assumptions that were made with the owner's knowledge and direction.

The OPR also serves as a guide to the building operating staff on how the facility was intended to operate and the features designed into the project. Development guidelines for the OPR are contained in ASHRAE Guideline 1, *The HVAC Commissioning Process* (latest approved version).

The design team described above is obviously more extensive than the traditional one. It is necessary to have a larger group involved to get everyone on board and pulling in the same direction. It also assists in achieving individual accountability for the goals.

The Team's Role

Green design requires clients to make decisions sooner, design documents to be more complete and comprehensive, the construction process better coordinated, and operators better trained and more diligent in maintaining facilities. All of this will impact the viability and success of a green project endeavor. Contractors may sound the cost and schedule alarm often due to their inexperience in new procedures. First-time application of sustainable development principles can result in slightly higher first costs, but this phenomenon will reverse itself as teams improve their learning curve. As the building industry becomes more familiar with applying these principles, lower costs of ownership will result.

In addition to the standard tasks associated with a design project, the design team is responsible for developing and implementing new concepts that will create a green project. For most, this will require learning on their own time, becoming familiar with new advances in software tools, green materials, and alternative systems. There is an abundance of information, and advances are occurring daily, requiring designers to add continuously to their knowledge base if they are going to be successful at developing green designs.

The greatest challenge to accomplishing green design is creating a team organizational structure that provides

- criteria for assessing how green the project is;
- strong leadership through the green design process to integrate team members;
- careful examination of design alternatives, costs, and schedule impacts; and
- documentation of success.

Strong leadership by experienced green building practitioners leading the team through the decision process can:

- Help overcome confusion about applying green principles
- Define what tasks are required to accomplish green design
- Identify who is responsible for each of the tasks
- Identify when tasks must be completed so as not to impede the design process or affect the project schedule
- Establish criteria for selection of green design features considered for incorporation into a project
- Assist with integrating selected green design goals into the construction documents
- Define the level of effort required for each of the green project goals
- Help contractors overcome psychological and physical constraints

- Establish how to track, measure, and document the success of accomplished project goals

The designers must also help inform their clients that there are costs for depletion of resources to be consumed beyond the cost of extraction. The practice of looking only at simple payback when analyzing alternatives based on extraction cost has never been realistic because there is no way to replace many resources at *any* cost.

Most design teams are eager to develop green designs when given the opportunity, but they lack the experience of actually integrating green design into their projects. They need assistance and guidance to integrate knowledge from each discipline and project member that, when combined, will result in a green design. In addition, most teams struggle with what makes a design green, how to incorporate green design principles, and the logistics of incorporating these principles into the design. Green design creates a need for a broader range of disciplines and experience and requires a process that focuses the team on achieving the goal of developing a green design. The process is necessary to ensure that a wider range of input and participation gets factored into the decision-making process.

The project team—from initial concept through construction documents, construction, commissioning, and building operations—must work as an integrated team if it is going to be successful at achieving better project performance, a basic principle of green design. This will require the project team to investigate new approaches and process more information than ever before as they strive to increase performance and lower the total cost of ownership. Their decision-making process must change from traditional emphasis on lowest first cost to emphasis on life-cycle cost.

This requires close collaboration of the project team combined with innovative thinking between disciplines. Supported by computer simulation tools, a process for selecting between alternatives should quantify first costs and life-cycle cost savings. Optimizing design tradeoffs, looking at all of the issues and principles contained in sustainable development as a whole instead of independently, are benefits that are often blurred by first cost.

Design team responsibility:

- Setting sustainability goals
- Energy optimization
- Life-cycle cost optimization
- Materials selections
- Systems integration

- Environmental impact minimization
- Documenting design intent
- Commissioning the building
- Training the operator

Team Leadership

The integrated building design process requires more effort between the team members to explore the various opportunities to incorporate sustainable principles into the project. For example, the architect, mechanical engineers, and electrical engineers must interact closely to develop a high-performance building that will provide an improved work environment, lower operating costs, and minimized consumption of natural resources. Strong leadership helps to meet these objectives.

Designers can elect to develop their own criteria, or they can use established criteria. The effort of deciding what should be considered green design is often made easier by using one of the established rating systems developed through a balanced consensus process.

THE ENGINEER'S ROLE

The HVAC&R engineer is a crucial player in the design of a "green building." In fact, it is virtually impossible (and certainly not cost-effective) to design a green building without major involvement of that engineer.

The HVAC&R engineer must get outside the normal "box" in which he or she lives and become much more involved. This means moving beyond just responding to questions asked by others. It is making positive contributions—even initiating discussions—on how project goals can be achieved. These discussions must move beyond what the most efficient mechanical systems or equipment for the project are.

Engineers help analyze the various options to be considered, create mathematical computer models that are used to judge alternatives, provide creative input, and develop new techniques and solutions. The HVAC engineer can be invaluable in helping the architect decide which type of glazing will provide the maximum quantity of natural light while at the same time analyzing the heat transfer characteristics of the glazing options. The HVAC engineer can also help the architect select structural systems and exterior walls to utilize thermal mass features to reduce equipment needs. Working with the electrical engineer and architect, the HVAC&R engineer can offer ideas and various options, such as incorporating daylighting and lighting controls to reduce artificial light when natural light is available, which, in turn, can

result in lower cooling requirements and lowered HVAC requirements to meet peak load. Lower equipment sizes translate into reduced structural and electrical requirements, lower operating and maintenance costs, and lower construction costs, all of which lower the total cost of ownership.

The plumbing engineer, working with the structural and civil engineers and landscape architect, can reduce the facility's potable water, sewer, and stormwater conveyance requirements. Some examples are waterless urinals or use of stormwater or graywater for irrigation of vegetation or to flush toilets. Depending on the type of building, water from condensate can be used for graywater applications or for cooling tower makeup. The design engineer must weigh the benefits of water-cooled condensers versus air-cooled condensers and the water versus electrical energy consumed by each. The engineer must examine the site climate and determine what alternatives and strategies can best be applied and develop life-cycle analysis to guide the owner through the decision process posed by the maze of complex issues surrounding green design.

SUCCESSFUL APPROACHES TO DESIGN

Universities throughout the country are successfully implementing changes in how projects are designed, constructed, and operated using green principles. Emory University's Whitehead Biomedical Research Building, for example, utilizes enthalpy wheels that recover 83% of the energy being exhausted by the general exhaust system; captures air-conditioning condensate to displace potable water otherwise used for cooling tower makeup; and captures all the rainwater from the roof for site irrigation, displacing over 3 million gallons of potable water usage per year.

The following two sections describe two approaches to the green building design process that have proved successful.

Low Energy Design Process: NREL's Experience

This energy design process was used to design and construct the Thermal Test Facility (TTF) at the National Renewable Energy Laboratory (NREL). The TTF is a 10,000 ft^2 (929 m^2) office and light laboratory building constructed in 1996 in Golden, Colorado. Actual performance data collected for more than one year show that the TTF costs 63% less to operate than an equivalent building that complies with ASHRAE Standard 90.1. The process used is summarized in "NREL's Nine-Step Process for Low-Energy Building Design" on page 33.

Further information may be obtained from an *ASHRAE Journal* article (Hayter, S., Torcellini, P., Judkoff, R., "Optimizing Building and HVAC Systems," *ASHRAE Journal*, December 1999).

Integrated Design Process: Canada's Experience

Recent building design experience in North America and Europe led to the recognition of key factors that are relevant to the achievement of very high levels of environmental performance. These include use of an integrated design process (IDP), which incorporates passive and bio-climatic approaches and also includes an iterative process. (For a description of a specific program developed to investigate the feasibility of designing high performance buildings using this process, see the sidebar on Canada's C-2000 program beginning on page 34 of this chapter.)

What Does "Integrated Design" Mean?

One of the key attributes of a well-designed, cost-effective green building is that it is designed in an "integrated" fashion, wherein all systems and components work together to produce overall functionality and environmental performance. This has a major impact on the design process for HVAC-related systems, as conceptual development must begin with HVAC system integration into the building form and into the approaches being taken to meet other green building aspects. For example:

- HVAC systems that employ natural ventilation and underfloor air distribution, often used in green buildings, can have major impacts on building form.

- Other building energy innovations, such as daylighting and passive solar, often have significant impacts on the design of the HVAC system.

- On-site energy systems that produce waste heat, such as fuel cells, engine-driven generators, or micro-turbines, will affect the design of HVAC systems in order for waste heat to be most effectively utilized.

Beyond these form-giving elements, there are many other specific features of a green building that

NREL's NINE-STEP PROCESS FOR LOW-ENERGY BUILDING DESIGN

1. Create a base case building model to quantify base case energy use and costs. The base case building is solar neutral (equal glazing areas on all wall orientations) and meets the requirements of applicable energy efficiency codes such as ASHRAE Standard 90.1 and 90.2.

2. Complete a parametric analysis to determine sensitivities to specific load components. Sequentially eliminate loads from the base case building, such as conductive losses, lighting loads, solar gains, and plug loads.

3. Develop preliminary design solutions. The design team brainstorms possible solutions that may include strategies to reduce lighting and cooling loads by incorporating daylighting or to meet heating loads with passive solar heating.

4. Incorporate preliminary design solutions into a computer model of the proposed building design. Energy impact and cost-effectiveness of each variant is determined by comparing the energy with the original base case building and with the other variants. Those variants having the most favorable results should be incorporated into the building design.

5. Prepare preliminary set of construction drawings. These drawings are based on the decisions made in step 3.

6. Identify an HVAC system that will meet the predicted loads. The HVAC system should work with the building envelope and exploit the specific climatic characteristics of the site for maximum efficiency. Often, the HVAC system is much smaller than in a typical building.

7. Finalize plans and specifications. Ensure the building plans are properly detailed and that the specifications are accurate. The final design simulation should incorporate all cost-effective features. Savings exceeding 50% from a base case building are frequently possible with this approach.

8. Rerun simulations before design changes are made during construction. Verify that changes will not adversely affect the building's energy performance.

9. Commission all equipment and controls. Educate building operators. A building that is not properly commissioned will not meet the energy efficiency design goals. Building operators must understand how to properly operate the building to maximize its performance.

CANADA'S C-2000 PROGRAM

The C-2000 Program was designed in 1993 by Natural Resources Canada, a government agency, to demonstrate the feasibility of achieving very high levels of building performance. The program's technical requirements cover energy performance,[1] environmental impacts, indoor environment, functionality, and a range of other related parameters.[2] It was therefore expected that incremental costs for design and construction would be substantial. After a preliminary analysis of then-prevalent project costs and an informal survey of designers, provision was made for support of incremental costs in both the design and construction phase. Contributions were provided according to a sliding scale, ranging from 7% in large projects to 12% in small projects.

Even though the program targeted a select group of clients known to have an interest in high performance, it was assumed that some level of financial incentive would be required to make the program a success. However, the extent of incentives required and the best point of intervention within the project development process were very much open to question.

The first two C-2000 projects received support according to this formula in the range of $400,000 to $750,000 CAN, and funding of this order of magnitude was also planned for subsequent projects. However, after the first six projects were designed and two of them had been completed, it was found that that incremental capital costs were less than expected, partly due to the fact that designers used technologies that were less sophisticated and expensive than anticipated.[3]

A careful investigation of the first two C-2000 projects constructed, Crestwood 8[4] and Green on the Grand,[5] indicated that the marginal costs for both projects, including design and constructio phases, was 7%-8% more than a conventional building, a rather modest increase. Even more interesting, the designers all agreed that application of the integrated design process required by the C-2000 program was the main reason why high levels of performance could still be reached. It also appeared that most of the benefit of intervention was achieved during the design process.

C-2000, now called the integrated design process (IDP) process, includes the key steps listed on page 35.

The design process itself emphasizes the following sequence:

- First minimize heating and cooling loads through orientation, building configuration, an efficient building envelope, and careful consideration of amount, type, and location of fenestration
- Meet these loads through the maximum use of renewables and the use of efficient HVAC systems;
- Iterate the process to produce at least two, and preferably three, design concept alternatives.

The integrated design process contains no elements that are radically new but, rather, integrates well-proven approaches into a systematic total process. From an engineering perspective, the integrated design process permits the skills and experience of mechanical, electrical, and other engineers to be integrated at the design concept level from the very beginning of the design process. For example, reduced cooling loads will result in smaller and more economical systems, which in turn can reduce capital and replacement costs. When carried out in a spirit of cooperation among key persons, this results in a design that is highly efficient with minimal, and sometimes zero, incremental capital costs, along with reduced long-term operating and maintenance costs.

Most project interventions are now focused on providing advice on the design process at the very early stage. Six projects have been constructed on this basis, and all have either achieved the C-2000 performance requirements or have come very close. Capital costs have been either slightly above or slightly below base budgets. The most hopeful sign that the IDP approach is taking root is that several owners have subsequently used the same process for buildings that have not benefitted from any subsidy.

Simple software design support tools have been produced to help design teams enrolled in the C-2000 program. One outlines generic design steps and provides a simple way for designers to record their performance targets and strategies; another facilitates the task of having the client and design team reach a consensus on the relative importance of various issues. The C-2000 IDP process is now being used as a model for development of a generic international model by Solar Heating and Cooling Task 23 of the International Energy Agency, and discussions are underway with the Royal Architectural Institute of Canada (RAIC) to see if the process can be accepted as an alternative form of delivery of professional services.

---

1. At the time, the energy requirement was 50% better than the ASHRAE 90.1 standard (the benchmark is now the Model National Energy Code for Buildings, MNECB). Both are North American standards for good practice.

2. *C-2000 Program Requirements*, N. Larsson, Editor; Natural Resources Canada; Ottawa, October 1993, updated April 1996.

3. The conservative approach of designers is based primarily on their perception that they might face legal liability problems if they use exotic and unproven technologies.

4. *Technical Report on Bentall Corporation Crestwood 8 C-2000 Building*, April 1996, CETC, Natural Resources Canada.

5. *Technical Report on Green on the Grand C-2000 Building*, April 1996, CETC, Natural Resources Canada.

affect (or are affected by) HVAC systems to achieve the best overall performance. Some of these strongly impact HVAC system conceptual design, and some require only minor adjustments to HVAC specifications. Such features might include:

- Effective use of ventilation (and IAQ sensors linked to the ventilation system) to improve indoor air quality.
- Provision of user controls for temperature and humidity control.
- Reduced system capacities to reflect lower internal loads and building envelope loads.
- Selection of non-ozone-depleting refrigerants.
- Reduction and optimization of building energy usage below the levels of ASHRAE Standard 90.1-based codes or other applicable state and local energy codes. (Levels of reduction of as much as 40% to 50% below Standard 90.1 are becoming more common and are encouraged.)
- Use of reclaimed water for cooling tower make-up, and minimization of cooling tower blow-down discharge to the sanitary sewer system.
- Commissioning of the key systems, especially the HVAC systems.

Key Steps

The integrated design process includes the following elements:

- Ensuring that as many of the interested parties as possible are represented on the design team as early as possible; this includes not only architects, engineers, and owner (client) but also construction specialist (contractor), cost estimator, operations/maintenance person, and other specialists (outlined below).
- Interdisciplinary work among architects, engineers, costing specialists, operations people, and other relevant persons right from the beginning of the design process
- Discussion of the relative importance of various performance and cost issues and the establishment of a consensus on these matters between client and designers and among the designers themselves
- Provision of a design facilitator (or environmental design consultant) to raise performance issues throughout the process and to bring specialized knowledge to the table
- Addition of an energy specialist to test various design assumptions through the use of energy simulations throughout the process, to provide relatively objective information on a key aspect of performance

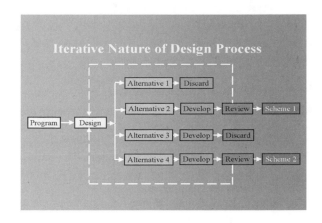

Figure 4-2 The iterative design process.

- Addition of subject specialists (e.g., for daylighting, thermal storage) for short consultations with the design team.
- Clear articulation of performance targets and strategies to be updated throughout the process by the design team.

Iterative Design Refinement

The design process requires the development of design alternatives. To come up with the most effective combination, these alternatives must be evaluated, refined, evolved, and finally optimized. This is the concept of *iterative design,* wherein the design is progressively refined over time, as shown in Figure 4-2.

Often fee and schedule pressures lead the designer to want to lock in a single design concept at the beginning of the project and stick with it throughout. But this precludes the opportunity to come up with a "better" system that reflects the unique combination of loads and design integration opportunities for this specific building. This better design usually evolves during schematics and early design development in the iterative process.

CONCEPT DEVELOPMENT

The Big Picture

Designers should always keep in mind the three major steps for achieving a green design:

- Reduce the loads
- Apply the most efficient systems
- Look for synergies.

Reduce the Loads. If you have a building with a normal 500-ton cooling load, is it possible to provide a more comfortable environment with, say, only 300 tons? The team would have to really work to achieve this: solar loads on the building would have to be reduced; lighting loads to the space would also have to be lowered; maybe the building could use daylight rather than electric light during the day, so the building shape would be influenced; the site for the building, its shape, its thermal mass, and its orientation could all work together to reduce the cooling load. Early and quick modeling can provide interesting information to assist decisions.

Similar things could be done with the heating load. Does the winter sun provide much of the building's heating needs during the day? With design changes, could the sun do more?

These considerations are usually not included in the world of the HVAC engineer, where the energy-efficient HVAC engineer gets the drawings, calculates the loads, and applies efficient systems. But one cannot achieve significant reductions by simply doing the same old job just a little bit better.

The HVAC or energy engineer can make a positive contribution to achievement of a green design. The value of the engineer to the project is significantly increased, and the results are reduced heating and cooling loads.

Someone once suggested an attidudinal approach to building design that says the designer should strive toward making the building inherently "work by itself." Building systems are there simply to fine tune the operation and pick up the extreme design conditions. In contrast, buildings traditionally are often designed like advanced fighter aircraft: if the flight computers are lost, the pilot cannot fly the plane.

Apply the Most Efficient Systems. This is the world of the energy-efficient engineer. This is the area where ASHRAE generally operates. While it is very important, it is not enough by itself.

Look for Synergies. The preceding two major steps have the potential of increasing capital costs. Therefore, you might have a wonderful, energy-efficient building that will not get built due to high first cost, or the "value-engineering knives" come out and cut the project back to a traditional, affordable project—proof perhaps that "green cannot work." Part of the solution to get around this syndrome is to look for synergies of how building elements can work *together*. This also relates to the cost transfer mentioned earlier.

If a building has a large southern exposure, exterior-shading devices might significantly reduce the summer solar load while still admitting lower angle winter sun. Daylight (but not direct sun) would allow shutting off the electric lights on sunny days. The HVAC system for the south perimeter zones could be significantly reduced in size and cost as the simultaneous solar and electric lighting loads are reduced. Indeed, the very nature of the HVAC system might

well be simplified due to the significant load reduction. Resulting cost savings can be used to pay for some or all of the additional treatments.

A major benefit to an integrated design that is on budget is you avoid wasting a lot of time on elemental payback exercises and value engineering (and cost cutting) because you are on budget. Many of the integrated solutions work—such that, if you save by cutting out an element such as the exterior shades, there is an additional cost in another area such as the size of the HVAC system.

The Nitty-Gritty

Success of green design starts with establishment of the project's goals and objectives, defining roles and responsibilities, establishing communication between design team members, developing a decision-making process, and establishing the level of effort that will be required by each member of the team. A workshop is often conducted to introduce the team to sustainable development principles, establish documentation requirements, and provide guidance in selecting project goals and tracking how well those goals are met. Commercially available software can assist in organizing process design.

The creation of documentation supporting both the decision-making process and the results of decisions is important in determining the success of green design efforts as well as establishing what was or was not successful and why. Like a business plan or construction plan, it is important to measure milestones so that adjustments can be made to correct course deviations in reaching the goals. A green design plan should also identify the assumptions made for life-cycle cost analysis, and the results should be documented for comparison against actual performance. Learning from the deviations that occur will allow teams as well as individuals to grow from the experience.

A green design and documentation plan provides the organizational structure required for successful projects. The software tools available today also increase communication within a team, help stimulate innovative thinking, and help teams optimize design trade-offs by grouping related issues.

The team must develop consensus criteria such as:

- Selecting a site that minimizes environmental impacts
- Utilizing existing infrastructure to the maximum extent possible to avoid building additional infrastructure to support the project
- Minimizing the impact of automobiles and the infrastructure required to support them, such as parking, roads and highways

- Developing high-performance buildings that enhance occupant productivity and comfort, minimize energy and water consumption, and are durable and recyclable at the end of their useful service life.

Based on the consensus criteria selected, identify potential goals. Once goals are identified, develop tasks necessary to obtain these goals, including studying the impacts these goals will have upon

- project cost, schedule, and energy and water usage;
- indoor environmental quality, operational and maintenance costs, life of the building, and occupant productivity;
- environmental impacts at the end of the building's or whole facility's useful service life.

Next, assign roles and responsibilities by identifying who is responsible for each task, when the task must be completed, and in what chronological order tasks must be completed so as to facilitate the tracking and management of the green design process.

A good green design and documentation plan provides the team the information needed to make informed decisions at specific milestones in the project.

OVERVIEW OF CHAPTERS 5 – 16

Chapters 5 through 16 are devoted to the various elements of the conceptual design process—from the design impact of architectural features and load determination, through the different major mechanical and electrical subsystems, and finally to analyzing, testing, and expressing these concepts. It is in these chapters that the reader will encounter the numerous ASHRAE GreenTips this guide offers, practical information that sets this guide apart from other green documents and should prove most useful to HVAC&R designers.

ONE FIRM'S GREEN BUILDING DESIGN PROCESS CHECKLIST

- ❑ Create an integrated, cross-disciplinary design team, committed to sustainability and aware of environmental issues, that includes all those impacted by the building.
- ❑ Pre-charrette and charrette meetings should include the project owner, architects and landscape architects, engineers, an energy engineer with experience in computer simulation of building energy consumption, facility occupants and users (including purchasing, human resources, and managers), facility manager, contractors when hired, interior designer, local utility representatives, cost consultant, and other specialty consultants.
- ❑ Review the client's unique operational characteristics. Decide what green design issues will make the most positive impact and the most sense for the corporation in order to provide focus and priority.
- ❑ Introduce environmental standards, goals, and strategies early in the design process and clearly state target requirements in the construction documents.
- ❑ Channel development to urban areas with existing infrastructures, protecting greenfields and preserving habitat and natural resources.
- ❑ Increase localized density to conform to existing or desired density goals by utilizing sites that are located within an existing minimum development density of 80,000 square feet per acre.

- ❑ Channel development to areas with existing transportation infrastructure that provides non-automobile-dependent choices.
- ❑ Select a location for the project within ½ mile of a rail station (commuter rail, light rail, or subway), within ¼ mile of two or more bus lines, or in a "live, work, walk, mixed use environment."
- ❑ Reduce the overall building footprint and use the space efficiently.
- ❑ Make important decisions on the mechanical load, daylighting, solar absorption, response to local climate and environment, and key building elements at the beginning in order to define subsequent decisions.
- ❑ Establish performance targets as a reference point.
- ❑ Integrate recycling systems into every aspect from reusing existing building materials to purchasing new materials.
- ❑ Design for disassembly at the end of the building's useful life.
- ❑ Educate contractor and subcontractor in sustainable practices.
- ❑ Evaluate and benchmark sustainable solutions at the same intervals as budgets and schedules.
- ❑ Appoint a team member to ensure sustainability goals are met at each stage, to gather research data, and to advocate for environmental choices during the course of the project.
- ❑ Tie compensation for the architect and design team to achieved building performance.

Chapter 5
Architectural Design Impacts

One of an architect's primary functions, as part of the design team, is to create an environment. This environment has both a psychological and a physiological effect on the occupants, which in turn impacts human productivity, building operational efficiency, and effectiveness of natural resource use.

Site location, building orientation and geometry, building envelope, arrangement of spaces, and local climatic characteristics are all elements the design team must address, and the result will have a distinct impact on both the occupants' environment and efficiency of the building. Buildings that use the attributes of their surroundings effectively as part of a project's design features, through the application of green design principles, generally provide psychological and physiological benefits for the occupants and tend to be more efficient.

As described in chapter 4, developing the owner's project requirements (OPR) is an essential precursor to identifying a project's green design goals and the functionality and performance the design team is charged with meeting. The OPR is the tool used in assessing the many options a design team develops during design. This chapter is intended to help designers understand the impacts some architectural decisions have and how these decisions affect green design goals.

Authors contributing to this chapter are Jay Enck and David Grumman.

SITE LOCATION

Consideration of the implications of site selection is essential to minimize the negative environmental impacts that may accompany a project, from construction activities to those that will occupy the facility. Prudent site selection can lower first cost, operating and maintenance costs, environmental cost, and people cost. Green design should consider the true cost of projects that encroach on animal habitats, prime farmland, or public parklands. Other considerations are transportation of materials and labor to construct the project; loss of land that supports bio-diversity; the highways, roads, and bridges required to provide access to the facility; the infrastructure needed to support operation of the facility; and the natural resources needed to transport occupants to and from the facility.

While design engineers may have little say about the above considerations, it is wise for the architect to involve the engineers early in the site selection process, when possible. Matters such as nearby pollution sources, ambient air quality, groundwater levels, site drainage, availability of or access to various energy sources (including renewables), and other not-so-obvious characteristics can have implications for a successful design in the later stages.

Further guidance is offered by the U.S. Green Building Council reference guide, which has a specific section on site selection.

SITE ORIENTATION

Building orientation affects many aspects of green design, ranging from energy performance to visual stimulation of the building occupant. Considerations of solar orientation; prevailing breezes; availability of natural light; shading created by natural vegetation, topography, or adjacent structures; and views—all impact the designer's choice of how to orient the building on a site. Site orientation can also affect landscaping choices and irrigation water consumption. The benefits, drawbacks, and trade-offs should be weighed when choosing the orientation, and the engineer members of the design team can be particularly helpful here.

Buildings that minimize east and west exposures, especially where a lot of glass is used, are generally more energy efficient because of the huge solar heat gains associated with east- and west-facing elevations during cooling months. If a goal of the owner is to use natural breezes to help meet cooling requirements, then the building needs to be oriented with operable windows and the dominant elevations perpendicular to the prevailing breezes to capture windward/leeward effects and better draw outside air through the building. (In some instances this may conflict with minimizing east and west elevations to limit solar heat gain.)

Here is where computer simulations, performed by an experienced energy analyst and yielding fast and factual results, can assist the design team by evaluating nuances in building orientation and the effect various stacking and massing options have on building performance.

BUILDING FORM/GEOMETRY

A building's form (stacking, massing, and overall geometry) has a significant impact on a building's functionality, energy efficiency, and occupant performance. One of the most important considerations in green design is the effect form has on natural lighting.

Glazing size, orientation, and an occupant's distance from glazing, in addition to glazing characteristics, determine the quality and quantity of natural light reaching a building's interior. The most desirable natural light comes from the north; it has the least solar heat gain associated with it and is composed of diffused light, which does not cause glare.

The distance natural light will travel into the interior of a building is dependent on window and ceiling height. The quantity of light is dependent on the glazing area. The quality of light is determined by orientation and glazing characteristics. The usefulness of natural light to meet task lighting requirements is a function of light quality on task surfaces. All of these factors affect the form a building takes to meet the requirement for natural daylighting.

Several sources of information are available to assist designers with daylighting strategies. First, chapter 11, "Lighting," in this guide offers some basic considerations on daylighting, concentrating on applicability, pros and cons, and cost. Two others, directed more toward architectural design aspects, are:

- "*Tips for Daylighting with Window,*" available at *eande.lbl.gov/BTP/pub/designguide/download.htm* and
- "Daylighting Design" by Benjamin Evans, in *Time-Saver Standards for Architectural Design Data*, McGraw-Hill, Inc., 1997.

Daylighting is only one of many green factors that may influence building geometry. Buildings designed for natural ventilation could be configured in a form to best capture prevailing breezes and direct them for most beneficial use. Stepping a building back as it rises in height could allow solar access to an adjacent property. The roof of a stepped building could also be vegetated, reducing the quantity and rate of stormwater to be treated.

BUILDING ENVELOPE

The building envelop performs the primary function of keeping the weather out (and, when feasible, letting its good aspects in), and its design is a key factor that defines how well a building and its occupants perform. (Examples of how the factors discussed in this chapter affect occupant performance are contained in Judith Heerwagen's productivity studies performed at a manufacturing facility designed to maximize the use of natural light [Heerwagen 2001].)

Daylighting and Energy

Access to outdoor views and natural light have positive psychological and physiological effect upon building occupants, but, as noted in Ms. Heerwagen's study, too much light and glare can have negative psychological and physiological impacts (Heerwagen 2001). Analysis of the building envelope utilizing daylighting simulation programs can help a design team optimize building geometry, define glazing characteristics based on glazing orientation, and provide essential information needed in performing an energy analysis of the facility.

Daylighting programs only provide one side of what a design team must consider when creating a building envelope. Honing it to minimize heating and cooling energy consumption requires energy modeling of the building, which is where the engineering side of the design team comes in during this phase of design.

Several software programs exist that allow the results of the daylighting model to be entered into the energy model. This combination of programs allows evaluation of different glazing characteristics, HVAC system types, and life-cycle costs of various combinations to determine which best meets project goals. (Programs such as *Radiance* and *e-quest* are available over the internet at no cost -- and are terrific tools in developing a green design.)

Moisture Intrusion

Although a primary function of the building envelop is protecting the building interior and its occupants from inclement weather, an astonishing fact is that 80% of insurance claims against architects are related to moisture intrusion through the building envelope. Further, moisture intrusion is a leading cause of sick building syndrome. Water can enter through the building envelope by three methods: direct rainwater intrusion, water vapor transmission, and negative pressurization (unwanted infiltration).

Design teams often use "belt-and-suspenders" approaches to try to avoid direct rainwater intrusion but then fail to test the design and installation to ensure that the design intent is met. Chapter 19 discusses in detail how commissioning helps ensure that the building performs as intended and verifies that this aspect of green design intent is met.

Often overlooked in design is water vapor transmission into and across the building envelope. Appropriate members of the design team should examine each proposed building envelope assembly type and conduct a vapor transmission analysis for each. Calculation methods for evaluating vapor transmission and determining the likelihood of moisture collecting within the building envelope can be found in ASHRAE's *Handbook—Fundamentals*. Indoor air quality problems and building failure resulting from moisture collecting within the building envelope has occurred in most areas of the United States and Canada.

While negative pressurization of a building in an arid climate generally has little air quality impact, indoor air quality problems *can* result when it occurs in a hot and humid—and sometimes even a moderate—climate. The resulting infiltration of humid air, in addition to being an added air-conditioning cost, can result in condensation in unexpected—and sometimes unseen—places. The ensuing problems (such as mold, mildew, spore production, etc.) can be so severe as to result in building evacuation and exten-

sive remedial costs, sometimes even exceeding the original cost of the building. (Having to build a building twice is not green!) Design teams need to be very conscious of building pressurization and ensure that the building envelope is appropriately pressurized for the climate and intended building use. Here in particular, coordination of HVAC design with building envelope design is critical to achieving good indoor environmental quality.

ARRANGEMENT/GROUPING OF SPACES

Although the owner's program, functional needs, daylighting constraints, aesthetics, and many non-engineering green factors go into an architect's determination of how spaces are grouped and arranged in a building, what results can also impact how efficiently the HVAC system performs.

Avoiding unnecessary energy use by shutting down or scaling back the operation of systems serving building areas not being used is a basic green design principle (use only what is needed), and doing this depends in part on how spaces are arranged or grouped. If a department or group of occupants is known to work on a different schedule than most others, having that area served by a separate air-handling system, for instance, would avoid the need to run one or more large air-handling systems to accommodate the needs of that one group.

While this is only one factor of many an architect must consider, there is no reason why the HVAC engineer should not ensure that the architect is aware of this factor where it may be applicable.

CLIMATIC IMPACTS

Climatic factors are those conditions, features, or influences external to the building that can have an impact on the building. Some are natural, and some are man-made. The key characteristics are: ambient temperature and humidity patterns, ambient air quality, potential pollution sources, solar availability and intensity, wind patterns, soil conditions, freshwater availability and quality, and site drainage.

The climatic characteristics of a site obviously have an impact on how the building performs, especially its energy performance and impact on its surroundings. The design team should be aware of such key characteristics, with each member examining them from the standpoint of his or her own expertise: How will each affect my portion of the design? the overall design? Can any be utilized or accommodated in a way to further the goal of green design for this building?

Chapter 6

Conceptual Engineering Design— Load Determination

The traditional load determination methods, such as the CLTD/SCL/CLF method or rules of thumb, are rough first approximations based on old correlations or simplified heat transfer calculations. Designing low energy buildings requires the engineer to have a thorough understanding of the dynamic nature of the interactions of the building with the environment and the occupants. To optimize the design, detailed computer simulations allow the engineer to model accurately the major loads and interactions.

Loads can be divided into those stemming from the envelope and those from internal sources. Envelope loads include the impacts of the architectural features; heat and moisture transfer through the walls, roof, floor, and windows; and infiltration. Internal loads include lights, equipment, people, and process equipment. Examine all of the loads in two ways: separately, to determine their relative impacts, and together, to determine their interactions.

The engineer must also understand the energy sources and flows in the building and their location, magnitude, and timing. Once the engineer understands these sources and flows, he/she can be creative in coming up with solutions. The charts in Figure 6-1 show how average energy use breaks

Authors contributing to this chapter are Michael Deru, David Grumman, Malcolm Lewis, Blair McCarry, Ron Perkins, and Mick Schwedler.

down in typical office buildings at three different climatic locations in the United States. As designs are developed, breakdowns such as these should be kept in mind so that the energy-using areas that matter most are given priority in the design process.

Figure 6-1 shows how buildings use energy differently in different climatic zones. When trying to minimize energy use in buildings, the first step is to identify which aspects of building operation offer the greatest energy-saving opportunities. For example, as shown in the pie charts, in Chicago, the reduction of space heating energy would be the first priority, whereas in Miami and Philadelphia, the first priority would be reduction of energy used in lighting. In Philadelphia the second priority would be space heating, but in Miami it would be space cooling.

To find energy end-use statistics for many types of buildings (office, education, health care, lodging, retail, etc.) based on building location, age, size, and principal energy sources, consult the *Commercial Buildings Energy Consumption Tool* found at *http://www.eere.energy.gov/buildings/energydata.cfm*.

ENERGY IMPACTS OF ARCHITECTURAL FEATURES

For economic reasons, it is very important to focus your efforts in the following sequence: *Reduce loads first.*

Work with architects to improve the thermal envelope, especially in areas of external shading of

43

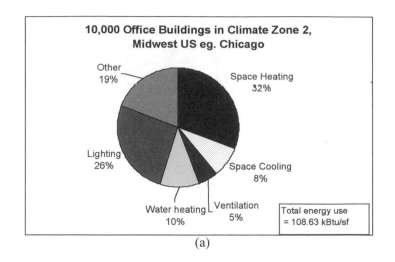

(a)

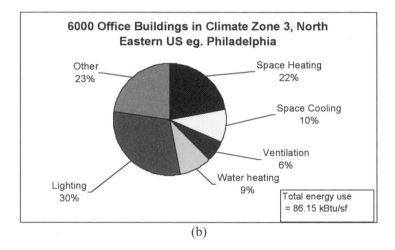

(b)

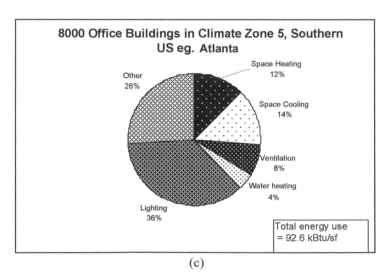

(c)

Figure 6-1 Average office building energy use in U.S.

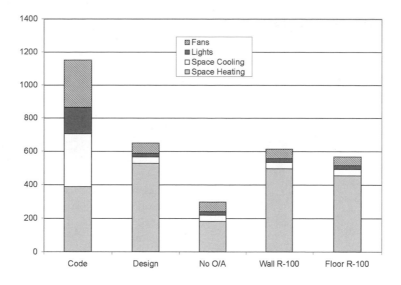

Figure 6-2 Sample parametric analysis to determine relative impacts of building envelope.

glazing; spectrally selective glazing, appropriately placed and sized; good roof and wall insulation with a radiant barrier; and orientation of building (east-west long axis).

To gain an understanding of how the proposed design of the building affects energy use, the engineer should perform a series of parametric simulations on the building in the specific location. In the first pass, take each load out of the energy balance one at a time and note the effect on overall energy use.

For instance, set the wall thermal resistance to a very high value (such as R-100) to effectively remove wall conductive heat transfer from the energy balance. Continue to do this individually with the floors, roofs, and windows. Then remove the window solar gain and the daylighting. The final envelope load is infiltration, which may or may not be important depending on whether the building is pressurized by the outside air ventilation. Then look at the effect of outside air by setting it to zero. Plot the results for each case by annual energy use or by peak load to compare the impacts, as illustrated in Figure 6-1. A "code" building would be the building that meets the minimum requirements of the current ASHRAE/IESNA Standard 90.1, and the "design" building is a proposed building design.

Look for creative solutions to minimize the impact of each load, starting with those with the largest impact or those that are the easiest to implement. From the parametric analysis example in Figure 6-1, outside air has the largest impact on the annual energy use. One solution to this problem may be to

monitor CO_2 levels to reduce the ventilation requirements. If solar gain through the windows is a large problem, look at orientation, size, and location of the windows, glass type, and possibly external shading.

THERMAL/MASS TRANSFER OF ENVELOPE

Basic, steady-state energy transfer through building envelopes is well known, well understood, and easy to calculate. Increased R-values are certainly beneficial in heating climates, with recommended amounts spelled out in ASHRAE's energy standard (Standard 90.1, latest approved edition). While values above those recommended can be beneficial in simple structures, high values can be counterproductive over a heating/cooling season in more complex structures. It is always wise to evaluate R-value benefits through the application of load and energy simulation programs.

The effects of thermal mass are sometimes not as easy to gauge intuitively, so the above-mentioned simulation programs, properly applied, are very useful in this regard. If thermal mass is significant in the building being planned (or if increased mass would be easy to vary as optional design choices), then such programs are almost essential for evaluating the "flywheel" effects of thermal mass on both loads and longer-term energy use.

ASHRAE GreenTip 1 describes a technique for combining nighttime ventilation with a building's thermal mass to achieve load and/or energy savings.

ASHRAE GreenTip #1: Night Precooling

GENERAL DESCRIPTION

Night precooling involves the circulation of cool air within a building during the nighttime hours with the intent of cooling the structure. The cooled structure is then able to serve as a heat sink during the daytime hours, reducing the mechanical cooling required. The naturally occurring thermal storage capacity of the building is thereby utilized to smooth the load curve and for potential energy savings. More details on the concept of thermal mass on building loads are included in the chapter on "Architectural Design Impacts."

There are two variations on night precooling. One, termed *night ventilation precooling*, involves the circulation of outdoor air into the space during the naturally cooler nighttime hours. This can be considered a passive technique except for any fan power requirement needed to circulate the outdoor air through the space. The night ventilation precooling system benefits the building indoor air quality through the cleansing effect of introducing more ventilation air. With the other variation, *mechanical precooling*, the building mechanical cooling system is operated during the nighttime hours to precool the building space to a setpoint usually lower than that of normal daytime hours.

Consider these key parameters when evaluating either concept:

- local diurnal temperature variation,
- ambient humidity levels, and
- the thermal coupling of the circulated air to the building mass.

The electric utility rate structure for peak and off-peak loads also is important to determine the cost-effectiveness, in particular for a mechanical precooling scheme.

A number of published studies show significant reductions in overall operating costs by the proper precooling and discharge of building thermal storage. The lower overall costs result from load shifting from the day to the nighttime with its associated off-peak utility rates. For example, Braun (1990) showed significant energy cost savings of 10% to 50% and peak power requirements of 10% to 35% over a traditional nighttime setup control strategy. The percent savings were found to be most significant when lower ambient temperatures allowed night ventilation cooling to be performed.

For a system incorporating precooling to be considered truly a green design concept, the total energy used through the entire 24-hour day should be lower than without precooling. A system that uses outdoor air to do the precooling only requires the relatively lower power needed to drive the circulation fans, compared to a system that incorporates mechanical precooling. Electrical energy provided by the utility during peak demand periods also may be "dirtier" than that provided during normal periods, depending on the utility and circumstances.

The system designer needs to be aware of the introduction of additional humidity into the space with the use of night ventilation. Thus, the concept of night ventilation precooling is better suited for drier climates. A mechanical nighttime precooling system will prevent the introduction of additional humidity into the space by the natural dehumidification it provides, but at the expense of greater energy usage compared to night ventilation alone.

Both variations (night ventilation and night mechanical precooling) are not 100% efficient in the thermal energy storage in the building mass, particularly if the building is highly coupled (thermally) with the outside environment. Certain building concepts used in Europe are designed to increase the exposure of the air supply or return with the interior building mass (see, for example, Andersson et al. 1979). This concept will increase the overall efficiency of the thermal storage mass.

For either type of system, the designer must carefully analyze the structure and interaction with the HVAC system air supply using transient simulations in order to assess the feasibility with their particular project. A number of techniques and commercially available computer codes exist for this analysis (Balaras 1995).

WHEN/WHERE IT'S APPLICABLE

Night precooling would be applicable in the following circumstances:

- When the ambient nighttime temperatures are low enough to provide sufficient opportunity to cool the building structure through ventilation air. Ideally, a low ambient humidity level would also occur. A hot, dry environment, such as the southwestern United States, is an ideal potential area for this concept.

The author of this GreenTip is Thomas Lawrence.

ASHRAE GreenTip #1: Night Precooling (continued)

- When the building occupants would be more tolerant of the potential for slightly cooler temperatures during the morning hours.
- When the owner and design team are willing to include such a system concept and to commit to (1) a proper analysis of the dynamics of the building thermal performance and (2) the refinement of the control strategy upon implementation to fine-tune the system performance.
- More massive buildings, or those built with heavier construction materials such as concrete or stone as compared to wood, have a greater potential for benefits. Just as important is the interaction of the building mass with the building internal and HVAC system circulating air. This interaction may allow for more efficient transfer of thermal energy between the structure and the air space.

PROS AND CONS

Pro

1. Night ventilation precooling has a good potential for net energy savings because the power requirements to circulate the cooler nighttime air through the building are relatively low compared to the power required to mechanically cool the space during the daytime hours.
2. Mechanical precooling could lead to net energy savings, although there will likely be a net increase in total energy use due to the less-than-100% thermal energy storage efficiency in the building mass.
3. Both variations require only minor, if any, change to the overall building and system design. Any changes required are primarily in the control scheme.
4. Night ventilation can provide a better indoor air quality environment due to increased circulation of air during the night. A greater potential exists with the ventilation precooling concept. Both will be better than if the system were completely shut off during unoccupied hours.

Con

1. Temperature control should be monitored carefully. The potential exists for the building environment to be too cool for the occupant's comfort during the early hours of the occupied period. This will result in increased service calls or complaints and may end with the night precooling being bypassed or turned off.

2. The increased run time on the equipment could lead to lower equipment life expectancy or increased frequency in maintenance. Careful attention should be given to the resulting temperature profile through the day during the commissioning process. Adjustments may be needed to the control schedule to keep the building within the thermal comfort zone.
3. Proper orientation must be given to the building operator to understand how the control concept affects the overall system operation throughout the day.
4. Future turnovers in building ownership or operating personnel could negatively affect how successfully the system performs.
5. Occupants would probably need at least some orientation so that they would understand and be tolerant of the differences in conditions that may prevail with such a system. Future occupants may not have benefit of such orientation.

KEY ELEMENTS OF COST

The following provides a possible breakdown of the various cost elements that might differentiate a nighttime precooling scheme from a conventional one and gives an indication of whether the net cost for the precooling option is likely to be lower (L), higher (H), or the same (S). This assessment is only a perception of what might be likely, but it may not be correct in all situations. **There is no substitute for a detailed cost analysis as part of the design process.** The listings below may also provide some assistance in identifying the cost elements involved.

First Cost

- Mechanical ventilation system elements   S
- Architectural design features   S
- System controls   H
- Analysis and Design Fees   H

Recurring Cost

- Energy for mechanical portion of system
  Ventilation precooling   L
  Mechanical precooling   S/H
- Total cost to operate cooling systems   L
- Maintenance of mechanical ventilation and cooling system   S/H
- Training of building operators   H
- Orientation of building occupants   H
- Commissioning cost   H
- Occupant productivity   S

ASHRAE GreenTip #1: Night Precooling (continued)

SOURCES OF FURTHER INFORMATION

The following is a sampling of representative papers that can provide further background information:

Andersson, L.O., K.G. Bernander, E. Isfält, and A.H. Rosenfeld. 1979. Storage of heat and coolth in hollow-core concrete slabs. Swedish experience and application to large, American style buildings. Second International Conference on Energy Use and Management, Lawrence Berkeley National Laboratory, LBL-8913.

Balaras, C.A. 1995. The role of thermal mass on the cooling load of buildings. An overview of computational methods. *Energy and Buildings* 24(1): 1-10.

Braun, J.E. 1990. Reducing energy costs and peak electrical demand through optimal control of building thermal storage. *ASHRAE Transactions* 96(2): 876-888.

Keeney, K.R., and J.E. Braun. 1997. Application of building precooling to reduce peak cooling requirements. *ASHRAE Transactions* 103(1):463-469.

Kintner-Meyer, M., and A.F. Emery. 1995. Optimal control of an HVAC system using cold storage and building thermal capacitance. *Energy and Buildings* 23:19-31.

Ruud, M.D., J.W. Mitchell, and S.A. Klein. 1990. Use of building thermal mass to offset cooling loads. *ASHRAE Transactions* 96(2):820-829.

ENGINEERING LOAD-DETERMINING FACTORS

Parametric simulations should be completed for the internal loads as well. Set the lighting load to zero, set the equipment load to zero, and then take all the people out of the building. In this manner, the engineer can understand what is driving the energy use in the building. For office buildings, lights are usually the major culprits. Therefore, optimize the daylighting and electric lighting design.

Likewise, evaluate office equipment loads. Make recommendations about the effects of the choices of computers, monitors, printers, and other types of equipment. In many offices, this equipment is left on all night. An office building should have very few loads when the building is unoccupied. Leaving an office full of equipment on all night and on weekends can easily add up to large energy consumption.

For example, assume one 34,000 ft^2 office building has nighttime plug loads of 10 kW, and assume the building is unoccupied for 14 hours a day during the week and 24 hours a day on the weekend. This adds up to around 6000 hours per year and 60,000 kWh—or $4200 (at $0.07/kWh)—of electricity that could have easily been reduced. It is important for the engineer to bring up these issues during the design stage (and later, during the operation) of the building because no one else may be paying attention to such details. Designing and building a great building is only half the job; operating it in the correct manner is the other, and often more important, half. The engineer can make better operation possible by designing piping, wiring, and controls capable of easily turning things off when not being used

Educate owners about efficient office equipment and appliances to reduce plug loads, covering such things as flat screen computer monitors, laptops vs. desktop CPUs, copy machines, refrigerators, and process equipment. Consider measuring usage in one of the clients' existing buildings to get an accurate picture of load distribution and population profiles. Attempt to develop a total building electric load profile for every minute of one week.

SYSTEM/EQUIPMENT EFFICIENCIES

It is important to use the right-size cooling and heating equipment. The old rule of thumb of 250-350 gross ft^2/ton cooling load does not apply to sustainable buildings. Recent high-performance building projects operate between 600 and 1000 GSF/ton. Set cooling equipment and system performance targets in terms of kW/ton, such as:

Chiller	0.51	kW/ton
Cooling tower	0.011	kW/ton
Chilled water pump	0.026	kW/ton
Condenser water pump	0.021	kW/ton
Air-handling unit	0.05	kW/ton

Industry standards such as ASHRAE 90.1 (latest approved version) give minimum requirements for equipment efficiencies and system design and installation. Understand that these represent the least efficient end of the spectrum of energy-conserving buildings that should be built! To be considered green, a building must exceed these standards.

There are a number of sources for information on green building design in addition to ASHRAE, some of which are listed below. This guide does not endorse any of them; the list is presented for informational purpose only. Readers should be aware that the sources use various methods to arrive at their final recommendations and that some of the guidance offered may have a hidden (or not so hidden) agenda. Some may use economics as a basis; however, the underlying economic assumptions should be understood prior to using the information. Others attempt to push energy efficiency to its technical limits. Therefore, before using any of these sources for guidance, investigate the premises used, the methods of analysis, and the background of the author.

Governmental Agencies

- U.S. EPA's Energy Star program
  http://www.energystar.gov
- U.S. Department of Energy's Federal Energy Management Program
  http://www.eere.energy.gov/femp
- U.S. Department of Energy's High Performance Buildings Institute
  http://www.highperformancebuilding.gov
- California Energy Commission
  http://www.energy.ca.gov

Environmental Groups

- American Council for an Energy Efficient Economy
  http://www.aceee.org
- Alliance to Save Energy
  http://www.ase.org

Industry Groups

- American Gas Cooling Center
  http://www.gascooling.org
- Geothermal Heat Pump Consortium
  http://www.geoexchange.org
- Air-Conditioning and Refrigeration Institute
  http://www.ari.org

Installing efficient pieces of equipment alone does not make a building green. It only creates the opportunity for the building to operate with reduced energy consumption. Integrating those pieces into a system is discussed in the following literature (use latest edition published):

- ASHRAE *Applications Handbook*
- ASHRAE's *Fundamentals of Water System Design*

- McQuay's *Chilled Water System Manual*
- Trane's *Multiple-Chiller-System Design and Control Manual*
- *CoolTools Chilled Water Plant Design Guide*.

In addition to system integration, the comfort and process heating and cooling systems should be integrated with the building.

As the building design changes, so should the systems. For example, lighting or glazing retrofits can greatly reduce system cooling requirements. In addition, reduction in the space load may change the characteristics of the load. When the space sensible load is drastically reduced, the space sensible heat ratio becomes much steeper. In such cases, the applicability of the system must be investigated. Both air and water systems should be revisited when major building retrofits occur.

LIGHTING

Good sustainable designs should not increase first costs over typical designs. More expensive equipment, glazing, and lighting should yield lower capacity requirements to offset those extra costs. Smaller equipment translates into smaller wiring, transformers, fuses, switchgear, etc.

The paragraphs below briefly outline some key considerations in lighting design, especially those involved in daylighting. Chapter 11 contains additional information for HVAC&R designers on lighting system design.

Electric Lighting

Work with electric lighting designers to lower connected and actual lighting loads while improving visual acuity. Set budget at less than 1 watt per gross square foot connected load. Consider indirect, low ambient lighting levels, task lights at workstations, and accent lighting for relief, color, and interest.

Daylighting

Studies on Daylighting. One of the principal rationales for the use of daylighting is the beneficial impact it has on the occupants of the building in terms of improved productivity and well-being.

- A study of daylighting impacts on retail sales[1] showed a 40% improvement in sales.
- A study of daylighting impacts on school performance[1] showed a 20% improvement in math scores and a 26% improvement in reading scores.

---

1. Heschong Mahone Group for Pacific Gas and Electric Company (*http://www.h-m-g.com*).

KEY CONSIDERATIONS IN THE HVAC DESIGN PROCESS

DESIGN INTENT

- Set Goals for Performance
  - Energy Performance
  - Environmental Performance
  - Comfort
  - Operating Cost
  - Determine How to Achieve the Goals
- System by system
  - Integrated Design.

VERIFY THAT DESIGN INTENT IS MET

- In Design
  - Verification of Px Goals in Design
  - Coordination between Design Disciplines
  - Including Cx in Design Documents
- In Construction
  - Procurement of Equipment and Materials
  - Installation
- At Start-Up and Testing
- In Operations

DESIGN INTEGRATION

- Integration with Other Disciplines
  - Architecture, Lighting, Interiors, Structural
  - Daylighting
  - Underfloor Air Distribution
  - "Form-follows-Function" Design
- Increased Emphasis on HVAC Performance
  - Thermal Comfort
  - IAQ
  - Energy Efficiency

H.V.A.C. SYSTEMS

- High-Efficiency Equipment
- Systems Responsive to Partial Loads
  - 80% of year, system operates at <50% of peak capacity.
- Emphasis on "Free" Cooling and Heating

- Economizers (air, water)
- Evaporative Cooling (cooling towers, pre-cooling)
- Heat Recovery
- Emphasis on Indoor Air Quality (IAQ)
- Under-floor Air Distribution is new wave

LOAD REDUCTION

- Reduce Envelope Loads
  - Solar Loads
- Reduce Lighting Loads
  - 1.5 watts/ft^2
- Reduce Power Loads
  - 1.5 watts/ft^2
- Reduced A/C Tonnage
  - Can Provide Higher A/C Efficiency for same cost

COOLING & HEATING LOAD REDUCTION

- Envelope Loads
  - Shading
  - Glass Selection
  - Glass Percentage
- Internal Loads
  - Lighting LPD
  - Equipment Loads (Energy Star)
  - Controls/Occupancy Sensors

DESIGN INTEGRATION

- Integration with Other Disciplines
  - Architecture, Lighting, Interiors, Structural
  - Daylighting
  - Underfloor Air Distribution
  - "Form-follows-Function" Design
- Increased Emphasis on HVAC Performance
  - Thermal Comfort
  - IAQ
  - Energy Efficiency

Daylighting Design Process: Some Key Points.

Design Process / Design Options
- Prospect in the schematic design phase.
- Integrate the design of all systems:
  -Envelope
  -HVAC
  -Lighting
  -Interiors
- Take credit for HVAC downsizing to "pay" for daylighting.
- Physical modeling can be useful.
- Address *all* the problems of daylit buildings:
  -Direct insolation and glare control
  -Daylighting central cores
  -Heat gain – glazing selection, low-E glass
  -Heat loss – glazing selection, double-pane, interior shading,
  -Owner awareness of design assumptions

Energy Conservation Regulation Compliance
- Prescriptive path vs. performance path (energy budget)
- A well-designed daylit building will comply with Title 24 energy budgets

Daylighting Considerations
- Envelope
- HVAC
- Lighting/controls
- Interiors/operations
- Implementation

Envelope
- Sitting and Orientation
- Fenestration/effective aperture area
  -Glass type
  -Area
- Shading and window management
  -External shading wherever possible
- Fenestration location

HVAC Loads
- Ensure realistic load assumptions among the design team
- Design for actual load, not "imaginary worst case"
- Take advantage of reduced internal loads to downsize
- Select appropriate HVAC system
- Capture skin loads before they enter the space
  - Return air grilles over windows
  - Returns or exhaust fans over skylights

HVAC Zonation
- Upsize cooling capacity in zones near daylighting fenestration, if warranted
- May need to upsize heating in such zones as well
- Perimeter HVAC zones should be sized to be similar to daylighting zones (15-18 feet deep)

Implementation

- Entire design has to be implemented
- Can't take out daylighting and not upsize HVAC to compensate
- Can't delete shading devices
- Can't delete controls
- Can't paint interiors black

Methods of operation need to be explained to occupants of the building.

DON'Ts in the daylighting process:

- (Avoid) partial design and specification
- (Avoid) partial implementation
- (Avoid) counter-productive building operation

Cost-benefit considerations:

- Lighting energy savings
- Energy savings due to reduced HVAC loads
- Capital savings due to reduced equipment size
- Capital savings from SCE "Savings by Design" (more info at *http://www.savingsbydesign.com*)
- Improved comfort
- Improved productivity and sales
- "Delight" factor sells the space

Chapter 7
Space Thermal/Comfort Delivery Systems

Occupant comfort and health are important in green building design. Sacrificing the quality of the indoor environment in the name of green design is not a viable strategy, since maintaining maximum human productivity and performance is paramount.

Thermal

To provide for a thermally comfortable environment that supports the productive performance of the building occupants,

- comply with ASHRAE Standard 55 (latest approved edition) plus approved addenda for thermal comfort, including humidity control, within established ranges for the climatic zone, and

- install a permanent temperature and humidity monitoring system configured to provide operators control over thermal comfort performance and effectiveness of humidification and/or dehumidification systems in the building.

Indoor Air Quality (IAQ)

Reduce the amount of indoor and exterior air contaminants that have adverse impacts on the environment and human health with the following steps:

Authors contributing to this chapter are Kevin Dickens, David Grumman, Michael Haggans, Thomas Lawrence, and Mick Schwedler.

- Evaluate and preferentially specify materials that are low-emitting, nontoxic, and chemically inert.
- Do not install combustion appliances unless they are sealed-combustion or power-vented; avoid gas ranges.
- Prevent exposure of building occupants and systems to environmental tobacco smoke (ETS).

Utilize effective moisture control to curb humidity and prevent mold problems.

Avoid using hard-to-seal building cavities, such as dropped ceiling plenums, for air movement unless these areas can be properly constructed and sealed.

Establish minimum IAQ performance to prevent the development of indoor air quality problems in the building, maintaining the health and well being of the occupants.

- Meet the minimum requirements of voluntary consensus standard ASHRAE Standard 62, *Ventilation for Acceptable Indoor Air Quality* (latest approved edition) and approved addenda.

- Provide indoor air quality (IAQ) monitoring to sustain long-term occupant health and comfort.

ENERGY EXCHANGE

Distributing energy throughout a building is usually accomplished through the flow of steam or a hydronic fluid, air, electrons (electricity), and sometimes a refrigerant. Air and hydronic flows in particular also serve the function of disposition of used air (exhaust) or liquid waste. That the air and hydronic media being so moved are often at different thermal levels (i.e., warm, cold) offers opportunities to incorporate green design techniques. There are several practical techniques whereby energy from one flow stream can be transferred usefully to another.

GreenTips 2 and 3 describe two such techniques involving energy exchange between airstreams follow directly. GreenTip 4 involves both air and water streams.

ENERGY DELIVERY METHODS

Media Movers (Fans/Pumps)

Basics: Power, Flow and Pressure. If air conditioning (heating/cooling) could be produced exactly where it is needed throughout a building, overall system efficiency would increase because there would be no additional energy used to move (distribute) conditioned water or air. For acoustic, aesthetic, logistic, and a variety of other reasons, this ideal seldom is realized. Therefore, fans and pumps are used to move energy in the form of water and air. Throughout this process, the goal is to minimize *system* energy consumption.

Minimization of a media mover's power at full-load and part-load conditions is the goal. Understanding how fan and pump power change with flow and pressure is imperative. (Note: Refer also to chapter 3, "Background and Fundamentals.")

$$Power \sim Flow \times \Delta Pressure$$

As flow drops, so does the pressure differential through pipes, chillers, and coils.

Pressure drop through these devices varies approximately with $(flow)^{1.85}$. This, in turn, means that the power required to cause flow through these devices varies approximately as $(flow)^{2.85}$. (In an ideal world, power changes with the cube of the flow. While the 2.0 and 3.0 exponent is not fully achieved in practical application, it is nevertheless clear that reducing flow can drastically reduce energy use.)

However, there are some pressure drops in typical systems that do *not* change as flow decreases. These are:

- The pressure differential setpoint that many system controls use
- Cooling tower static lift
- Pressure drop across balancing devices

Therefore, for flow through these system components, power will vary *directly* with flow.

To reduce pressure drop, the pipe or duct size should be maximized and valve and coil resistance minimized. (Duct and pipe sizes are discussed in the distribution section below.) Coil sizes should be maximized within the space allowed to reduce pressure drop on both the water-side and air-side. The ideal selection will require striking an economic balance between first cost and projected energy savings (operating cost).

Chilled water pumps. The most commonly used design conditions in the industry today are a chilled water ΔT of 10°F, which equates to 2.4 gpm/ton. In recent years, the 60% increase in required minimum chiller efficiency from a 3.8 COP (ASHRAE Standard 90-75) to 6.1 COP (ASHRAE Standard 90.1-1999) has led to a reexamination of the assumptions used in designing hydronic media flow paths and in selecting movers (pumps) with an eye to reducing energy consumption.

The CoolTools team came to the following conclusion:

"...the trend for most applications is that higher chilled water delta-Ts result in lower energy costs, and they will always result in the same or lower first costs." (*CoolTools Chilled Water Plant Design Guide*).

Simply stated, increase the temperature difference in the chilled water system to reduce chilled water pump flow rate. This reduces installed cost and operating costs. The *CoolTools Chilled Water Plant Design Guide* recommends starting with a chilled water temperature difference of 12°F to 20°F.

Condenser water pumps. In the same manner, design for condenser water flow has traditionally been based on a 10°F ΔT, which equates to 3 gpm/ton. Today's chillers will give approximately a 9.4°F ΔT with that flow rate. The guide states, "Higher delta-Ts will reduce first costs (because pipes, pumps, and cooling towers are smaller), but the net energy-cost impact may be higher or lower depending on the specific design of the chillers and tower."

The CoolTools team, in their summary, state:

In conclusion, there are times you can "have your cake and eat it too." In most cases larger ΔT's and the associated lower flow rates will not only save installation cost but will usually save energy over the course of the year. This is especially true if a portion of the first cost savings is reinvested in more efficient chillers. With the same cost chillers, at worst, the annual operating cost with the lower flows will be about equal to "standard" flows but still at a lower first cost (*CoolTools Chilled Water Plant Design Guide*).

The *CoolTools Chilled Water Plant Design Guide* recommends a design method that starts with a condenser water temperature difference of 12°F to 18°F.

Thus, reducing chilled and condenser water flow rates (conversely, increasing the ΔTs) can not only reduce operating cost but, more important, can free funds from being applied to the less efficient infrastructure and allow them to be applied toward increasing overall efficiency elsewhere.

Variable Flow Systems. The above discussion suggests that variable flow air and water systems are an excellent way to reduce system energy consumption. Variable flow (either air or water) is required by ASHRAE/IESNA 90.1 for many applications, but it may be beneficial in even more applications than the standard requires. Today's most used technology for reducing flow is the variable-frequency drive.

Distribution Paths (Ducts/Pipes/Wires)

Ducts, pipes, and wires are used to move media. Proper sizing is a balancing act between energy use and cost, material use and first cost. In terms of space consumed in running these carriers, in terms of the energy carried for the cross section of the carrier involved, wires (electricity) have the capacity for carrying the most, followed by pipes (hydronics), followed in turn by ducts (air). Another consideration is that the different energy-carrying media have different characteristics and capabilities in terms of meeting the requirements of the spaces served. The above factors will have some influence on determining the type of HVAC system to be used.

Sizing Considerations. The previous section ("Media Movers") stated that reducing flow rates may reduce both installed cost (by reducing duct, pipe, fan, and pump sizes) and operating cost (by reducing pump and fan energy use). Decreased duct and pipe sizes also lead to less insulation. However, the design professional may want to leave pipe and duct sizes larger to minimize energy cost if the incremental installed cost savings would be relatively small. The best designs begin with generalized ranges (as were stated above for chilled and condenser water) that are fine tuned for the specific application. This fine tuning may be done with commonly available analysis and design software.

To reduce pressure drop, pipes and ductwork should be laid out prior to locating pumps, chillers, and air handlers.

Hydronic Fluid Selection. Fluid properties can greatly affect system performance. Antifreeze generally increases pressure drop and decreases heat transfer effectiveness. This leads to reduced system efficiency and perhaps increased cost due to the need

for larger components. So the design professional should first examine the system to determine if antifreeze is an absolute necessity or whether water, with proper antifreeze safeguards, could not be used.

If antifreeze is truly necessary:

- Determine whether it is *freeze* or *burst* protection that is being sought. If an affected component (such as a chiller) does not need to be operated during freezing conditions, perhaps only burst protection is necessary. The amount of antifreeze needed can be greatly reduced, although slush may form in the pipes.
- Use only the minimum antifreeze necessary to provide protection; higher concentrations will simply reduce performance.
- Balance all environmental aspects of the antifreeze. Understand that, while some antifreezes are viewed as "less toxic," they can significantly increase system installed and operating costs. Often the greatest "environmental cost" of a particular antifreeze is the increased energy consumption.
- For more information on burst and freeze protection, consult the manufacturer. (e.g., *http://www.dow.com*).

Air Quality Considerations.

- Determine condition of ductwork system and develop methodologies to meet current standards for occupant comfort and well being.
- Inspect, evaluate, and document hygiene factors, microbial contamination, leakage, and thermal qualities according to ACGHI's *Bioaerosols: Assessment and Control*. If the standard is not met, proceed with required remediation.
- Clean ductwork in accordance with the National Air Duct Cleaning Association's (NADCA) *General Specification for the Cleaning of Commercial Heating, Ventilating and Air Conditioning Systems*.
- Achieve ductwork leakage class as described in Table 7 of the *2001 ASHRAE Handbook—Fundamentals*, chapter 34.

OCCUPIED-SPACE ENERGY DELIVERY MEANS (AIR TERMINALS/CONDUCTIVE/CONVECTIVE/RADIANT DEVICES)

Employ architectural and HVAC design strategies to increase ventilation effectiveness and prevent short-circuiting of airflow delivery.

For mechanically or naturally ventilated spaces, design ventilation systems that result in an air change effectiveness (E) of at least 0.9 under both heating and cooling modes using accepted reference standards of testing, design, or analysis. This requires special attention when heating from overhead.

Install a permanent carbon dioxide (CO_2) or an HVAC flow rate monitoring system that provides visual and/or auditory feedback on space ventilation performance by indicating when indoor carbon dioxide levels are greater than outdoor levels by more than 530 parts per million at any time. Or, monitor ventilation rates to not drop below those specified in ASHRAE 62-2001, Table 2. (Note: This reference is for a typical office building. Other building types or activity levels may require different values. Refer to ASHRAE 62-2001, appendices or the references.)

PROVISION OF OUTSIDE AIR VENTILATION

Mechanical Ventilation

Design the HVAC system so that the rate of outside air intake can be measured.

- In buildings with VAV ventilation systems, special controls may be required to maintain minimum outside air intake at all times. VAV control units must have a minimum open position to ensure required distribution of outside air to all portions of the building.

- Locate air intakes away from sources of pollution.

Natural Ventilation

- Provide natural ventilation in combination with air conditioning, using operable windows, cross-ventilation, and the stack effect. Provide interlocking controls to avoid simultaneous operation. (See ASHRAE GreenTip #8)

- Consider designing the building with no mechanical cooling and provide windows or other natural means such as evaporative cooling, earth, or groundwater contact without refrigeration.

- Install operable windows; include window frame switches to shut off mechanical air conditioning to rooms with open windows.

ASHRAE GreenTip #2: Air-to-Air Heat Recovery— Heat Exchange Enthalpy Wheels

GENERAL DESCRIPTION

A heat exchange enthalpy wheel, also known as a rotary energy wheel, has a revolving cylinder filled with an air-permeable medium with a large internal surface area. Adjacent airstreams pass through opposite sides of the exchanger in a counterflow pattern. Heat transfer media may be selected to recover heat only or sensible plus latent heat. Because rotary exchangers have a counterflow configuration and normally use small-diameter flow passages, they are quite compact and can achieve high transfer effectiveness.

Cross-contamination, or mixing, of air between the airstreams occurs in all rotary exchangers by one of two methods: carryover or leakage. Carryover occurs as air is entrained within the medium and is carried into the other airstream. Leakage occurs because the differential pressure across the two airstreams drives air from the high-pressure to the low-pressure airstream. Because cross-contamination can be detrimental, a purge section can be installed to reduce carryover.

Two control methods are commonly used to regulate wheel energy recovery. In the first, an air bypass damper controlled by a wheel supply air temperature sensor regulates the proportion of air that is permitted to bypass the exchanger. The second, and more common, method regulates the energy recovery rate by varying the wheel's rotational speed.

WHEN/WHERE IT'S APPLICABLE

In general, rotary air-to-air energy recovery systems can be used in process-to process, process-to-comfort, and comfort-to-comfort applications, where energy in the exhaust stream would otherwise be wasted. Regions with higher energy costs favor higher levels of energy recovery; however, the economics of scale often favor larger installations. Energy recovery is most economical when there are large temperature differences between the airstreams, the source of supply is close to the exhaust, and they are both relatively constant throughout the year. Applications with a large central energy source and a nearby waste energy use are more favorable than applications with several scattered waste energy sources and uses. Rotary energy wheels are best applied when cross-contamination is not a concern.

The author of this GreenTip is Kevin Dickens.

PROS AND CONS

Pro

1. The total HVAC system installed cost may be lower because central heating and cooling equipment may be reduced in sized.
2. With a total energy wheel, humidification costs may be reduced in cold weather and dehumidification costs may be lowered in warm weather.
3. Rotary wheels require little maintenance and are simple to operate.

Con

1. Energy recovery requires that the supply and exhaust airstreams be within close proximity.
2. Cross-contamination can occur between the airstreams.
3. Energy wheel adds pressure drop to the system.

KEY ELEMENTS OF COST

The following provides a possible breakdown of the various cost elements that might differentiate the above system from a conventional one – and an indication of whether the net cost for the alternative option is likely to be lower (L), higher (H), or the same (S). This assessment is only a perception of what might be likely, but it obviously may not be correct in all situations. **There is no substitute for a detailed cost analysis as part of the design process.** The listings below may also provide some assistance in identifying the cost elements involved.

First Cost

• Central equipment costs	L
• Co-locating exhaust and supply sources	S/H
• Ductwork	S/H
• Design fees	S

Recurring Cost

• Overall energy cost	L
• Maintenance of system	S/H
• Training of building operators	S/H
• Filters	H

SOURCES OF FURTHER INFORMATION

ASHRAE. 2003. *2003 ASHRAE Handbook—HVAC Systems and Equipment.*

Trane Company. 2000. Energy Conscious Design Ideas—Air-to-Air Energy Recovery. *Engineers Newsletter*, Vol. 29, No. 5. Publication ENEWS-29/5.

ASHRAE GreenTip #3: Air-to-Air Heat Recovery—Heat Pipe Systems

GENERAL DESCRIPTION

A heat pipe heat exchanger is a completely passive energy recovery device with an outward appearance of an ordinary extended surface, finned tube coil. The tubes are divided into evaporator and condenser sections by an internal partition plate. Within the permanently sealed and evacuated tube filled with a suitable working fluid, there is an integral capillary wick structure. The working fluid is normally a refrigerant, but other fluorocarbons, water, and other compounds are used in applications with special temperature requirements.

Heat transfer occurs when hot air flowing over the evaporator end of the heat pipe vaporizes the working fluid. A vapor pressure gradient drives the vapor to the condenser end of the heat pipe tube, where the vapor condenses, releasing the latent energy of vaporization. The condensed fluid is wicked back to the evaporator where it is re-vaporized, thus completing the cycle. Using this mechanism, heat transfer along a heat pipe is 1000 times faster than through copper.

Heat pipes typically have zero cross-contamination, but constructing a vented double-wall partition can provide additional protection. Changing the slope or tilt of a heat pipe controls the amount of heat it transfers. Operating the heat pipe on a slope with the hot end below (or above) the horizontal improves (or retards) the condensate flow back to the evaporator. By utilizing a simple temperature sensor-controlled actuator, the output of the exchanger can be modulated by adjusting its tilt angle to maintain a specific leaving temperature.

WHEN/WHERE IT'S APPLICABLE

In general, air-to-air energy recovery systems can be used in process-to-process, process-to-comfort, and comfort-to-comfort applications, where energy in the exhaust stream would otherwise be wasted. Regions with higher energy costs favor higher levels of energy recovery; however, the economics of scale often favor larger installations. Energy recovery is most economical when there are large temperature differences between the airstreams, the source of supply is close to the exhaust, and they are both relatively constant throughout the year. Applications with a large central energy source and a nearby waste energy use are more favorable than applications with several scattered waste energy sources and uses.

The author of this GreenTip is Kevin Dickens.

PROS AND CONS

Pro

1. The total HVAC system installed cost may be lower because central heating and cooling equipment may be reduced in sized.
2. They require little maintenance and are simple to operate.
3. Cross-contamination is not a significant concern.

Con

1. The system requires that the supply and exhaust airstreams be within close proximity.
2. Heat pipe adds pressure drop to the system.
3. Decomposition of the thermal fluid can deteriorate performance.

KEY ELEMENTS OF COST

The following provides a possible breakdown of the various cost elements that might differentiate a building with a heat pipe system from one without – and an indication of whether the net cost is likely to be lower (L), higher (H), or the same (S). This assessment is only a perception of what might be likely, but it obviously may not be correct in all situations. **There is no substitute for a detailed cost analysis as part of the design process.** The listings below may also provide some assistance in identifying the cost elements involved.

First Cost

• Central equipment costs	L
• Co-locating exhaust and supply sources	S/H
• Ductwork	S/H
• Design fees	S

Recurring Cost

• Overall energy cost	L
• Maintenance of system	S/H
• Training of building operators	S/H
• Filters	H

SOURCES OF FURTHER INFORMATION

ASHRAE. 2003. *2003 ASHRAE Handbook—HVAC Systems and Equipment.*

Trane Company. 2000. Energy Conscious Design Ideas—Air-to-Air Energy Recovery. *Engineers Newsletter*, Vol. 29, No. 5. Publication ENEWS-29/5.

ASHRAE GreenTip #4: Air-to-Air Heat Recovery—Run-Around Systems

GENERAL DESCRIPTION

A typical coil energy recovery loop places extended surface, finned tube coils in the supply and exhaust airstreams of a building or process. The coils are connected in a closed loop via counterflow piping through which an intermediate heat transfer fluid (typically water or an antifreeze solution) is pumped. An expansion tank must be included to allow fluid expansion and contraction.

The coil energy recovery loop cannot transfer moisture from one airstream to another. However, indirect evaporative cooling can reduce the exhaust air temperature, which significantly reduces cooling loads. And in comfort-to-comfort applications, the energy transfer is seasonally reversible. Specifically, the supply air is preheated when the outdoor air is cooler than the exhaust and precooled when the outside air is warmer.

Complete separation of the airstreams eliminates cross-contamination as a concern, but freeze protection must be considered. A dual-purpose three-way control valve can prevent freeze-ups by controlling the temperature of the solution entering the exhaust coil to 30°F or above. This condition is maintained by bypassing some of the warmer solution around the coil. This valve can also ensure that a prescribed air temperature from the supply coil is not exceeded.

WHEN/WHERE IT'S APPLICABLE

In general, air-to-air energy recovery systems can be used in process-to process, process-to-comfort, and comfort-to-comfort applications, where energy in the exhaust stream would otherwise be wasted. Regions with higher energy costs favor higher levels of energy recovery; however, the economics of scale often favor larger installations. Energy recovery is most economical when there are large temperature differences between the airstreams, and the source of supply is close to the exhaust and they are both relatively constant throughout the year. Runaround loops are highly flexible and well suited to renovation and industrial applications. The loop accommodates remote supply and exhaust ducts and allows the simultaneous transfer of energy between multiple sources and uses.

The author of this GreenTip is Kevin Dickens.

PROS AND CONS

Pro

1. The total HVAC system installed cost may be lower because central heating and cooling equipment may be reduced in sized.
2. The loop accommodates remote supply and exhaust duct locations.
3. Cross-contamination is not a concern.

Con

1. It requires a pump, which offsets some energy recovery savings.
2. It adds pressure drop to the system.
3. Relative to passive air-to-air heat exchangers (i.e., heat wheels or heat pipes), it requires more maintenance and controls.

KEY ELEMENTS OF COST

The following provides a possible breakdown of the various cost elements that might differentiate a building with a run-around coil system from one without and an indication of whether the net cost is likely to be lower (L), higher (H), or the same (S). This assessment is only a perception of what might be likely, but it obviously may not be correct in all situations. **There is no substitute for a detailed cost analysis as part of the design process.** The listings below may also provide some assistance in identifying the cost elements involved.

First Cost

• Central equipment costs	L
• Hydronics (piping, pumps, and controls)	H
• Ductwork	S
• Design fees	S

Recurring Cost

• Overall energy cost	L
• Maintenance of system	S/H
• Training of building operators	S/H
• Filters	H

SOURCES OF FURTHER INFORMATION

ASHRAE. 2003. *2003 ASHRAE Handbook—HVAC Systems and Equipment.*

Trane Company. 2000. Energy Conscious Design Ideas—Air-to-Air Energy Recovery. *Engineers Newsletter*, Vol. 29, No. 5. Publication ENEWS-29/5.

ASHRAE GreenTip #5: Displacement Ventilation

GENERAL DESCRIPTION

With a ceiling supply and return air system, the ventilation effectiveness may be compromised if sufficient mixing does not take place. While there are no data suggesting that cold air supplied at the ceiling will short circuit, it is possible that a fraction of the supply air may bypass directly to the return inlet without mixing at the occupied level when heating from the ceiling. For example, when heating with a typical overhead system with supply temperatures exceeding 15°F above room temperature, ventilation effectiveness will approach 80% or less. In compliance with Table 6.2, addendum *n* of ASHRAE Standard 62-2001, ventilation rates must be multiplied by 1/0.8 or 1.25. While proper system design and diffuser selection can alleviate this problem, another potential solution is displacement ventilation.

In displacement ventilation, conditioned air with a temperature slightly lower than the desired room temperature is supplied horizontally at low velocities at or near the floor. Returns are located at or near the ceiling. The supply air is spread over the floor and then rises by convection as it picks up the load in the room. Displacement ventilation does not depend on mixing. Instead, you are literally displacing the stale polluted air and forcing it up and out the return or exhaust grille. Ventilation effectiveness may actually exceed 100%, and Table 6.2 of Addendum n, ASHRAE Standard 62-2001, indicates a ventilation effectiveness of 1.2 shall be used.

Displacement ventilation is common practice in Europe, but its acceptance in North America has been slow primarily because of the conventional placement of ductwork at the ceiling level and more extreme climatic conditions.

WHEN/WHERE IT'S APPLICABLE

Displacement ventilation is typically used in industrial plants and data centers, but it can be applied in almost any application where a conventional overhead forced air distribution system could be utilized and the load permits.

Because the range of supply air temperatures and discharge velocities is limited to avoid discomfort to occupants, displacement ventilation has a limited ability to handle high heating or cooling loads if the space served is occupied. Some designs use chilled ceilings or heated floors to overcome this limitation. When

The author of this GreenTip is Kevin Dickens.

chilled ceilings are used, it is critical that building relative humidity be controlled to avoid condensation. Another means of increasing cooling capacity is to recirculate some of the room air.

Some associate displacement ventilation solely with underfloor air distribution and the perceived higher costs associated with it. In fact, most underfloor pressurized plenum, air distribution systems do not produce true displacement ventilation but, rather, well-mixed airflow in the lower part of the space. It can, however, be a viable alternative when considering systems for modern office environments where data cabling and flexibility concerns may merit a raised floor.

PROS AND CONS

Pro
1. Displacement ventilation offers improved thermal comfort and IAQ due to increased ventilation effectiveness.
2. There is reduced energy use due to extended economizer availability associated with higher supply temperatures.

Con
1. It may add complexity to the supply air ducting.
2. It is more difficult to address high heating or cooling loads.
3. There are perceived higher costs.

KEY ELEMENTS OF COST

The following provides a possible breakdown of the various cost elements that might differentiate a system utilizing displacement ventilation from one that does not and an indication of whether the net cost is likely to be lower (L), higher (H), or the same (S). This assessment is only a perception of what might be likely, but it obviously may not be correct in all situations. **There is no substitute for a detailed cost analysis as part of the design process.** The listings below may also provide some assistance in identifying the cost elements involved.

First Cost

• Controls	S
• Equipment	S
• Distribution ductwork	S/H
• Design fees	S

ASHRAE GreenTip #5: Displacement Ventilation (continued)

Recurring Cost

- Energy cost   L
- Maintenance of system   S
- Training of building operators   S/H
- Orientation of building occupants   S/H
- Commissioning cost   S

SOURCES OF FURTHER INFORMATION

ASHRAE. 2001. *2001 ASHRAE Handbook—Fundamentals.*

ASHRAE. 2001. *ASHRAE Standard 62-2001, Venti-lation for Acceptable Indoor Air Quality.*

Bauman, F., and T. Webster. 2001. Outlook for underfloor air distribution. *ASHRAE Journal* 43(6).

Interpretation IC-62-1999-30 of ASHRAE Standard 62-1999: *Ventilation for Acceptable Indoor Air Quality*, ASHRAE, August 2000.

Public Technology Inc., U.S. Department of Energy and the U.S. Green Building Council. 1996. *Sustainable Building Technical Manual—Green Building Design, Construction and Operations.* http://www.advancedbuildings.org

---

ASHRAE GreenTip #6: Dedicated Outdoor Air Systems

GENERAL DESCRIPTION

ASHRAE Standard 62 describes in detail the ventilation required to provide a healthy indoor environment as it pertains to indoor air quality (IAQ). Traditionally designers have attempted to address both thermal comfort and IAQ with a single mixed-air system. But ventilation becomes less efficient when the mixed air system serves multiple spaces with differing ventilation needs. If the percentage of outdoor air is simply based on the critical space's need, then all other spaces are overventilated. If the outdoor air percentage is determined using the multiple spaces procedure (ASHRAE 62-2001, Section 6.1.3.1), then all spaces are effectively underventilated. In turn, providing a separate dedicated outdoor air system (DOAS) may be the only reliable way to meet the true intent of ASHRAE Standard 62.

A DOAS uses a separate air handler to condition the outdoor air before delivering it directly to the occupied spaces. The air delivered to the space from the DOAS should not adversely affect thermal comfort (i.e., too cold, too warm, too humid); therefore, many designers call for systems that deliver neutral air. However, there is a strong argument for supplying cool dry air and decoupling the latent conditioning as well as the IAQ components from the thermal comfort (sensible only) system.

The only absolute in a DOAS is that the ventilation air must be delivered directly to the space from a separate system. Control strategy, energy recovery, and leaving air conditions are all variables that can be fixed by the designer.

WHEN/WHERE IT'S APPLICABLE

While a DOAS can be applied in any design, it is most beneficial in a facility with multiple spaces with differing ventilation needs. A DOAS can be combined with any thermal comfort conditioning system including, but not limited to, all-air systems, fan coil units, and hydronic radiant cooling. Note, however, that a design incorporating a separate 100% outdoor air unit delivering air to the mixed air intakes of other units is not a DOAS as defined here. While this type of system may have benefits, such as using less energy or providing more accurate humidity control, it still suffers from the multiple space dilemma described above.

PROS AND CONS

Pro

1. A DOAS ensures compliance with ASHRAE 62-1999 for proper multiple space ventilation and adequate IAQ.

2. It reduces a building's energy use when compared to mixed air systems that require overventilation of some spaces.

3. It allows the designer to decouple the latent load from the sensible load, hence providing more accurate space humidity control.

The author of this GreenTip is Kevin Dickens.

ASHRAE GreenTip #6: Dedicated Outdoor Air Systems (continued)

4. It allows easy airflow measurement and balance, and keeps ventilation loads off main HVAC units.

Con

1. Depending on overall design (thermal comfort and IAQ), it may add additional first cost associated with providing parallel systems.
2. Depending on overall design, it may require additional materials with their associated embodied energy costs.
3. Depending on overall design, there may be more systems to maintain.
4. With two airstreams, proper mixing may not occur when distributed to the occupied space.
5. The total airflow of two airstreams may exceed airflow of a single system.

KEY ELEMENTS OF COST

The following provides a possible breakdown of the various cost elements that might differentiate a building with a DOAS from one with another system and an indication of whether the net cost is likely to be lower (L), higher (H), or the same (S). This assessment is only a perception of what might be likely, but it obviously may not be correct in all situations. **There is no substitute for a detailed cost analysis as part of the design process.** The listings below may also provide some assistance in identifying the cost elements involved.

First Cost

• Controls	H
• Equipment	S/H
• Distribution ductwork	S/H
• Design fees	S/H

Recurring Cost

• Energy cost	S/L
• Maintenance of system	S/H
• Training of building operators	S/H
• Orientation of building occupants	S
• Commissioning cost	S/H

SOURCES OF FURTHER INFORMATION

ASHRAE. 2001. *ASHRAE Standard 62-2001: Ventilation for Acceptable Indoor Air Quality.*

Coad, W.J. 1999. Conditioning Ventilation Air for Improved Performance and Air Quality. *Heating/Piping/Air Conditioning*, September.

Morris, Wayne. 2003. The ABCs of DOAS. *ASHRAE Journal* 45(5).

Mumma, S.A. 2001. Designing Dedicated Outdoor Air Systems. *ASHRAE Journal* 43(5).

ASHRAE GreenTip #7: Ventilation Demand Control Using CO_2

GENERAL DESCRIPTION

A significant component of indoor environmental quality is the indoor air quality (IAQ). ASHRAE Standard 62-2001 describes in detail the ventilation required to provide a healthy environment. However, providing ventilation based strictly on the peak occupancy using the Ventilation Rate Procedure (Section 6.1) will result in overventilation during periods. Any positive impact on IAQ brought on by overventilation will be outweighed by the costs associated with the energy required to condition the ventilation air.

CO_2 can be used to measure or control the per-person ventilation rate and, in turn, allow the designer to introduce a ventilation demand control strategy. Simply put, the amount of CO_2 present in the air is an indicator of the number of people in the space and, in turn, the amount of ventilation air that is required. CO_2-based ventilation control does not affect the peak design ventilation capacity required to serve the space (Table 2 in ASHRAE 62-2001), but it does allow the ventilation system to modulate in sync with the building's occupancy.

The key components of a CO_2 demand-based ventilation system are CO_2 sensors and a means by which to control the outdoor fresh air intake, i.e., a damper with a modulating actuator. There are many types of sensors and the technology is evolving while at the same time costs are dropping. Sensors can be wall mounted or mounted in the return duct, but it is recommended that the sensor be installed within the occupied space whenever possible.

WHEN/WHERE IT'S APPLICABLE

CO_2 demand control is best suited for buildings with a variable occupancy. The savings will be greatest in spaces that have a wide variance, such as gymnasiums, large meeting rooms, and auditoriums. For buildings with a constant occupancy rate, such as an office building or school, a simple nighttime setback scenario may be more appropriate for ventilation demand control, but CO_2 monitoring may still be utilized for verification that high IAQ is achieved.

PROS AND CONS

Pro

1. CO_2 demand control reduces a buildings energy use as it relates to overventilation.

The author of this GreenTip is Kevin Dickens.

2. It assists in maintaining adequate ventilation levels regardless of occupancy.

Con

1. There is an added first cost associated with the sensors and additional controls.
2. There are additional materials and their associated embodied energy costs.
3. Evolving sensor technology may not be developed to full maturity.

KEY ELEMENTS OF COST

The following provides a possible breakdown of the various cost elements that might differentiate a building utilizing a CO_2 ventilation demand control strategy from one that does not and an indication of whether the net cost is likely to be lower (L), higher (H), or the same (S). This assessment is only a perception of what might be likely, but it obviously may not be correct in all situations. **There is no substitute for a detailed cost analysis as part of the design process.** The listings below may also provide some assistance in identifying the cost elements involved.

First Cost

• Controls	H
• Design fees	S/H

Recurring Cost

• Energy cost	L
• Maintenance of system	S/H
• Training of building operators	S/H
• Orientation of building occupants	S/H
• Commissioning cost	S/H

SOURCES OF FURTHER INFORMATION

ASHRAE Standard 62-2001: *Ventilation for Acceptable Indoor Air Quality.* ASHRAE.

ASTM D 6245-1998: *Standard Guide for Using Indoor Carbon Dioxide Concentrations to Evaluate Indoor Air Quality and Ventilation.* ASTM, 1998.

Schell, M., and D. Int-Hout. 2001. Demand Control Ventilation Using CO_2. *ASHRAE Journal* 43(2).

Trane Company. *A Guide to Understanding ASHRAE Standard 62-2001. http://trane.com/commercial/issues/iaq/ashrae2001.asp*

U.S. Green Building Council. 2001. *LEED Reference Guide*, Version 2.0.

http://www.advancedbuildings.org

ASHRAE GreenTip #8: Hybrid Ventilation

GENERAL DESCRIPTION

A hybrid ventilation system allows the controlled introduction of outside air ventilation into a building by both mechanical and passive means; thus, it is sometimes called mixed-mode ventilation. It has built-in strategies to allow the mechanical and passive portions to work in conjunction with one another so as to not cause additional ventilation loads compared to what would occur using mechanical ventilation alone. It thus differs from a passive ventilation system, consisting of operable windows alone, which has no automatic way of controlling the amount of outside air load.

Two variants of hybrid ventilation are the *changeover* (or *complementary*) type and the *concurrent* (or *zoned*) type. With the former, spaces are ventilated either mechanically or passively, but not both simultaneously. With the latter variant, both methods provide ventilation simultaneously, though usually to zones discrete from one another.

Control of hybrid ventilation is obviously an important feature. With the changeover variant, controls could switch between mechanical and passive ventilation seasonally, diurnally, or based on a measured parameter. In the case of the concurrent variant, appropriate controls are needed to prevent "fighting" between the two ventilation methods.

WHEN/WHERE IT'S APPLICABLE

A hybrid ventilation system may be applicable in the following circumstances:

- When the owner and design team are willing to explore employing a nonconventional building ventilation technique that has the promise of reducing ongoing operating costs as well as providing a healthier, stimulating environment.
- When it is determined that the building occupants would accept the concept of using the outdoor environment to determine (at least, in part) the indoor environment, which may mean greater variation in conditions than with a strictly controlled environment.
- When the design team has the expertise and willingness—and has the charge from the owner —to spend the extra effort to create the integrated design needed to make such a technique work successfully.

The author of this GreenTip is David Grumman.

- Where extreme outside conditions—or a specialized type of building use—do not preclude the likelihood of the successful application of such a technique.

Buildings with atriums are particularly good candidates.

PROS AND CONS

Pro

1. Hybrid ventilation is an innovative and potentially energy-efficient way to provide outside air ventilation to buildings and, in some conditions, to cool them, thus reducing energy otherwise required from conventional sources (power plant).
2. Corollary to the above, it could lead to a lower building life-cycle cost.
3. It could create a healthier environment for building occupants.
4. It offers a greater sense of occupant satisfaction due to the increased ability to exercise some control over the ventilation provided.
5. There is more flexibility in the means of providing ventilation; the passive variant can act as backup to the mechanical system and vice versa.
6. It could extend the life of the equipment involved in providing mechanical ventilation since it would be expected to run less.

Con

1. Failure to integrate the mechanical aspects of a hybrid ventilation system with the architectural design could result in a poorly functioning system. Some architectural design aspects could be constrained in providing a hybrid ventilation system, such as building orientation, depth of occupied zones, grouping of spaces
2. Additional first costs could be incurred since two systems are being provided where only a single one would be provided otherwise, and controls for the passive system could be a major portion of the added cost.
3. If automatic operable window openers are utilized, these could result in security breaches if appropriate safeguards and overrides are not provided.

4. If integral building openings are utilized in lieu of, or in addition to, operable windows, pathways for the entrance of outside pollutants and noise or of unwanted insects, birds, and small animals would exist. If filters are used to prevent this, they could become clogged or could be an additional maintenance item to keep clear.

5. Building operators may have to have special training to understand and learn how best to operate the system. Future turnovers in building ownership or operating personnel could negatively affect how successfully the system performs.

6. Occupants would probably need at least some orientation so that they would understand and be tolerant of the differences in conditions that may prevail with such a system. Future occupants may not have the benefit of such orientation.

7. Special attention would need to be given to certain safety issues, such as fire and smoke propagation in case of a fire.

8. Although computer programs (computational fluid dynamics or CFD) exist to simulate, predict, and understand airflow within the building from passive ventilation systems, it would be difficult to predict conditions under all possible circumstances.

9. Few codes and standards in the U.S. recognize and address the requirements for hybrid ventilation systems. This would likely result in local code enforcement authorities having increased discretion over what is acceptable or not.

KEY ELEMENTS OF COST

The following provides a possible breakdown of the various cost elements that might differentiate a hybrid ventilation system from a conventional one and an indication of whether the net cost for the hybrid option is likely to be lower (L), higher (H), or the same (S). This assessment is only a perception of what might be likely, but it obviously may not be correct in all situations. **There is no substitute for a detailed cost analysis as part of the design process.** The listings below may also provide some assistance in identifying the cost elements involved.

First Cost

Mechanical ventilation system elements	S
Architectural design features	H/L
Operable window operators	H
Integral opening operators/dampers	H
Filters for additional openings	H
Controls for passive system/coordination with mechanical system	H
Design fees	H

Recurring Cost

Energy for mechanical portion of system	L
Maintenance of above	L
Energy used by controls, mechanical operators	H
Maintenance of passive system	H
Training of building operators	H
Orientation of building occupants	H
Commissioning cost	H
Occupant productivity	H

SOURCES OF FURTHER INFORMATION

Kosik, W.J. 2001. Design strategies for hybrid ventilation. *ASHRAE Journal* 43(10).

Chapter 8
Energy Distribution Systems

For there to be heating, cooling, lighting, and electric power throughout a building, the energy required by these functions is usually distributed from one or more central points. The most common media used to distribute energy are steam, hydronics, air, and electricity. Refrigerants are also used as a means of energy transfer between components of refrigeration equipment. Usually, except for industrial and certain specialized applications, the length of refrigerant piping runs is not great.

Discussion here will concentrate primarily on steam, hydronics, and air systems.

STEAM

Advantages

- Steam flows to the terminal usage without aid of external pumping.
- Steam systems are not greatly affected by the height of the distribution system, which has a significant impact on a water system.
- Steam distribution can readily accommodate changes in the system terminal equipment.
- Major steam distribution repair does not require piping drain-down.
- The thermodynamics of steam utilization are effective and efficient.

Authors contributing to this chapter are David Grumman and Charles Wilkin.

With these advantages, steam is often a logical choice for commercial and industrial processes and for large-scale distribution systems, such as on campuses and in large or tall buildings. However, steam traps require periodic maintenance and can become a source of significant energy waste. (See subsequent section on steam traps.)

Classification

Steam distribution is either one-pipe or two-pipe. One-pipe distribution is defined to be where both the steam supply and the condensate travel through a single pipe connecting the steam source and the terminal heating units. Two-pipe distribution is defined to be where the steam supply and the steam condensate travel through separate pipes. Two-pipe steam systems are further classified as gravity return or vacuum return.

Steam systems are also classified according to system operating pressure:

- Low pressure is defined to be 15 PSIG or less.
- High pressure is defined to be over 15 PSIG.

Selection of steam pressure is based on the constraints of the process served. The level of system energy rises with the system pressure. Higher steam pressure may allow smaller supply distribution pipe sizes, but it also increases the temperature difference across the pipe insulation and may result in more heat loss. Higher steam pressure also dictates the use of pipe, valves, and equipment that can withstand the higher pressure. This translates to higher installation cost.

Piping

Supply and return piping must be installed to recognize the thermodynamics of steam and to allow unencumbered steam and condensate flow. Piping that does not slope correctly—that is, is installed with unintended water traps, or that has leaks—will not function properly and will increase system energy use. Careful installation will result in efficient and effective operation. If steam or condensate leaks from the piping system, additional water must be added to make up for the losses. Makeup water is chemically treated and is an operating cost.

Control

Control of steam flow at the terminal equipment is very important. Steam control valves are selected to match the controlled process. If steam flow varies over a wide range, it may be necessary to have multiple control valves. On large terminal heat exchange units, a single control valve usually cannot provide effective control; in such cases, multiple control valves of various sizes operated in a sequential manner are used. Consult sizing data available from manufacturers.

Steam Traps

Selection of steam traps is related to the function of the terminal device or pipe distribution served. Steam traps have the function of draining condensate from the supply side of the system to the condensate return side of the system without allowing steam to flow into the return piping. The flow of steam into return piping unnecessarily wastes energy, and significant energy waste can occur if periodic maintenance is not performed. Properly sized and installed steam traps allow terminal heat exchange equipment to function effectively. If condensate is not fully drained from the terminal heat exchange equipment, heat transfer area is reduced, resulting in a loss of capacity.

Sources of Further Information

Manufacturers of equipment—control valves, steam traps, and other devices—are valuable resources. There are multiple web sites that contain system design information. Perform a search on the Internet for "steam piping design." "Steam Systems" is chapter 10 of the *ASHRAE Handbook—HVAC Systems and Equipment.*

HYDRONICS

Pumping heated water and chilled water is common system design practice in many buildings. Water is often diluted with an antifreeze fluid to avoid water freezeup in extremely cold conditions (thus referring to these systems as *hydronic.*) There are many approaches in utilizing these systems.

Classification

Hot water heating systems are classified as low-temperature water, medium-temperature water, or high-temperature water.

- Low-temperature water systems operate at temperatures of 250°F and below.
- Medium-temperature water systems operate at temperatures above 250°F to 350°F.
- High-temperature water systems operate at temperature above 350°F.

Chilled water systems distribute cold water to terminal cooling coils to provide dehumidification and cooling of conditioned air or cooling of a process. They can also serve cooling panels in occupied spaces. Chilled water panels, which serve as a heat sink for heat radiated from occupants and other warm surfaces to the radiant panel, can be used to reduce the sensible load normally handled solely by mechanical air cooling. The percentage by which the load can be reduced depends upon the panel surface area and dew point limitations, which are necessary to avoid any possibility of condensation.

Condenser water systems connect mechanical refrigeration equipment to outdoor heat dissipation devices such as cooling towers or water- or air-cooled condensers. These, in turn, reduce the temperature of the condenser water by rejecting heat to the outdoor environment.

Piping, Flow Rates, and Pumping

Each of these systems uses two pipes—a supply and a return—to make up the piping circuit, and each uses one or more pumps to move the water through the circuit. Information on the design and characteristics of these various systems can be found in chapters 12, 13, and 14 of the *ASHRAE Handbook—HVAC Systems and Equipment.*

Cost-effective design depends on consideration of the system constraints. Piping must be sized to provide the required load capacities and arranged to provide necessary flow at full and part-load conditions. Design will be determined by several system characteristics and selections.

- Supply and return water temperatures
- Flow rates at individual heat transfer units
- System flow rate at design condition
- Piping distribution arrangement
- System water volume
- Equipment selections for pumps boilers, chillers, and coils
- Temperature control strategy.

Pumping energy can be a significant portion of the energy used in a building. Traditionally, it was common to select heating water flow for coils based on a temperature difference of 20°F between the supply and return. Flow rate in gallons per minute (gpm) was calculated by dividing the heating load in Btu per hour by 10,000 (1 Btu per lb °F × 8.33 lb per gallon × 60 minutes per hour × 20°F temperature difference). As long as the cost of energy was cheap, this method was widely used.

Flow rate can easily be reduced by one-half of the 20°F value by using a 40°F temperature difference. The impact on pump flow rate is significant. The temperature difference selected depends upon the ability of the system to function with lower return water temperatures. Certain types of boilers can function with the low return water temperatures, while others cannot. Care must be taken in selecting the boiler type, coupled with supply and return water design temperatures. In specific instances, a low return water temperature could damage the boiler due to the condensation of combustion gases.

Lower flow rates could allow smaller pipe sizes, and pipe size, along with flow, affects pumping energy. A goal should be established for the pump horsepower to be selected. A small increase in some or all of the pipe distribution sizes could reduce the pump horsepower needed for the system. When this goal is established and attained in the finished design, the concept and energy usage will be achieved.

At times, reductions in pipe sizes to reduce first cost are suggested as "value engineering." However, energy usage of the building may be greatly impacted: pump size and horsepower could well be increased. In order to be truly valid, "value engineering" should also include refiguring the life-cycle cost of owning and operating the building. These factors can also be applied to chilled water systems, except that chilled water systems have a smaller range of temperatures within which to work.

System Volume

In small buildings, water system volume may relate closely to boiler or water chiller operation. When pipe distribution systems are short and of small water volume, both boilers and water chillers may experience detrimental operating effects. Manufacturers of water chillers state that system water volume should be a minimum of 3 to 10 gallons per installed ton of cooling. In a system less than this and under light cooling load conditions, thermal inertia coupled with the reaction time of chiller controls may cause the units to short-cycle or shut down on low-temperature safety control.

Similar detrimental effects may occur with small modular boilers in small systems. Under light load conditions, boilers may experience frequent short cycles of operation. An increase in system volume may eliminate this condition.

Energy Usage

There are many opportunities to reduce energy usage in the design of hydronic systems:

- Reduction of flow rates by using larger supply-to-return temperature differences.
- Reduction of pipe sizes by using larger supply-to-return temperature differences.
- Reduction in pumping horsepower based on flow reduction and responsible sizing of piping.

Sources of Further Information

Manufacturers of equipment—pumps, boilers, water chillers, control valves, and other devices—are valuable sources. There are also multiple web sites that contain system design information. (Perform a search on the Internet for "hydronic piping design.") Hydronic systems are also discussed in chapters 12, 13, and 14 of the *ASHRAE Handbook—HVAC Systems and Equipment*.

AIR

Using air as a means of energy distribution is almost universal in buildings, especially as a means of providing distributed cooling to spaces that need it. A key characteristic that makes air so widely used, however, is its importance in maintaining good indoor air quality (IAQ). Thus, air distribution systems are not only a means for energy distribution, they serve the essential role of providing fresh or uncontaminated air to occupied spaces.

Air distribution systems are often challenging to design because, for the energy carried per cross sectional area, they take up the most space in a ceiling cavity and are frequent causes of space "conflicts" between disciplines (structural members, plumbing lines, heating/cooling pipes, light fixtures, etc.). Many approaches have been tried to better coordinate duct runs with other services—or even to integrate them in some cases.

Another tricky aspect of air system design is that there are temperature limitations on supply air due to the fact that air is the energy medium that directly impacts space occupants. While care must always be taken in how air is introduced into an occupied space, it is especially critical the colder that the supply temperature gets. Low temperature air supply systems offer many advantages in terms of green design, but an especially critical design aspect is avoiding occupant discomfort at the supply air/occupant interface.

Most of the same principles that were discussed under hydronic energy distribution systems apply to air systems with respect to temperature differences, carrier size, and driver power and energy. Thus, there are plenty of opportunities for applying green design techniques to such systems and for seeking innovative solutions.

ELECTRIC

From the standpoint of space consumed, distribution of energy by electric means (wire, cables, etc.) is the most efficient. This advantage has often overcome the usual higher cost of electricity (per energy unit) as an energy form and has been one of the major reasons for electing to design all-electric buildings.

Since electric distribution systems are under the purview of the electrical engineer, further comment is not provided here.

ASHRAE GreenTip #9: Variable Flow/Variable Speed Pumping Systems

GENERAL DESCRIPTION

In most hydronic systems, variable flow with variable speed pumping can be a significant source of energy savings. Variable flow is produced in chilled and hot water systems by using two-way control valves and in condenser-water cooling systems by using automatic two-position isolation valves interlocked with the chiller machinery's compressors. In most cases, variable flow alone can provide energy savings at a reduced first cost since two-way control valves cost significantly less to purchase and install than three-way valves. In condenser water systems, even though two-way control valves may be an added first cost, they are still typically cost-effective, even for small (one- to two-ton) heat pump and air-conditioning units. (ASHRAE Standard 90.1-1999 requires isolation valves on water-loop heat pumps and *some* amount of variable flow on all hot-water and chilled-water systems.)

Variable speed pumping can dramatically increase energy savings, particularly when it is combined with demand-based pressure reset controls. Variable speed pumps are typically controlled to maintain the system pressure required to keep the most hydraulically remote valve completely open at design conditions. The key to getting the most savings is placement of the differential pressure transducer as close to that remote load as possible. If the system serves multiple hydraulic loops, multiple transducers can be placed at the end of each loop, with a high-signal selector used to transmit the signal to the pumps. With DDC control systems, the pressure signal can be reset by demand and controlled to keep at least one valve at or near 100% open. If valve position is not available from the control system, a "trim-and-respond" algorithm can be employed.

Even with constant-speed pumping, variable flow designs save some energy, as the fixed-speed pumps ride up on their impeller curves, using less energy at reduced flows. For hot water systems, this is often the best life-cycle cost alternative, as the added pump heat will provide some beneficial value. For chilled water systems, it is typically cost-effective to control pumps with variable speed drives.

The author of this GreenTip is Mark Hydeman.

WHEN/WHERE IT'S APPLICABLE

Variable flow design is applicable to chilled water, hot water, and condenser water loops that serve water-cooled air-conditioning and heat pump units. The limitations on each of these loop types are as follows:

- Chillers require a minimum flow through the evaporators. (Chiller manufacturers can specify flow ranges if requested.) Flow minimums on the evaporator side can be achieved via hydronic distribution system design using either a primary/secondary arrangement or primary-only variable flow with a bypass line and valve for minimum flow.
- Some boilers require minimum flows to protect the tubes. These vary greatly by boiler type. Flexible bent water-tube and straight water-tube boilers can take huge ranges of turn-down (close to zero flow). Fire-tube and copper-tube boilers, on the other hand, require a constant flow primary pump.

Variable speed drives on pumps can be used on any variable flow system. As described above, they should be controlled to maintain a minimum system pressure. That system pressure can be reset by valve demand on hot-water and chilled-water systems that have DDC control of the hydronic valves.

PROS AND CONS:

Pro

1. Both variable flow and variable speed control save significant energy.
2. Variable speed drives on pumps provide a "soft" start, extending equipment life.
3. Variable speed drives and two-way valves are self balancing.
4. Application of demand-based pressure reset significantly reduces pump energy and decreases the occurrence of system overpressurization, causing valves near the pumps to lift.
5. Variable speed systems are quieter than constant speed systems.

Con

1. Variable speed drives add cost to the system. (They may not be cost-effective on hot water systems.)

ASHRAE GreenTip #9: Variable Flow/Variable Speed Pumping Systems (continued)

2. Demand-based supply pressure reset can only be achieved with DDC (direct digital control) of the heating/cooling valves.
3. Variable flow on condenser water systems with open towers requires that supplementary measures be taken to keep the fill wet on the cooling towers.

KEY ELEMENTS OF COST

The following provides a possible breakdown of the various cost elements that might differentiate a variable flow/variable speed system from a conventional one and an indication of whether the net cost for the hybrid option is likely to be lower (L), higher (H), or the same (S). This assessment is only a perception of what might be likely, but it obviously may not be correct in all situations. **There is no substitute for a detailed cost analysis as part of the design process.** The listings below may also provide some assistance in identifying the cost elements involved.

First Cost

*   Hydronic system terminal valves: two-way vs. three-way (applicable to heating water and chilled water systems) L
*   Bypass line with two-way valve or alternative means (if minimum chiller flow is required) H
*   Hydronic system isolation valves: two-position vs. none (applicable to condenser water systems) H
*   Cooling tower wet-fill modifications (condenser water systems) H
*   Variable speed drives and associated controls H
*   DDC system (may need to allow demand-based reset) or pressure transducers H
*   Design fees H

Recurring Cost

*   Pumping energy   L
*   Testing and balancing (TAB) of hydronic system   L
*   Maintenance   H
*   Commissioning   H

SOURCES OF FURTHER INFORMATION

Taylor, S., P. Dupont, M. Hydeman, B. Jones, T. Hartman. 1999. *The CoolTools™ Chilled Water Plant Design and Performance Specification Guide.* PG&E Pacific Energy Center, San Francisco, CA.

Optimizing the Design and Control of Chilled Water Plants. Professional Development Seminar (PDS), ASHRAE Learning Institute.

CEC. 2002. *Part II: Measure Analysis and Life-Cycle Cost 2005, California Building Energy Standards,* P400-02-012. California Energy Commission, Sacramento CA. May 16, 2002.

Taylor, S. 2002. Primary-Only vs. Primary-Secondary Variable Flow Chilled Water Systems. *ASHRAE Journal,* February.

Taylor, S, and J. Stein. 2002. Balancing Variable Flow Hydronic Systems. *ASHRAE Journal,* October.

Chapter 9
Energy Conservation Systems

HEAT GENERATORS (HEATING PLANTS)

Considerable improvements in the seasonal efficiency of conventional heating plant equipment, such as boilers and furnaces, have been made over the last several decades. Designers should verify claims of equipment manufacturers by reviewing documented data of this equipment demonstrating the efficiency ratings.

Some nonconventional equipment/techniques to achieve greater efficiency or other possible green building design goals are described in the ASHRAE GreenTips at the end of this chapter.

COOLING GENERATORS (CHILLED WATER PLANTS)

Chilled water plants are most often used in large facilities. Their benefits include higher efficiency and reduced maintenance costs in comparison to decentralized plants.

Generally, a chilled water plant consists of:

- Chillers
- Chilled water pumps
- Condenser water pumps (for water-cooled systems)
- Cooling towers (for water-cooled systems) or air-cooled condensers
- Associated piping, connections, and valves.

Authors contributing to this chapter are David Grumman, Malcolm Lewis, and Mick Schwedler.

Because chilled water temperature can be closely controlled, chilled water plants have an advantage over direct-expansion systems because they allow air temperatures to be closely controlled also.

Often chilled water plant equipment will be in a single central location, allowing system control, maintenance, and problem diagnostics to be performed efficiently. Chilled water plants also allow redundancy to be easily designed into the system by adding one (or more) extra chillers, chilled water pumps, condenser water pumps, and cooling tower fans.

Chiller Types

Electric chillers used within chiller plants employ either a scroll, reciprocating, screw, or centrifugal type compressor (in order of increasing size). Models can be offered with both air-cooled or water-cooled condensers, with the exception that centrifugal compressors today are water-cooled only. Absorption chillers, powered by steam, hot water, natural gas, or other hot gases, are used in some plants to offset high electric demand or consumption charges.

The various chiller types are used most often, though not exclusively, in the following situations.

Electric chillers:

- Where low to moderate electric consumption and demand charges prevail
- Where air-cooled heat dissipation is preferred
- Where condenser heat recovery is desired

Absorption chillers:

- Where low fuel (e.g., natural gas) costs prevail
- Where high electric demand charges prevail
- Where there is a plentiful source of heat available, its main use usually being for other functions.

Heat Pumps. A heat pump is another means of generating cooling as well as heating using the same piece of equipment. There is usually an array of them used for a project, and they are generally distributed throughout the building (i.e., not part of a central plant). See the GreenTips at the end of this chapter on various heat pump system types.

Thermal Energy Storage. Thermal energy storage is a technique that has been encouraged by electricity pricing schedules where the off-peak rate is considerably lower than the on-peak rate. Cooling, in the form of chilled water or ice, is generated during off-peak hours and stored for use on-peak. Although not refrigeration equipment per se, the technique can usually reduce the size of refrigeration equipment – or obviate the need for adding a chiller to an existing plant.

The characteristics, merits, and cost factors of thermal energy storage for cooling, as well as numerous reference sources are presented in GreenTip #15.

System Design Considerations

When a designer puts together a chilled water plant, there are many design parameters to optimize. They include fluid flow rates and temperatures, pumping options, plant configuration, and control methods. For each specific application, the design professional should understand the client's needs and desires and implement the chiller plant options that best satisfy them.

Fluid Flow Rates. Flow rates were discussed in the "Media Movers" section of chapter 7.

Fluid Temperatures. To allow the aforementioned lower flow rates, the chiller must be able to supply colder chilled water temperatures and to tolerate higher condenser leaving temperatures.

Pumping Options. Pumps may be selected to operate with a specific chiller or they may be manifolded.

Pump-per-chiller arrangement advantages include:

- Hydronic simplicity
- Chiller and pump are controlled together
- Pumps and chillers may be sized for one another.

Manifolded-pump arrangement advantages include:

- Simpler redundancy
- Pumps may be centrally located.

Plant Configuration (Multiple Chillers). Today, the most prevalent chiller plant configuration is the *primary-secondary* (decoupled) system. This system allows the flow rate through each chiller to be constant, yet it accommodates a reduction in pumping energy since the system water flow rate varies with the load.

Becoming more common are *variable primary flow* systems that also vary the flow through the chiller evaporators. New chiller controls allow this. Often these systems can be installed at a reduced cost when compared to primary-secondary systems since fewer pumps (and their attendant piping, connections, valves, fittings, and electrical draws) are required. These systems also save energy in comparison to the primary-secondary configuration.

[The subjects of plant configuration, pumping options, and control methods are discussed in detail in ASHRAE's *Fundamentals of Water System Design*, McQuay's *Chilled Water System Manual*, Trane's *Multiple-Chiller-System Design and Control Manual* and Pacific Gas and Electric's *Chilled Water Plant Design Guide*.]

The designer should always review the overall use of energy within a facility and employ systems (including heat recovery systems) that interact with one another so as to minimize the overall energy consumption of the entire chilled water plant.

DISTRIBUTED ELECTRICITY GENERATION

One of the major opportunities for energy conservation in buildings is the use of on-site generation systems to provide both distributed electric power and thermal energy (otherwise wasted heat from the generation process), which can be used to meet the thermal loads of the building.

Distributed generation (DG) provides electricity directly to the building's electrical systems to offset loads that would otherwise have to be met by the utility grid (see Figure 9-2). The waste heat from that generation process goes through a heat recovery mechanism where it may be provided as heat to meet loads for conventional heating (such as space heating, reheat, domestic water heating) or for specialized processes. Alternatively, that heat energy, if at a sufficiently high temperature, can be used to power an

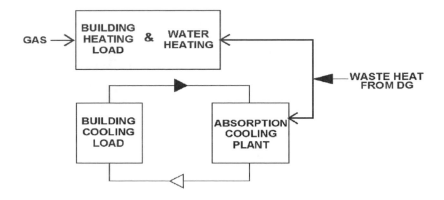

Figure 9-1 Thermal uses of waste heat.

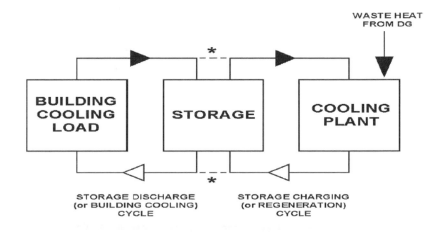

Figure 9-2 Thermal energy storage and waste heat usage.

absorption chiller to produce chilled water to meet either space cooling or process cooling loads. This is shown in Figure 9-1.

Any timing differences between the generation of the waste heat from the DG system and the thermal needs of the building can be handled utilizing a chilled-water thermal energy storage system. This concept may also permit downsizing the absorption cooling system (so it does not need to be sized for the peak cooling load).

The overall usable energy value from the fuel input to the generation process is only about 30% (or less) if there is no waste heat recovery, but it can be over 70% if most or all the waste heat is able to be utilized. This increased system efficiency can have a radical impact on the economics of the energy systems because almost two-and-one-half times the useful value is obtained from the fossil fuel purchased. System sizing is generally done by evaluating the relative electrical and thermal loads over the course of the typical operating cycle and then selecting the system capacity to meet the *lesser* of the thermal or electrical loads. See Figure 9-3 showing comparative thermal and electrical energy for typical office buildings.

If it is sized for the greater of the two, then there will result a net waste of energy produced since it is seldom economical to sell electricity back to the grid. A key design issue that arises here is whether or not the system is being designed to improve efficiency, as discussed above, or as a baseload on-site generation system for purposes of improving the reliability of the electric and/or thermal energy supply. Either of these is a legitimate design criterion, although the goal, from a green design standpoint, almost always focuses on the energy-efficient strategy.

Distributed Generation Technologies

Technologies that can be used for this type of gen-

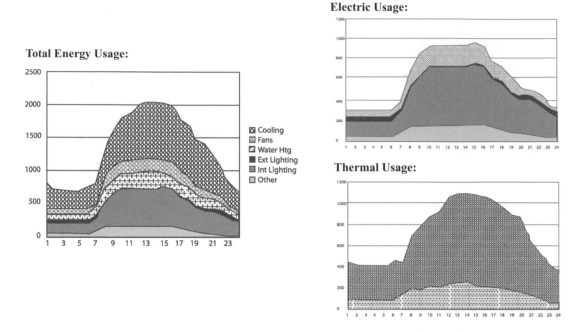

Figure 9-3 Relationship of electric and thermal energy.

Table 9-1. Comparison of Power Generation Options

Generation Option	Efficiency (%)	Typical Size	Installed Costs ($/kW)	O&M Costs ($/kWh)	Life-Cycle Costs (LCC assumes 20 year life-cycle) ($/kWh)
Wind Turbine	NA	5 kW - 600 kW	$750 - $1250	$0.001 - $0.007	$0.036
Hybrid Fuel Cell - Gas Turbine with Heat Recovery*	56-80%	5 KW - 3 MW	$1300 - $1500	$0.005 - $0.010	$0.048
Natural Gas Cogen on-site with Heat Recovery	40-48%	30 KW -300 KW	$600 - $1000	$0.003 - $0.010	$0.052
Natural Gas Power Plant (Combustion Turbine)	28-45%	500 KW - 150 MW	$600-$900	$0.003-$0.008	$0.052
Fuel Cell without Heat Recovery	30-60%	5 KW - 3 MW	$1900-$3500	$0.005-$0.010	$0.072
Natural Gas Cogen on-site without Heat Recovery	20-28%	30 KW - 300 KW	$600-$1000	$0.003-$0.010	$0.072
Photovoltaics (PV)	8%-13%	1 KW - 50 KW	$3500-$6000†	$0.003-$0.005	$0.166

Note: Life-cycle costs assume the same cost for gas as for all technologies. Central technologies will likely have lower rates.
* Hybrid fuel cell microturbine plant is still in testing stage of development, not commercially available, and costs are projected costs for 2004.
† Does not include balance of system components, such as the inverter (AC to DC power), wiring, and controls.

eration include engine-driven generators, micro-turbine-driven generators, or fuel cells. Typically, each uses natural gas as the input fuel. There are advantages and disadvantages associated with these technologies, which are summarized briefly below.

Engine-Driven Generator (EDG). This technology has been around the longest of the three and is in many ways the least expensive option. It produces a relatively high temperature of waste heat that can be more effectively utilized by the heat recovery systems. Disadvantages, however, include air pollution, acoustical impacts, and noise/vibration from the engines. EDG sets are available in sizes ranging from approximately 40 kW to several thousand kW.

Micro-Turbine Generator (MTG). MTGs are at the moment somewhat more expensive in first cost than EDGs, but they have less air pollution and less severe acoustic and vibration impacts than EDGs. They also have longer operating lives and a projected lower cost. However, they are only available at the moment in sizes less than 100 kW per unit as compared to EDGs, which can be up in the several-hundreds-per-unit range.

Fuel Cells. Fuel cells are the most advanced form of power generation in terms of being a "clean and green" technology. They generate virtually no air pollution, have minimal acoustic and vibration impacts, and are considered the "wave of the future." At this point (early in the 2000s decade), however, the cost of fuel cell equipment is still so high as to make it the least attractive of these options from an economic standpoint. It is anticipated that this will change as continued development of the technology evolves over the next several years.

Summary

All the pros and cons of these generation technologies must be taken into account in determining the most appropriate for a specific project. The key point, from a green design perspective, is that any of them are substantially "greener" than utilizing utility grid power for the simple reason that they afford the opportunity to use the waste heat from the electrical generation process.

ASHRAE GreenTip #10: Low-NO$_x$ Burners

GENERAL DESCRIPTION

Low-NO$_x$ burners are natural gas burners with improved energy efficiency and lower emissions of nitrous oxides (NO$_x$).

When fossil fuels are burned, nitric oxide and nitrogen dioxide are produced. These pollutants initiate reactions that result in the production of ozone and acid rain. The NO$_x$ come from two sources: high-temperature combustion (thermal NO$_x$) and nitrogen bound to the fuel (fuel NO$_x$). For clean-burning fuels such as natural gas, fuel NO$_x$ generation is insignificant.

In most cases, NO$_x$ levels are reduced by lowering flame temperature. This can be accomplished by modifying the burner to create a larger (and therefore lower temperature) flame, injecting water or steam into the flame, recirculating flue gases, or limiting the excess air in the combustion process. In many cases a combination of these approaches is used. In general, reducing the flame temperature will reduce the overall efficiency of the boiler. However, recirculating flue gases and controlling the air-fuel mixture can improve boiler efficiency, so that a combination of techniques may improve total boiler efficiency.

Natural-gas-fired burners with lowered NO$_x$ emissions are available for commercial and residential heating applications. One commercial/residential boiler has a burner with inserts above the individual burners; this design reduces NO$_x$ emissions by 30%. The boiler also has a "wet base" heat exchanger to capture more of the burner heat and reduce heat loss to flooring.

NO$_x$ production is of special concern in industrial high-temperature processes because thermal NO$_x$ production increases with temperature. These processes include metal processing, glass manufacturing, pulp and paper mills, and cement kilns. Although natural gas is the cleanest-burning fossil fuel, natural gas can produce NO$_x$ emissions as high as 100 ppm or more.

A burner developed by MIT and the Gas Research Institute combines staged introduction combustion air, flue gas recirculation, and integral reburning to control NO$_x$ emissions. These improvements in burner design result in a low-temperature, fuel-rich primary zone, followed by a low-temperature, lean secondary zone; these low temperatures result in lower NO$_x$ formation. In addition, any NO$_x$ emission present in the recirculated flue gas is reburned, further reducing emissions. A jet pump recirculates a large volume of flue gas to the burner; this reduces NO$_x$ emissions and improves heat transfer.

The low-NO$_x$ burner used for commercial and residential space heating is larger in size than conventional burners, although it is designed for ease of installation.

WHEN/WHERE IT'S APPLICABLE

Low NO$_x$ burners are best applied in regions where air quality is affected by high ground-level ozone and where required by law.

PROS AND CONS

Pro

1. Lowers NO$_x$ and CO emissions, where that is an issue
2. Increases energy efficiency

Con

1. High cost
2. Higher maintenance

KEY ELEMENTS OF COST

The following provides a possible breakdown of the various cost elements that might differentiate a low-NO$_x$ system from a conventional one and an indication of whether the net cost for the alternative system is likely to be lower (L), higher (H), or the same (S). This assessment is only a perception of what might be likely, but it obviously may not be correct in all situations. **There is no substitute for a detailed cost analysis as part of the design process.** The listings below may also provide some assistance in identifying the cost elements involved.

First Cost

- Conventional burner   L
- Low NO$_x$ burner   H

Recurring Cost

- Maintenance   H
- Possible avoidance of pollution fines   L

SOURCES OF FURTHER INFORMATION

American Gas Association, Washington DC 20001. *http://www.aga.org*

The author of this GreenTip is Stephen Carpenter.

ASHRAE GreenTip #11: Combustion Air Preheating

GENERAL DESCRIPTION

For fuel-fired heating equipment, one of the most potent ways to improve efficiency and productivity is to preheat the combustion air going to the burners. The source of this heat energy is the exhaust gas stream, which leaves the process at elevated temperatures. A heat exchanger, placed in the exhaust stack or duct-work, can extract a large portion of the thermal energy in the flue gases and transfer it to the incoming combustion air.

With natural gas, it is estimated that for each 50°F that the combustion air is preheated, overall boiler efficiency increases by approximately 1%. This provides a high leverage boiler plant efficiency measure because increasing boiler efficiency also decreases boiler fuel usage. And, since combustion airflow decreases along with fuel flow, there is a reduction in fan power usage as well.

There are two types of air preheaters: recuperators and regenerators. Recuperators are gas-to-gas heat exchangers placed on the furnace stack. Internal tubes or plates transfer heat from the outgoing exhaust gas to the incoming combustion air while keeping the two streams from mixing. Regenerators include two or more separate heat storage sections. Flue gases and combustion air take turns flowing through each regenerator, alternatively heating the storage medium and then withdrawing heat from it. For uninterrupted operation at least two regenerators and their associated burners are required: one regenerator is needed to fire the furnace while the other is recharging.

WHEN/WHERE IT'S APPLICABLE

While theoretically any boiler can use combustion preheating, flue temperature is customarily used as a rough indication of when it will be cost-effective. However, boilers or processes with low flue temperatures but a high exhaust gas flow may still be good candidates and must be evaluated on a case-by-case basis. Financial justification is based on energy saved, rather than on temperature differential. Some processes produce dirty or corrosive exhaust gases that can plug or attack an exchanger, so material selection is critical.

The author of this GreenTip is Kevin Dickens.

PROS AND CONS

Pro
1. Lowers energy costs
2. Increasing thermal efficiency lowers CO_2 emissions.

Con
1. There are additional material and equipment costs
2. Corrosion and condensation can add to maintenance costs.
3. Low specific heat of air results in relatively low U-factors and less economical heat exchangers.
4. Increasing combustion temperature also increases NO_x emissions.

KEY ELEMENTS OF COST

The following provides a possible breakdown of the various cost elements that might differentiate a building with a combustion preheat system from one without and an indication of whether the net cost is likely to be lower (L), higher (H), or the same (S). This assessment is only a perception of what might be likely, but it obviously may not be correct in all situations. **There is no substitute for a detailed cost analysis as part of the design process.** The listings below may also provide some assistance in identifying the cost elements involved.

First Cost

• Equipment costs	H
• Controls	S
• Design fees	H

Recurring Cost

• Overall energy cost	L
• Maintenance of system	H
• Training of building operators	H

SOURCES OF FURTHER INFORMATION

Fiorino, D.P. 2000. Six Conservation and efficiency measures reducing steam costs. *ASHRAE Journal* 42(2).

Office of Industrial Technologies, Energy Efficiency, and Renewable Energy, U.S. Department of Energy. *Energy Tip Sheet #1*, May 2002.

ASHRAE GreenTip #12: Combination Space/Water Heaters

GENERAL DESCRIPTION

Combination space and water heating systems consist of a storage water heater, a heat delivery system (for example, a fan coil or hydronic baseboards), and associated pumps and controls. Typically gas-fired, they provide both space and domestic water heating. The water heater is installed and operated as a conventional water heater. When there is a demand for domestic hot water, cold city water enters the bottom of the tank, and hot water from the top of the tank is delivered to the load. When there is a demand for space heating, a pump circulates water from the top of the tank through fan coils or hydronic baseboards.

The storage tank is maintained at the desired temperature for domestic hot water (e.g., 140°F). Because this temperature is cooler than conventional hydronic systems, the space heating delivery system needs to be slightly larger than typical. Alternatively, the storage tank can be operated at a higher water temperature; this requires tempering valves to prevent scalding at the taps.

The water heater can be either a conventional storage type water heater (either naturally venting or power vented) or a recuperative (condensing) gas boiler. Conventional water heaters have an efficiency of approximately 60%. By adding the space heating load, the energy factor increases because of longer run times and reduced standby losses on a percentage basis. Recuperative boilers can have efficiencies approaching 90%.

WHEN/WHERE IT'S APPLICABLE

These units are best suited to buildings that have similar space and water heating loads, including dormitories, apartments, and condos. They are suited to all climate types.

PROS AND CONS

Pro

1. Reduces floor space requirements
2. Lowers capital cost
3. Improves energy efficiency
4. Increases tank life

Con

1. They are only available in small sizes
2. All space heating piping has to be designed for potable water
3. No ferrous metals or lead-based solder can be used
4. All components must be able to withstand prevailing city water pressures.

KEY ELEMENTS OF COST

The following provides a possible breakdown of the various cost elements that might differentiate a combination space and water heating system from a conventional one and an indication of whether the net cost for the hybrid option is likely to be lower (L), higher (H), or the same (S). This assessment is only a perception of what might be likely, but it obviously may not be correct in all situations. **There is no substitute for a detailed cost analysis as part of the design process.** The listings below may also provide some assistance in identifying the cost elements involved.

First Cost

• Conventional heating equipment	L
• Combination space/domestic water heater	H
• Sanitizing/inspecting space heating system	H
• Piping and components able to withstand higher pressures	H
• Floor space used	L

Recurring Cost

• Heating energy	L
• Maintenance	L

SOURCES OF FURTHER INFORMATION

Combo Heating Systems: A Design Guide. Union Gas, Chatham ON, CAN N7M5M1. *http://www.uniongas.com*

Sustainable Sources. *http://www.greenbuilder.com/sourcebook/GasWaterHeat.html*

U.S. Department of Energy. *http://www.eere.energy.gov/consumerinfo/refbriefs/ad6.html.*

The author of this GreenTip is Stephen Carpenter.

ASHRAE GreenTip #13: Ground-Source Heat Pumps

GENERAL DESCRIPTION

A ground-source heat pump extracts solar heat stored in the upper layers of the earth; the heat is then delivered to a building. Conversely, in the summer season, the heat pump rejects heat removed from the building into the ground rather than into the atmosphere or a body of water.

Ground-source heat pumps (GSHP) can reduce the energy required for space heating, cooling, and service water heating in commercial/institutional buildings by as much as 50%. Ground-source heat pumps replace the need for a boiler in winter by utilizing heat stored in the ground; this heat is upgraded by a vapor-compressor refrigeration cycle. In summer, heat from a building is rejected to the ground. This eliminates the need for a cooling tower or heat rejector and also lowers operating costs because the ground is cooler than the outdoor air.

Water-to-air heat pumps are typically installed throughout a building with ductwork serving only the immediate zone; a two-pipe water distribution system conveys water to and from the ground-source heat exchanger. The heat exchanger field consists of a grid of vertical boreholes with plastic U-tube heat exchangers connected in parallel.

Simultaneous heating and cooling can occur throughout the building, as individual heat pumps, controlled by zone thermostats, can operate in heating or cooling mode as required.

Unlike conventional boiler/cooling tower type water-loop heat pumps, the heat pumps used in GSHP applications are generally designed to operate at lower inlet-water temperature. GSHP are also more efficient than conventional heat pumps, with higher COPs and EERs. Because there are lower water temperatures in the two-pipe loop, piping needs to be insulated to prevent sweating; in addition, a larger circulation pump is needed because the units are slightly larger in the perimeter zones requiring larger flows.

Ground-source heat pumps reduce energy use and, hence, atmospheric emissions. Conventional boilers and their associated emissions are eliminated since no supplementary form of energy is usually required. Typically, single packaged heat pump units have no field refrigerant connections and thus have significantly lower refrigerant leakage compared to central chiller systems.

GSHP units have life spans of 20 years or more. The two-pipe water-loop system typically used allows for unit placement changes to accommodate new tenants or changes in building use. The plastic piping used in the heat exchanger should last as long

The author of this GreenTip is Stephen Carpenter.

as the building itself.

When the system is disassembled, attention must be given to the removal and recycling of the HCFC or HFC refrigerants used in the heat pumps themselves and the antifreeze solution typically used in the ground heat exchanger.

WHEN/WHERE IT'S APPLICABLE

The most economic application of ground-source heat pumps is in buildings that require significant space/water heating and cooling over extended hours of operation. Examples are retirement communities, multi-family complexes, large office buildings, retail shopping malls, and schools. Building types not well-suited to the technology are buildings where space and water heating loads are relatively small or where hours of use are limited.

PROS AND CONS

Pro

1. Requires less mechanical room space
2. Requires less outdoor equipment
3. Does not require roof penetrations, maintenance decks, or architectural blends
4. Has quiet operation
5. Reduces operation and maintenance costs
6. Requires simple controls only
7. Requires less space in ceilings
8. Loop piping, carrying low-temperature water, does not have to be insulated
9. Installation costs are lower than for many central HVAC systems

Con

1. Requires surface area for heat exchanger field
2. Higher initial cost overall
3. Requires additional site coordination and supervision

KEY ELEMENTS OF COST

The following provides a possible breakdown of the various cost elements that might differentiate a ground-source heat pump system from a conventional one and an indication of whether the net cost for it is likely to be lower (L), higher (H), or the same (S). This assessment is only a perception of what might be likely, but it obviously may not be correct in all situations. **There is no substitute for a detailed cost analysis as part of the design process.** The listings below may also provide some assistance in identifying the cost elements involved.

ASHRAE GreenTip #13: Ground-Source Heat Pumps (continued)

First Cost

- Conventional heating/cooling generators   L
- Heat pumps   H
- Outside piping system   H
- Heat exchanger field   H
- Operator training   H
- Design fees   H

Recurring Cost

- Energy cost (fossil fuel for conventional)   L
- Energy cost (electricity for heat pumps)   H
- Maintenance   L

SOURCES OF FURTHER INFORMATION

ASHRAE. 1995. *Commercial/Institutional Ground-Source Heat Pump Engineering Manual.* Atlanta: American Society of Heating, Refrigerating and Air-Conditioning Engineers, Inc.

Caneta Research Inc. GS-2000TM (a computer program for designing and sizing ground heat exchangers for these systems). Caneta Research Inc., Mississauga, ON, CAN L5N 6J7.

Canadian Earth Energy Association, Ottawa ON, CAN K1P 6E2. *http://www.earthenergy.org.*

The Energy Outlet. *http://www.energyoutlet.com*

RETScreen (software for renewable energy analysis), Natural Resources Canada. *retscreen.gc.ca*

Kavanaugh, Stephen P., and Kevin Rafferty. 1997. *Ground-Source Heat Pumps: Design of Geothermal Systems for Commercial and Institutional Buildings.* Atlanta: Amercian Society of Heating, Refrigerating and Air-Conditioning Engineers, Inc.

ASHRAE GreenTip #14: Water-Loop Heat Pump Systems

GENERAL DESCRIPTION

A water-loop heat pump system consists of multiple water-source heat pumps serving local areas within a building and tied in to a neutral-temperature (usually 60-90°F) water loop that serves as both heat source and heat sink. The loop is connected to a central heat source (e.g., small boiler) and a central heat dissipation device (e.g., closed-circuit evaporative condenser or open-circuit cooling tower isolated from building loop via heat exchanger). These operate to keep the temperature of the loop water within range.

The water-source heat pump itself is an electric-driven, self-contained, water-cooled heating and cooling unit with a reversible refrigerant cycle (i.e., a water-cooled air-conditioning unit that can run in reverse). Its components include heat exchanger, heating/cooling coil, compressor, fan, and reversing controls, all in a common casing. The heat exchanger and coil are designed to accept hot and cold refrigerant liquid or gas. The units can be located either within the space (e.g., low, along outside wall) or remotely (e.g., in a ceiling plenum or in a separate nearby mechanical room).

Piping all of the water-to-refrigerant heat exchangers together in a common loop yields what is essentially an internal source heat recovery system. In effect, the system is capable of recovering heat energy (through the cooling process) and redistributing it where it is needed.

During the cooling mode, heat energy is extracted from room air circulated across the coil (just like a room air-conditioner) and rejected to the water loop. In this mode, the unit's heat exchanger acts as a condenser and the coil as an evaporator. In the heating mode, the process is reversed: specifically, a reversing valve allows the heat exchanger to function as the evaporator and the coil as the condenser so that heat extracted from the water loop is "rejected" to the air being delivered to the occupied space, thus heating the space.

In addition to the components mentioned above, the system includes equipment and specialties normally associated with a closed hydronic system (e.g., pumps, filters, air separator, expansion tank, make-up system, etc.)

The authors of this GreenTip are Kevin Dickens and David Grumman.

ASHRAE GreenTip #14: Water-Loop Heat Pump Systems (continued)

WHEN/WHERE IT'S APPLICABLE

A water-source heat pump system is well qualified for applications where simultaneous heating and cooling needs/opportunities exist. (An example might be a building where, in certain seasons, south side or interior rooms need cooling at the same time north side rooms require heating.) Appropriate applications may include office buildings, hotels, schools, apartments, extended care facilities, and retail stores.

The system's characteristics may make it particularly suitable when a building is to be air-conditioned in stages, perhaps due to cost constraints; once the basic system is in, additional heat pumps can be added as needed and tied in to the loop. Further, since it uses low-temperature water, this system is an ideal candidate for mating with a hydronic solar collection system (since such solar systems are more efficient the lower the water temperature they generate).

PROS AND CONS

Pro

1. It can make use of energy that would otherwise be rejected to atmosphere.
2. Loop piping, carrying low-temperature water, does not have to be insulated.
3. When applied correctly, the system can save energy. (Note: Some factors tend to decrease energy cost, and some tend to increase it; which prevails will determine whether savings result.)
4. It is quieter than a system utilizing air-cooled condensers (i.e., through-the-wall room air conditioners).
5. Failure of one heat pump unit does not affect others.
6. It can condition (heat or cool) local areas of a building without having to run the entire system.

Con

1. Multiple compressors located throughout a building can be a maintenance concern because of their being noncentralized and sometimes difficult to access (e.g., above the ceiling).

2. Effective water filtration is critical to proper operation of heat exchangers.
3. There is an increased potential for noise within the conditioned space from heat pump units.
4. Some of the energy used in the heating cycle is derived from electricity (used to drive the heat pump compressors), which may be more expensive than energy derived from fossil fuel.

KEY ELEMENTS OF COST

The following provides a possible breakdown of the various cost elements that might differentiate the above system from a conventional one and an indication of whether the net incremental cost for the alternative option is likely to be lower (L), higher (H), or the same (S). This assessment is only a perception of what might be likely, but it obviously may not be correct in all situations. **There is no substitute for a detailed cost analysis as part of the design process.** The listings below may also provide some assistance in identifying the cost elements involved.

First Cost

• Equipment costs (will vary depending on what type of conventional system would otherwise be used)	S/L
• Controls	S
• Design fees	S

Recurring Cost:

• Overall energy cost	L
• Maintenance of system	H
• Training of building operators	H

SOURCES OF FURTHER INFORMATION

Trane Water-Source Heat Pump System Design Application Engineering Manual. 1994. Publication SYS-AM-7, Trane, Lacrosse, WI.
Web sites:
http://cipco.apogee.net/ces/hucw.asp
http://www.heatpumpcentre.org/tutorial/building.htm
http://tristate.apogee.net/cool/cchc.asp

ASHRAE GreenTip #15: Thermal Energy Storage for Cooling

GENERAL DESCRIPTION

Active thermal storage systems utilize a building's cooling equipment to remove heat, usually at night, from an energy storage medium for later use as a source of cooling. The most common energy storage media are ice and chilled water. These systems decouple the production of cooling from the demand for cooling, i.e., plant output does not have to match the instantaneous building cooling load. This decoupling increases flexibility in design and operations, thereby providing an opportunity for a more efficient air-conditioning system than with a non-storage alternative. Before applying active thermal storage, however, the design cooling load should be minimized.

Although many operating strategies are possible, the basic principle of a thermal energy storage system is to reduce peak building cooling loads by shifting a portion of peak cooling production to times when the building cooling load is lower. Energy is typically charged, stored, and discharged on a daily or weekly cycle. The net result is an opportunity to run a chiller plant at peak efficiency during the majority of its operating period. A non-storage system, on the other hand, has to follow the building cooling load, and the majority of its operation is at part-load conditions. Part-load operation of chiller plants comes at the expense of efficiency.

Several buildings have demonstrated site energy reductions with the application of thermal energy storage as discussed in both the "Pro" and "Sources of Further Information" sections following.

In addition to the potential of site energy reduction, operation of thermal energy storage systems can reduce energy resource consumption. This reduction is due to a shift toward using energy during periods of low aggregate electric utility demand. As a result, transmission and distribution losses are lower and power plant generating efficiencies can be higher because the load is served by base-load plants. Thermal storage can also have beneficial effects on combined heat and power systems by flattening thermal and electric load profiles.

The ASHRAE *Design Guide for Cool Thermal Storage* (Dorgan and Elleson 1993) covers cool storage application issues and design parameters in some detail.

WHEN/WHERE IT'S APPLICABLE

Thermal energy storage systems tend to perform well in situations where there is variability in loads.

Successful applications of thermal energy storage systems have included commercial office buildings, schools, worship facilities, convention centers, hotels, health care facilities, industrial processes, and turbine inlet air cooling.

PROS AND CONS

Pro

1. **Capital cost savings.** Because thermal energy storage allows downsizing the refrigeration system, the resulting cost savings (which may include *avoiding* having to add such equipment on an existing project) may substantially or entirely cover the added incremental cost of the storage system proper (see also Con #1 below).

2. **Reduced size of refrigerating equipment**. The addition of a thermal energy storage system allows the size of refrigerating equipment to be reduced since it will have to meet an average cooling load rather than the peak cooling load. Reduced refrigeration equipment size means less on-site refrigerant usage and lower probability of environmental impacts due to direct effects.

3. **Factors increasing energy efficiency.** Because thermal energy storage allows operation of the refrigeration system at or near peak efficiency during all operating hours, the annual energy usage may be lower than non-storage systems that must operate at lower part-load ratios to meet instantaneous loads. In addition, since off-peak hours are usually at night when lower ambient temperatures prevail, lower condensing temperatures required for heat rejection would tend to increase refrigeration efficiency. A number of carefully documented examples of energy savings can be found in the literature, including Bahnfleth and Joyce (1994), Fiorino (1994), and Goss et al. (1996).

4. **Reduced environmental impacts.** Because thermal energy storage systems shift the consumption of site energy from on-peak to off-peak periods, the total energy resources required to deliver cooling to the facility will be lower (Reindl et al. 1995 and Gansler et al. 2001). In addition, in some electric grids, the last generation plants to be used to meet peak loads may be the most polluting per kW of energy produced (Gupta 2002); in such cases, emissions would be further reduced by the use of thermal energy storage.

The author of this GreenTip is Douglas Reindl.

ASHRAE GreenTip #15: Thermal Energy Storage for Cooling (continued)

5. **Related high-efficiency technologies.** Thermal energy storage enables the practical incorporation of other high-efficiency technologies such as cold-air distribution systems and nighttime heat recovery.

6. **Electric power infrastructure.** Thermal energy storage can be effective at preventing or delaying the need to construct additional power generation and transmission equipment.

Con

1. **Capital cost increases.** Compared to a conventional system, the thermal storage element proper (water tank or ice tank) and any associated pumping, piping accessories, and controls add to the incremental capital cost. If the system's refrigeration equipment can be reduced in size sufficiently (see Pro #1), this burden may be mitigated substantially or balanced out.

2. **Factors decreasing energy efficiency.** The need to generate cooling at evaporator temperatures lower than conventional ones tends to decrease refrigeration efficiency. This reduction may be overcome, however, by factors that increase efficiency (see Pro #3 above).

3. **Engineering.** Successful thermal energy storage systems require additional efforts in the design phase of a project.

4. **Space.** Thermal energy storage systems will require increased site space usage. The impact of site space usage can be mitigated by considering ice storage technologies.

5. **Operations.** Because a thermal storage system departs from the norm of system operation, continued training of facility operations staff is required as well as procedures for propagating system knowledge through a succession of facilities personnel.

KEY ELEMENTS OF COST

The following provides a possible breakdown of the various cost elements that might differentiate the system above from a conventional one and an indication of whether the net cost for the alternative option is likely to be lower (L), higher (H), or the same (S). This assessment is only a perception of what might be likely, but it obviously may not be correct in all situations. **There is no substitute for a detailed cost analysis as part of the design process.** The listings

below may also provide some assistance in identifying the cost elements involved.

First Cost

• Storage element (CHW tank or ice tank)	H
• Additional pumping/piping re storage element	H
• Chiller/heat rejection system	L
• Controls	H
• Electrical (re chiller/heat rejection system)	S/L
• Design fees	H
• Operator training	H
• Commissioning	S/H
• Site space	H

Recurring Cost

• Electric energy	L
• Operator training (on-going)	H

SOURCES OF FURTHER INFORMATION

Bahnfleth, W.P., and W.S. Joyce. 1994. Energy use in a district cooling system with stratified chilled water storage. *ASHRAE Transactions* 100(1): 1767-1778.

California Energy Commission. 1996. Source Energy and Environmental Impacts of Thermal Energy Storage. Tabors, Caramanis & Assoc.

Dorgan, C., and J.S. Elleson. 1993. *Cool Storage Design Guide,* Atlanta: ASHRAE.

Elleson, J.S. 1996. *Successful Cool Storage Projects: From Planning to Operation.* ASHRAE.

Fiorino, D.P. 1994. Energy conservation with stratified chilled water storage. *ASHRAE Transactions* 100(1): 1754-1766.

Goss, J.O., L. Hyman, and J. Corbett. 1996. Integrated heating, cooling and thermal energy storage with heat pump provides economic and environmental solutions at California State University, Fullerton. *EPRI International Conference on Sustainable Thermal Energy Storage,* pp. 163-167.

Gupta, A. Director of Energy, NRDC. *New York Times*, March 17, 2002.

Lawson, 1988. Computer facility keeps cool with ice storage. *HPAC*, August.

Mathaudhu, S.S. 1999. Energy conservation showcase. *ASHRAE Journal* 41(4): 44-46.

Reindl, D.T., R.A. Gansler, and T.B. Jekel. 2001. Simulation of source energy utilization and emissions for HVAC systems. *ASHRAE Transactions* 107(1): 39-51.

ASHRAE GreenTip #15: Thermal Energy Storage for Cooling (continued)

Reindl, D.T., D.E. Knebel, and R.A. Gansler. 1995. Characterising the marginal basis source energy and emissions associated with comfort cooling systems. *ASHRAE Transactions* 101(1): 1353-1363.

O'Neal, E.J. 1996. Thermal sorage system achieves operating and first-cost savings (Technology Award case study). *ASHRAE Journal* 38(4).

Galuska, E.J. 1994. Thermal storage system reduces costs of manufacturing facility (Technology Award case study). *ASHRAE Journal*, March.

Duffy, G. 1992. Thermal storage shifts to saving energy. *Eng. Sys.*

Links to Other Efficient Buildings Utilizing Thermal Energy Storage

Centex—Most efficient building in U.S. in 1999: *http://www.energystar.gov/index.cfm?fuseaction=labeled_buildings.showProfile&profile_id=1306*

LEED Gold Building Hewlett Foundation: *http://www.usgbc.org/Docs/Certified_Projects/Cert_Reg67.pdf*

ASHRAE GreenTip #16: Double-Effect Absorption Chillers

GENERAL DESCRIPTION

Chilled water systems that use fuel types other than electricity can help offset high electric prices, whether those high prices are caused by consumption or demand charges. Absorption chillers use thermal energy (rather than electricity) to produce chilled water. A double-effect absorption chiller using high-pressure steam (115 psig) has a COP of approximately 1.20. Some double-effect absorption chillers use low-pressure steam (60 psig) or 350-370°F hot water, but with lower efficiency or higher cost.

Double-effect absorption chillers are available from several manufacturers. Most are limited to chilled water temperatures of 40°F or above, since water is the refrigerant. The interior of the chiller experiences corrosive conditions; therefore, the manufacturer's material selection is directly related to the chiller life. The more robust the materials, the longer the life.

WHEN/WHERE IT'S APPLICABLE

Double-effect absorption chillers can be used in the following applications:

- When natural gas prices (used to produce steam) are significantly lower than electric prices.
- When the design team and building owner wish to have fuel flexibility to hedge against changes in future utility prices.

- When there is steam available from an on-site process; an example is steam from a turbine.
- When a steam plant is available but lightly loaded during the cooling season. Many hospitals have large steam plants that run at extremely low loads, low efficiency, during the cooling season. By installing an absorption chiller, the steam plant efficiency can be increased significantly during the cooling season.
- At sites that have limited electric power available.
- In locations where district steam is available at a reasonable price (e.g., New York City).

PROS AND CONS

Pro

1. Reduces electric charges.
2. Allows fuel flexibility, since (e.g.) natural gas, No. 2 fuel oil, propane, or waste steam may be used to supply thermal energy for the absorption chiller.
3. Uses water as the refrigerant, making it environmentally friendly.
4. Allows system expansion even at sites with limited electric power.
5. When the system is designed and controlled properly, it allows versatile use of various power sources.

The author of this GreenTip is Mick Schwedler.

ASHRAE GreenTip #16: Double-Effect Absorption Chillers (continued)

Con

1. Cost of an absorption chiller will be roughly double that of an electric chiller of the same capacity as opposed to 25% more for a single-effect absorption machine.
2. Size of an absorption chiller is larger than an electric chiller of the same capacity.
3. Although absorption chiller efficiency has increased in the past decade, the amount of heat rejected is significantly higher than that of a similar capacity electric chiller. This requires larger cooling towers, condenser pipes, and cooling tower pumps.
4. Few plant operators are familiar with absorption technology.

KEY ELEMENTS OF COST

The following provides a possible breakdown of the various cost elements that might differentiate an absorption chiller system from a conventional one—and an indication of whether the net cost for the hybrid option is likely to be lower (L), higher (H), or the same (S). This assessment is only a perception of what might be likely, but it obviously may not be correct in all situations. **There is no substitute for a detailed cost analysis as part of the design process.** The listings below may also provide some assistance in identifying the cost elements involved.

First Cost

• Absorption chiller	H
• Cooling tower and associated equipment	H
• Electricity feed	L
• Design fees	H
• System controls	H

Recurring Cost

• Electric costs	L
• Chiller maintenance	S
• Training of building operators	H

SOURCES OF FURTHER INFORMATION

Trane Co. 1999. *Trane Applications Engineering Manual, Absorption Chiller System Design, SYS-AM-13.*

ASHRAE. 2000. *2000 ASHRAE Handbook—HVAC Systems and Equipment*, p. 4.1.

ASHRAE. 2002. *2002 ASHRAE Handbook—Refrigeration*, chapter 41.

ASHRAE GreenTip #17: Gas-Engine-Driven Chillers

GENERAL DESCRIPTION

Chilled water systems that use fuel types other than electricity can help offset high electric prices, whether those high prices are caused by consumption or demand charges. Gas engines can be used in conjunction with electric chillers to produce chilled water.

Depending on chiller efficiency, a gas engine-driven chiller may have a cooling coefficient of performance (COP) of 1.6 to 2.3.

Some gas engines are directly coupled to a chiller's shaft. Another option is to use a gas engine and switchgear. In such cases, the chiller may either be operated using electricity from the engine or from the electric utility.

WHEN/WHERE IT'S APPLICABLE

A gas engine is applicable in the following circumstances:

- When natural gas prices are significantly lower than electric prices.
- When the design team and building owner wish to have fuel flexibility to hedge against changes in future utility prices.
- At sites that have limited electric power available.

PROS AND CONS

Pro

1. Reduces electric charges.
2. Allows fuel flexibility if installed as a hybrid system (part gas engine and part electric chiller, so the plant may use either gas engine or electricity from utility).
3. Allows system expansion even at sites with limited electric power.
4. When the system is designed and controlled properly, allows versatile use of various fuel sources.
5. May be used in conjunction with an emergency generator if switchgear provided.

The author of this GreenTip is Mick Schwedler.

Con

1. Added cost of gas engine.
2. Additional space required for engine.
3. Due to amount of heat rejected being significantly higher than for similar capacity electric chiller, larger cooling towers, condenser pipes, and cooling tower pumps may be required.
4. Site emissions are increased.
5. Noise from engine may need to be attenuated, both inside and outside.
6. Significant engine maintenance costs.

KEY ELEMENTS OF COST

The following provides a possible breakdown of the various cost elements that might differentiate a gas-engine-driven chiller from a conventional one and an indication of whether the net cost is likely to be lower (L), higher (H), or the same (S). This assessment is only a perception of what might be likely, but it obviously may not be correct in all situations. **There is no substitute for a detailed cost analysis as part of the design process.** The listings below may also provide some assistance in identifying the cost elements involved.

First Cost

• Gas engine	H
• Cooling tower and associated equipment	H
• Electricity feed	L
• Site emissions	H
• Site acoustics	H
• Design fees	H
• System controls	H

Recurring Cost

• Electric costs	L
• Engine maintenance	H
• Training of building operators	H
• Emissions costs	H

SOURCES OF FURTHER INFORMATION

New Buildings Institute. 1998. *Gas Engine Driven Chillers Guideline.* Fair Oaks, Calif.: New Buildings Institute and Southern California Gas Company. *http://www.newbuildings.org/downloads/guidelines/GasEngine.pdf*

ASHRAE GreenTip #18: Gas-Fired Chiller/Heaters

GENERAL DESCRIPTION

Chilled water systems that use fuel types other than electricity can help offset high electricity prices, whether those high prices are caused by consumption or demand charges. Absorption chillers use thermal energy (rather than electricity) to produce chilled water. Some gas-fired absorption chillers can provide not only chilled water but also hot water. They are referred to as "chiller-heaters."

A gas-fired absorption chiller has a cooling COP of approximately 1.0 and heating efficiency in the range of about 80%.

Gas-fired chiller-heaters are available from several manufacturers. Most are limited to chilled water supply temperatures of 40°F or above, since water is the refrigerant. Some manufacturers offer dual-fuel capability (natural gas or No. 2 fuel oil).

WHEN/WHERE IT'S APPLICABLE

Gas-fired chiller-heaters are applicable in the following circumstances:

- When natural gas prices are significantly lower than electric prices.
- At sites where a boiler can be eliminated by using the chiller-heater.
- When the design team and building owner wish to have fuel flexibility to hedge against changes in future utility prices.
- At sites that have limited electric power available.

PROS AND CONS

Pro

1. Reduces electric charges.
2. Allows fuel flexibility, since either natural gas or No. 2 fuel oil may be used to supply thermal energy for the absorption chiller.
3. May allow a boiler to be eliminated.
4. Uses water as the refrigerant, making it environmentally friendly.
5. Allows system expansion even at sites with limited electric power.
6. When the system is designed and controlled properly, allows versatile use of various fuel sources.

Con

1. Cost will be roughly double that of the same capacity electric chiller.

2. Size of absorption chiller will be larger than the same capacity electric chiller and added space is required.
3. The amount of heat rejected is significantly higher than from a similar capacity electric chiller, approximately double that of a single-stage absorption machine, 50% greater for a two-stage unit.
4. Larger cooling towers, condenser pipes, and cooling tower pumps are required compared with electric-drive machines.
5. Few plant operators are familiar with absorption technology.

KEY ELEMENTS OF COST

The following provides a possible breakdown of the various cost elements that might differentiate the above system from a conventional one and an indication of whether the net cost for the hybrid option is likely to be lower (L), higher (H), or the same (S). This assessment is only a perception of what might be likely, but it obviously may not be correct in all situations. **There is no substitute for a detailed cost analysis as part of the design process.** The listings below may also provide some assistance in identifying the cost elements involved.

First Cost

- Absorption chiller   H
- Possible boiler elimination   L
- Cooling tower and associated equipment   H
- Electricity feed   L
- Design fees   H
- System controls   H

Recurring Cost

- Electric costs   L
- Chiller maintenance   S
- Training of building operators   H

SOURCES OF FURTHER INFORMATION

Applications Engineering Manual for Direct-Fired Absorption. American Gas Cooling Center. January 1994.

Trane Applications Engineering Manual, "Absorption Chiller System Design," SYS-AM-13. Trane Company, May 1999.

ASHRAE. 2000. *2000 ASHRAE Handbook—HVAC Systems and Equipment,* p. 4.1.

ASHRAE. 2002. *2002 ASHRAE Handbook—Refrigeration,* chapter 41.

The author of this GreenTip is Mick Schwedler.

ASHRAE GreenTip #19: Desiccant Cooling and Dehumidification

GENERAL DESCRIPTION

Rotary desiccant dehumidifiers use solid desiccants such as silica gel to attract water vapor from the moist air. Humid air, generally referred to as the process air, is dehumidified in one part of the desiccant bed while a different part of the bed is dried for reuse by a second airstream known as reactivation air. The desiccant rotates slowly between these two airstreams so that dry, high-capacity desiccant leaving the reactivation air is available to remove moisture from the moist process air.

Process air that passes through the bed more slowly is dried more deeply, so for air requiring a lower dew point, a larger unit (slower velocity) is required. The reactivation air inlet temperature changes the outlet moisture content of the process air. In turn, if the designer needs dry air, it is generally more economical to use high reactivation temperatures. On the other hand, if the leaving humidity need not be especially low, inexpensive low-grade heat sources such as waste heat or rejected cogeneration heat can be used.

The process air outlet temperature is higher than the inlet temperature primarily because the heat of sorption of the moisture removed is converted to sensible heat. The outlet temperature rises roughly in proportion to the amount of moisture that is removed. In most comfort applications, provisions must be made to remove excess sensible heat from the process air following reactivation. Cooling is accomplished with cooling coils, and the source of this cooling affects the operating economics of the system.

WHEN/WHERE IT'S APPLICABLE

In general, applications that require a dew point at or below 40°F may be candidates for active desiccant dehumidification. Examples include facilities handling hygroscopic materials; film drying; the manufacture of candy, chocolate, or chewing gum; the manufacture of drugs and chemicals; the manufacture of plastic materials; packaging of moisture-sensitive products; and the manufacture of electronics. Supermarkets often use desiccant dehumidification to avoid condensation on refrigerated casework. And when there is a need for a lower dew point and a convenient source of low-grade heat for reactivation is available, rotary desiccant dehumidifiers can be especially economical.

PROS AND CONS

Pro

1. Desiccant equipment tends to be very durable.
2. Often this is the most economical means to dehumidify below a 40°F dew point.
3. It eliminates condensate in the airstream, in turn limiting the opportunity for mold growth.

Con

1. Desiccant usually must be replaced, replenished, or reconditioned every 5 to 10 years.
2. In comfort applications, simultaneous heating and cooling may be required.
3. The process is not especially intuitive and the controls are relatively complicated.

KEY ELEMENTS OF COST

The following provides a possible breakdown of the various cost elements that might differentiate a building with a rotary desiccant dehumidification system from one without and an indication of whether the net cost is likely to be lower (L), higher (H), or the same (S). This assessment is only a perception of what might be likely, but it obviously may not be correct in all situations. **There is no substitute for a detailed cost analysis as part of the design process.** The listings below may also provide some assistance in identifying the cost elements involved.

First Cost

• Equipment costs	H
• Regeneration (heat source and supply)	H
• Ductwork	S
• Controls	H
• Design fees	S

Recurring Cost

• Overall energy cost	S/H
• Maintenance of system	H
• Training of building operators	H
• Filters	H

SOURCES OF FURTHER INFORMATION

ASHRAE. 2000. 2000 *ASHRAE Handbook—HVAC Systems and Equipment.*

The author of this GreenTip is Kevin Dickens.

ASHRAE GreenTip #20: Indirect Evaporative Cooling

GENERAL DESCRIPTION

Evaporative cooling of supply air can be used to reduce the amount of energy consumed by mechanical cooling equipment. Two general types of evaporative cooling—direct and indirect—are available. The effectiveness of either of these methods is directly dependent on the extent that dry-bulb temperature exceeds wet-bulb temperature in the supply airstream.

Direct evaporative cooling introduces water directly into the supply airstream, usually with a spray or wetted media. As the water absorbs heat from the air, it evaporates. While this process lowers the dry-bulb temperature of the supply airstream, it also increases the air moisture content.

By contrast, *indirect evaporative cooling* uses an additional water-side coil to lower supply air temperature. The added coil is placed ahead of the conventional cooling coil in the supply airstream and is piped to a cooling tower where the evaporative process occurs. Because evaporation occurs elsewhere, this method of "precooling" does not add moisture to the supply air, but it is somewhat less effective than direct evaporative cooling.

A conventional cooling coil provides any additional cooling required.

WHEN/WHERE IT'S APPLICABLE

In climates with low wet-bulb temperatures, significant amounts of cooling are available. In such climates, the size of the conventional cooling system can be reduced as well.

In more humid climates, indirect evaporative cooling can be applied during non-peak seasons. It is especially applicable for loads that operate 24 hours a day for many days of the year.

PROS AND CONS

Pro

1. Indirect evaporative cooling can reduce the size of the conventional cooling system.
2. It reduces cooling costs during periods of low wet-bulb temperature.

3. It does not add moisture to the supply airstream (in contrast, direct evaporative cooling does add moisture).
4. It may be designed into equipment such as self-contained units.

Con

1. Airside pressure drop (typically 0.2 to 0.4 inches water column) increases due to an additional coil in the airstream.
2. To make water cooler, the cooling tower fans operate for longer periods of time and consume more energy.
3. Condenser piping and controls must be accounted for during design process.

KEY ELEMENTS OF COST

The following provides a possible breakdown of the various cost elements that might differentiate an indirect evaporative cooling system from a conventional one and an indication of whether the net cost for the hybrid option is likely to be lower (L), higher (H), or the same (S). This assessment is only a perception of what might be likely, but it obviously may not be correct in all situations. **There is no substitute for a detailed cost analysis as part of the design process.** The listings below may also provide some assistance in identifying the cost elements involved.

First Cost

• Indirect cooling coil	H
• Decreased conventional cooling system capacity	L
• Condenser piping, valves, and control	H

Recurring Cost

• Cooling system operating cost	L
• Supply fan operating cost	H
• Tower fan operating cost	H
• Maintenance of indirect coil	S

SOURCES OF FURTHER INFORMATION

ASHRAE. 1999. *1999 ASHRAE Handbook—HVAC Applications*, p. 50.1-3.
ASHRAE. 2000. *2000 ASHRAE Handbook—Systems and Equipment*, p. 19.3-4; 44.7.

The author of this GreenTip is Mick Schwedler.

Chapter 10
Energy/Water Sources

RENEWABLE/NONRENEWABLE ENERGY SOURCES

There is often little choice in the selection of nonrenewable energy sources that may be needed at a given building site. The designer must deal with utility companies, who usually offer only one commodity (though there are some exceptions to this, and there may be alternative rate schedules that may be considered). Some purchased usage of electricity may be reduced by electing to generate on site, though this requires purchased energy in a different form.

Another consideration, also usually with little choice of options for the designer, is the nature of off-site energy resources from which the site energy source is derived. Whether electricity is generated from coal, imported oil, natural gas, or uranium, for example, may have broad implications for national or industry interests, the environment, or economics; however, there is little a designer can do about it—at least in choosing between conventional nonrenewable energy sources.

This subject is addressed in more detail in the "Energy Resources" chapter of the ASHRAE Handbook, and the designer is referred to that source for more specific data.

A choice a designer does have, however, is

Authors contributing to this chapter are Jay Enck and David Grumman.

whether to incorporate renewable energy resources to help energize the project, thereby reducing the energy needed from conventional nonrenewable sources. Inclusion of such renewable sources on a project can be done, most simply, in passive ways (few or no mechanical or electrical assists, such as solar-sensitive envelope design or natural ventilation) or, with greater complexity, in active ways (hybrid ventilation, solar collectors, wind turbines, geothermal heat pumps, for example). Consideration of active renewable systems should involve the entire design team, particularly the owner, because it can be costly up-front and because its success will depend on many design and post-design (operational) factors.

A key characteristic of most renewable energy sources is that, while "free," they are very "distributed" or low density – meaning not concentrated. The best way to illustrate this characteristic is to think of a gallon jug of, say, fuel oil compared to an array of hydronic solar collectors. The fuel oil could provide hot water, on demand, for hours in a simple water heater occupying a corner of a boiler room. The equivalent job done by solar collectors would require many square feet on a roof plus a tank, piping, and controls—and then some would say it's unsightly! And that's just to get the water to the point of the heater outlet, where it is then distributed to users. In other words, a lot of equipment—and space —is needed to collect and "concentrate" the solar energy because it's so scattered.

Another example of the distributed nature of renewable energy is the collection of wind energy farms covering acres and acres, almost as far as the eye can see, just outside of Palm Springs, California, one of the windiest places in the continental U.S. There are wind turbines of all vintages and designs there, of varying efficiencies and with some down for maintenance, and whatever electricity the ones running generate is always usable by the local power grid. On one edge of this array sits an industrial building, located within a small fenced-in area, about the size of a house. It contains a gas turbine generator, capable by itself of generating the equivalent amount of power, on demand, as acres and acres of wind turbines.

While consideration of renewables is a highly touted element of green design, the team should be well aware of the key characteristics of a particular renewable considered and develop creative strategies to make the most effective use of this free energy source.

Following is some additional discussion on the two main renewable energy sources (other than hydropower) in the world today.

SOLAR

Solar energy is the primary energy source that fuels the growth of the earth's natural capital and drives wind and ocean currents that also can provide alternative energy sources. Solar energy has successfully been harnessed for human use since the beginning of time. Early civilizations and some modern ones used solar energy for many purposes, food and clothes drying, heating water for baths, heating adobe and stone dwellings, etc. Solar energy is free and available to anyone who wishes to utilize it.

A key impediment to increased solar use is economics: its amortized cost vis-à-vis the cost of the energy source supplanted. (When fuel prices shot up in the late1970s and 1980s, a solar industry began to be developed. With prices down again at this writing, few seem willing to make the investment required without a better prospect of return.) Since the start of the industrial revolution, humans have only been concerned with the cost of extraction and conversion of natural resources, which does not include the cost of replacement or other "services" provided by nature, such as forests that convert carbon dioxide to oxygen.

If replacement costs were factored into the cost/ benefit analysis, alternatives such as solar would be easier to justify. It will require a paradigm shift in how humanity establishes its values—and a change from market-force economics to eco-economics—before alternatives to fossil fuel will be evaluated using replacement cost and environmental impacts. (See *Natural Capitalism*, by Hawken, Lovins, and Lovins for more on this subject.)

The first challenge to a design team wishing to utilize alternative energy is to minimize the use of energy by the building. Reducing the building's total energy requirements reduces the alternative energy requirements and the consequent first costs. Appropriate building geometry, orientation, and glazing selection can be used to control solar energy for daylighting, limit its contribution to cooling load, and utilize it for space heating in appropriate climatic locations. Green design integration requires the design team to assess design synergies: how various building elements can provide multiple functions.

Cost-effectiveness of solar and other energy alternatives can be bolstered when building design integrates these alternatives as part of the design using building elements as system components. The possibilities are limited only by the designer's imagination and project economics.

An example of this would be a concrete frame structure, a common building component, also used for thermal energy storage. Air circulated through the concrete structure storage could store heat or cooling energy, depending on the climate and season, to offset heating and cooling requirements. A second example could be using solar collectors that power absorption cooling to double as shading for roof, wall, and glass areas, thus reducing solar gain and cooling load.

As another example, in cool arid climates, solar energy can be used as a primary air mover to induce ventilation, minimizing the need for fan power to cool. Using a simple physics principle such as thermosiphon, fluid flow can be induced by a change in fluid density, which can result from a change in fluid temperature. Solar energy can be the motor that drives the flow. (Unfortunately, most projects will not have the luxury of being located in a cool, arid climate where use of solar in this way is optimal.)

Solar energy thermal applications range from low-temperature applications such as domestic water or swimming pool heating to medium-to-high temperature applications, such as absorption cooling or steam production for electrical generation. Solar electric applications convert solar radiation into direct current electrical energy through special cells in photovoltaic solar collectors.

The capital cost of solar thermal systems generally increases with higher working fluid temperatures. The higher the delivery temperature, the lower the efficiency and the more solar collector area is generally required to deliver the same net energy. This is due to parasitic thermal losses inherent in solar collector design. Different solar collector types provide advantages and disadvantages, depending on the application, and there are significant cost differences between each solar collector type. Some common collector types are discussed below.

Flat plate solar collectors are best suited for processes requiring working fluid temperatures from (80°F to 160°F) and can deliver 80°F fluid temperatures even during overcast conditions. The term "flat plate collector" generally refers to a hydronic coil-covered absorber housed in an insulated box with a glass cover that allows solar energy to heat the absorber. Heat is removed by a fluid running through the hydronic coils. Its design makes it more susceptible to parasitic losses than an evacuated tube collector but more efficient because flat plate collectors convert both direct and indirect solar radiation into thermal energy, making flat plate collectors the preferred choice for domestic hot water and other low-temperature heating applications. Coupling a water-source heat pump (low fluid temperatures) with solar collectors provides heating efficiencies higher than ground-source heat pump applications and standard natural gas furnaces.

The cost-effectiveness of thermal solar systems is also dependent on having a consistent need for the energy the solar system provides. Since heating requirements are generally seasonal in most climates, it is advisable that energy from the solar system have more uses than space heating alone. Domestic water heating is usually a much steadier year-round load, though often not very substantial. Cooling using solar can help meet this requirement as well. However, applying solar to absorption or dessicant cooling requires higher temperatures of fluid, adds additional cost and complexity, and requires a different type of solar collector. Changing from a flat plate collector to an evacuated tube or concentrating collector significantly raises the cost.

Evacuated tube collectors generally refer to a series of small absorbers consisting of approximately 3/8-inch copper tubing encased in a clear, cylindrical evacuated "thermos bottle" that minimizes parasitic losses even at elevated temperatures. Because of the relatively small absorber area, significantly more collector area is required than with the flat plate or concentrating collector.

Concentrating collectors generally refer to the use of a parabolic reflector that focuses the solar radiation falling within the reflector area onto a centrally located absorber. This type of collector converts only direct solar radiation, which varies dramatically with sky clarity and air quality (such as smog).

Pros and cons of different solar collector types and other limitations of active solar systems can be found in a number of sources. A preferred one is *Principles of Solar Engineering* by Frank Kreith and Jan Kreider.

The percentage of energy a solar system can provide is known as the solar fraction. Jan Kreider developed a mathematical model to predict the energy contribution a solar system can provide as part of his doctoral theses at the University of Wisconsin. The f-chart method developed by Kreider provides an accurate assessment of the amount of energy a solar thermal system will provide. This modeling provides the designer the ability to vary system parameters, such as collector area, storage volume, operating temperature, and load, to optimize system design.

Tying solar system component costs into utility energy costs allows the designer to determine the optimum system configuration based on life-cycle costs. This method is known as the f-chart. The f-chart method, however, neglects other positive benefits that can be derived by integrating a solar system into a building. Installation of solar collectors as an integral component of a building can lower solar gain through glazing or onto roof surfaces, lowering the cooling load on a building. This benefit is often overlooked, and the positive financial benefit is seldom considered when examining the cost benefit of a solar system.

Photovoltaic collectors are addressed in Green-Tip #21.

WIND

Using prevailing breezes and wind energy is one of the most promising alternative technologies today. Wind turbine design and power generation have become more reliable over the last 30 years. Consistency and velocity of available breezes are essential to successful application of wind for natural ventilation and electrical generation. Information on velocities, durations, and direction of winds in a projects area are generally available from National Oceanic and Atmospheric Administration (*http://www.noaa.gov*).

From a natural ventilation perspective, other factors, such as temperature and relative humidity, also must be taken into consideration. Many areas of the United States can use outside air/natural breezes to provide cooling only during a limited period of the year, requiring designers wanting to use natural ventilation to carefully analyze both climatic conditions and cost to implement. The benefits of using natural ventilation must be weighed against the consistency of breezes, potential for higher relative humidities (which may affect indoor air quality), and the impact on occupant comfort and HVAC operation.

There are many excellent examples where natural ventilation provides the cooling needed throughout the year, but most are located in cool, arid climates. Even in moderate climates, like Atlanta, Georgia, natural ventilation can provide cooling during much of the year, but in doing so, the designer must consider the impact on HVAC operation and building control. These elements may be very difficult to get to work effectively with operable windows. Additional programming and control points are required for successful operation. (See also GreenTip #8, "Hybrid Ventilation," in chapter 7.)

Incorporating one or more wind turbine generators at a building site is another, more active approach. Initially, it should be recognized that there is a disadvantage of scale: one or two wind turbines alone are destined to be less cost-effective than a wind farm with hundreds. If this drawback is recognized, then other key factors can be evaluated. First, sufficiently consistent wind velocity is required for electrical generation to be at all cost-effective. Noise, vibration, building geometry (if on the building), wind pattern interrupters, wildlife effect, periodic maintenance, safety, visual impact, and community acceptance must also be taken into account.

WATER

See chapter 12 for a discussion of water as a resource, as well as some specific measures for using it sparingly and prudently.

ASHRAE GreenTip #21: Solar Energy System—Photovoltaic

GENERAL DESCRIPTION

Light shining on a photovoltaic (PV) cell, which is a solid-state semi-conductor device, liberates electrons that are collected by a wire grid to produce direct current electricity.

The use of solar energy to produce electricity means that PV systems reduce greenhouse gas emissions, electricity cost, and resource consumption. Electrical consumption can be reduced. Because the peak generation of PV electricity coincides with peak air-conditioning loads (IF the sun shines then), peak electricity demands (from the grid) may be reduced, though it's unlikely without substantial storage capacity.

PV can also reduce electrical power installation costs where the need for trenching and independent metering can be avoided. The public appeal of using solar energy to produce electricity results in a positive marketing image for PV-powered buildings and thus can enhance occupancy rates in commercial buildings.

While conventional PV design has focused on the use of independent applications in which excess electricity is stored in batteries, grid-connected systems are becoming more common. In these cases, electricity generated in excess of immediate demand is sent to the electrical grid, and the PV-powered building receives a utility credit. Grid-connected systems are often integrated into building elements. Increasingly PV cells are being incorporated into sunshades on buildings for a doubly effective reduction in cooling and electricity loads.

PV power is being applied in innovative ways. Typical economically viable commercial installations include the lighting of parking lots, pathways, or signs, emergency telephones, and small outbuildings.

A typical PV module consists of 33 to 40 cells, which is the basic block used in commercial applications. Typical components of a module are aluminum, glass, tedlar, and rubber; the cell is usually silicon with trace amounts of boron and phosphorus.

Because PV systems are made from a few, relatively simple components and materials, the maintenance costs of PV systems are low. Manufacturers now provide 20-year warranties for PV cells.

Photovoltaic systems are adaptable and can easily be removed and re-installed in other applications. Systems can also be enlarged for greater capacity through the addition of more PV modules.

WHEN/WHERE IT'S APPLICABLE

PV is best suited for rural and urban off-grid applications and for grid-connected buildings with air-conditioning loads. The economic viability of PV depends on the distance from the grid, electrical load sizes, and power line extension costs. For example, a distance of two kilometres from the grid was the economic threshold for a typical residential application in 1997.

PV applications include prime buildings, outbuildings, emergency telephones, irrigation pumps, fountains, lighting for parking lots, pathways, security, clearance, billboards, bus shelters or signs, and remote operation of gates, irrigation valves, traffic signals, radios, telemetry, or instrumentation.

PV is typically not well suited to grid-connected buildings with peak wintertime loads.

Note that a portion of a PV system is direct current (DC), so appropriate fusing and breakers may not be readily available. A PV system is not solely an electrical installation. Other trades, such as roofing and light steel erectors, may be involved with a PV installation. When a PV system is installed on a roof or wall, it will result in envelope penetrations which will need to be sealed.

PROS AND CONS

Pro

1. Reduces greenhouse gas emissions
2. Reduces nonrenewable energy demand
3. Enhances green-image marketing
4. Lowers electricity consumption costs and may reduce peak electrical demand charges
5. Reduces infrastructure costs.

Con

1. May increase capital costs
2. Requires energy storage in batteries or a connection to electrical utility grid
3. May encounter regulatory barriers

The author of this GreenTip is Stephen Carpenter.

ASHRAE GreenTip #21: Solar Energy System—Photovoltaic (continued)

4. High-capacity systems require large building envelope areas that are clear of protuberances and have uninterrupted access to sunshine

5. Capacity to supply peak electrical demand can be limited, depending on sunshine during peak hours.

KEY ELEMENTS OF COST

The following provides a possible breakdown of the various cost elements that might differentiate a PV system from a conventional one and an indication of whether the net cost for this system is likely to be lower (L), higher (H), or the same (S). This assessment is only a perception of what might be likely, but it obviously may not be correct in all situations. **There is no substitute for a detailed cost analysis as part of the design process.** The listings below may also provide some assistance in identifying the cost elements involved.

First Cost

• Photovoltaic modules	H
• Wiring and various electrical devices	H
• Battery bank	H
• Instrumentation	H

Recurring Cost

• Electricity	L

SOURCES OF FURTHER INFORMATION

Photovoltaic Systems Design Manual. Natural Resources Canada, Office of Coordination and Technical Information, Ottawa ON CAN K1A 0E4.

WATSUN-PV (simulation software), University of Waterloo, Waterloo ON CAN.

RETSCREEN (renewable energy analysis software), Natural Resources Canada, Energy Diversification Research Laboratory, Varennes PQ CAN J3X 1S6; tel 1 450 652 4621
http://www.retscreen.gc.ca

Centre for Photovoltaic Engineering UNSW
http://www.pv.unsw.edu.au/solpages.html

Photovoltaic Resource Site
http://www.pvpower.com/

U.S. Department of Energy
http://www.eere.energy.gov/pv

Sustainable Sources
http://www.greenbuilder.com/sourcebook/Photvoltaic.html

Renewable Energy Deployment Initiative (REDI) (a Canadian federal program that supports the deployment of renewable technologies. Some technologies qualify for incentives).
http://www.nrcan.gc.ca/redi

Canadian Renewable Energy Network
http://www.canren.gc.ca/

Chapter 11
Lighting Systems

Coverage of the subject of lighting in a guide for HVAC&R designers is not intended to make them into lighting experts but rather to familiarize them with the basic process of lighting design and the materials involved so that they can interact effectively with lighting designers and architects in creating an effective system. Since lighting has such a big impact on building loads and energy use, it is important that the HVAC&R designer understand the role played by these other team members.

Proper lighting system design should always involve an experienced professional, preferably one who is a member of the green building design team.

ELECTRIC LIGHTING

Efficient Lighting Design

Lighting design as a practice and a profession has evolved considerably since the early days of interest in energy efficiency. Lower lighting levels (footcandles) have become common and, due to significant advances in lighting equipment efficiency, power levels are much lower than 25 years ago.

For any lighting designer setting out to perform a lighting design, consulting the Illuminating Engineering Society—North America (IESNA) Lighting Handbook is highly recommended. However, assuming some familiarity with the process, the following guidance should yield good results.

The author of this chapter is James Benya.

Many buildings can be efficiently lighted using carefully selected standard lighting systems. Assuming that some basic rules of spacing and lamp or luminaire wattage are followed, successful lighting designs with lighting power densities of 0.9-1.0 watts per square foot can be easily applied to most building types.

Most energy codes have lighting power limits between 1.0 and 1.5 watts per square foot. The primary exceptions are storage buildings (less), retail stores (more), and hospitality facilities (more). However, even in some stores and hospitality buildings, the same efficient lighting approaches suitable for schools, offices, and most other common building types can also be used.

Efficient Lighting Systems

Tables 11-1, 11-2, and 11-3 contain a listing of standard lighting systems and related criteria that will generally satisfy modern (IESNA) light level recommendations as well as comply with energy codes and meet a modest project budget.

*   Table 11-1 lists two common lighting systems that can be used for a wide variety of project types and at very low cost.

*   Table 11-2 lists lighting designs suitable for private and open office areas and similar spaces, such as exam rooms in clinics and hospitals.

Table 11-1. General Use Systems

Primary application	Luminaire type	Lamps or total lamp watts	Spacing between luminaries (In plan view)	Lamp ballast system
General use—spaces of all types	Nominal 4-ft recessed or surface-mounted fluorescent troffer (parabolic, basket, lensed, etc.) with high-efficiency electronic ballast	(2) F32T8 lamps	No less than 8 ft OC	Maximum 56 watts, 45-48 watt, low-ballast-factor ballast preferred
General use—spaces of all types	Nominal 2-ft recessed or surface-mounted fluorescent troffer (parabolic, basket, lensed, etc.) with electronic ballast	(3) F17T8 lamps	No less than 8 ft OC	Maximum 52 watts.

Table 11-2. Lighting for Offices, Including Commercial, Academic, and Institutional

Primary application	Luminaire type	Lamps or total lamp watts	Spacing between luminaires in plan view	Lamp ballast system
Open offices	Suspended linear fluorescent fixtures, consisting of nominal 4-ft sections in continuous rows with electronic ballast(s) Nominal 4-ft recessed or surface-mounted fluorescent troffers	One F54T5HO or two F32T8 or two F28T5 Two F32T8 lamps	Continuous rows no closer than 15 ft apart Regular grid 8 ft OC	Maximum 60 input watts per 4 ft unit, minimum ceiling height 10 ft Maximum 48 input watts per luminaire
Very small private offices <105 ft²	One recessed or suspended 4 ft linear fluorescent fixture	Three F32T8 lamps	One luminaire per office	Maximum 90 input watts Minimum ceiling height 9'-0" for suspended fixtures
Small private offices 105-125 ft²	Two recessed or suspended 4-ft linear fluorescent fixtures	Two F32T8 lamps per fixture	No less than 6 ft OC	Maximum 48 input watts to each luminaire; minimum ceiling height 9'-0" for suspended fixtures
Small private offices 126-160 ft²	Two recessed or suspended 4-ft linear fluorescent fixtures	Two F32T8 lamps per fixture	No less than 6 ft OC	Maximum 56 input watts to each luminaire; minimum ceiling height 9'-0" for suspended fixtures
Medium private offices 160- 200 ft²	Two recessed or suspended 4-ft linear fluorescent fixtures three recessed or suspended 4-ft linear fluorescent fixtures four recessed 2-ft linear fluorescent fixtures	Three F32T8 lamps per fixture Two F32T8 lamps per fixture Two F17T8 lamps per fixture	No less than 6 ft OC	Maximum 72 input watts to each luminaire Maximum 48 input watts to each luminaire Maximum 36 input watts per fixture
Executive offices and conference rooms 200-250 ft²	Four recessed or suspended 4-ft linear fluorescent fixtures four recessed 2-ft linear fluorescent fixtures	Two F32T8 lamps per fixture Two F32T8U lamps per fixture	No less than 8 ft OC	Maximum 48 input watts to each luminaire

Key to Table Abbreviations:
OC = on center
< = less than

Table 11-3. Other Common Lighting Systems

Primary application	Luminaire type	Lamps or total lamp watts	Spacing between luminaires in plan view	Lamp ballast system
Lobbies, atriums, etc. Industrial space	Metal halide, induction, or multiple compact fluorescent lamp (of equivalent lamp watts with electronic ballasts) downlights, pendants, etc.	100 watts or less 150 watts or less 250 watts or less 400 watts or less	No less than 12 ft OC No less than 15 ft OC No less than 18 ft OC Not less than 22 ft OC	Mounting height at least 12 ft AFF; only recommended for high bay spaces
Corridors, lobbies, meeting rooms, etc.	Compact fluorescent (including twin tube, quad tube, or triple tube) or metal halide downlights, wallwashers, monopoints, and similar directional luminaires Wall sconces using any of the above light sources	40 watts or less 60 watts or less 80 watts or less 100 watts or less	No less than 6 ft OC No less than 8 ft OC Not less than 10 ft OC No less than 12 ft OC	Any space height
Undercabinet and undershelf task lighting	Hardwired undercabinet or undershelf fluorescent luminaires, nom. 2 ft, 3 ft, or 4 ft in length and employing an electronic ballast	No greater than 8.5 watts per foot of luminaire	When mounted underneath permanent overhead cabinets.	Luminaires may be mounted end-to-end if needed to accommodate cabinet length
Lobbies, executive offices, and conference rooms accent lighting	Low-voltage downlights, accent lights, or monopoint lights having an integral transformer	Rated at 50 watts or less	No less than 8 ft OC	For accent lighting only – should not be used for general lighting
Copy room, storeroom, etc.	Nominal 4-ft recessed or surface-mounted fluorescent troffer, wraparound, strip lights, etc., with electronic ballast	One or two lamps totaling 64 watts or less	No less than 8 ft OC	Maximum 60 input watts to luminaire
Small utility, storage, and closet spaces	Single-lamp fluorescent with electronic ballast (strip, wrap, industrial, or other fixture.)	32 watts	One luminaire in a closet, electric room, or other small space	Maximum 35 input watts to luminaire
Storage and utility spaces	Industrials, wraparounds, strip lights, etc., consisting of nominal 4-ft sections	Two F32T8	Individual 12-lamp luminaires 8 ft OC Continuous single-lamp rows no closer than 8 ft apart	48 input watts per two lamps
Bathroom vanities and stairwells	Two-lamp fluorescent with electronic ballast (wrap, cove, troffer, corridor, vanity, valence, or other fixture)	Two F32T8	One luminaire per vanity in a toilet or locker room or one luminaire per landing in a stairwell	Maximum 48 input watts to luminaire
Exit signs	LED	No greater than 3.5 watts/sign		

Key to Table Abbreviations:
AFF = Above finished floor
LED = Light-emitting diode
OC = On centers
< = less than

- Table 11-3 lists a variety of common lighting systems that can be used in industrial and commercial applications

For most spaces, designers should employ lighting layouts that conform to these criteria. Spacing measurements are taken from the plan-view center of the luminaire. Luminaires should be mounted at least one-third of the indicated mounting distance away from any ceiling-high partition.

If more than one type of luminaire (excluding exit signs) is to be located within one space enclosed with ceiling high partitions, the spacing between different luminaires must be the larger of the required spacing for the two luminaires.

None of the following luminaires should be employed:

- Luminaires employing Edison (standard screw-in) baseline voltage sockets or halogen lamps using any sockets rated over 150 watts
- Luminaires designed for incandescent or halogen low-voltage lamps exceeding 75 watts
- Track lighting systems of any kind or voltage of operation
- Line-voltage monopoints permitting the installation of track luminaires.

However, for every 20 luminaires meeting these requirements, a single hardwired luminaire of any type (except track) rated not more than 150 lamp watts may be placed as desired. This permits architects, interior designers, and lighting designers the ability to add lighting for aesthetic effects or décor without an unreasonable energy burden. Note that if more than one such luminaire is permitted, any number of them may be located in any of the project's spaces. In other words, in a project with one hundred luminaires from Tables 11-1, 11-2, or 11-3, five decorative luminaires would be permitted, and they could all be installed over the receptionist's desk.

These lists are not intended to be comprehensive but rather straightforward and instructive. There are certainly other good (and efficient) designs not listed. Professional lighting design assistance may be needed to reach optimum performance for specific conditions.

In all cases, be certain to review the subsequent sections on other aspects of lighting for detailed information on product specifications and additional energy-saving ideas.

When/Where Applicable

The above systems are generally good for most conventional space types with ordinary ceiling systems. These include:

- Typical private offices
- Typical open office areas
- Office area corridors
- Conference rooms and classrooms
- Meeting and seminar rooms
- Most laboratories
- Equipment, server, cable, and equipment rooms
- Building lobbies
- Elevator lobbies
- Building "core" and circulation areas
- Industrial areas, shops, and docks
- "Big box" and grocery stores

For commercial buildings, these recommendations assume standard acoustical tile ceilings. For industrial buildings, open bar joist construction is assumed. Ceiling heights are assumed to be standard as well.

Efficient Lamps and Ballasts

The lighting industry has made significant improvements in technology over the last 25 years. Recent improvements, while not as widely publicized, continue to permit good lighting at decreasing power levels. Proper specification of lamps and ballasts are an important part of achieving these results.

Specifications. The following specifications are recommended to ensure the latest technology is being employed.

Ballasts. Ballasts for all fluorescent lamps and for HID lamps rated 150 watts and less should be electronic. Harmonic distortion should be less than 20%,

- *T-8 System Ballasts*

Four-foot T-8 fluorescent lighting systems should employ "high-efficiency" electronic ballasts. Because instant-start ballasts are the most efficient and least costly, they should be used in all longer duty cycle applications where the lights are turned on and off infrequently. Fluorescent systems controlled by motion sensors in spaces where the lights will be turned on and off frequently should employ program-start ballasts.

Designers are strongly encouraged to use low-ballast-factor ballasts (BF < 0.80) whenever possible. T-8 low-ballast-factor and normal-ballast-factor ballasts should be "high efficiency" electronic, not exceeding 28 input watts per 4 ft lamp at BF > 0.85 and not exceeding 24 input watts for BF > 0.70 (ANSI free air rating).

In lieu of the above, electronic dimming ballasts may be used as needed.

- *Metal Halide Ballasts*

Metal halide ballasts 150 watts and less should be electronic.

Table 11-4. Common Lamp Types

Generic Lamp Types	Applications	Requirements
4-ft T-8 lamps F32T8	Primary lighting systems in commercial, institutional, and low bay industrial spaces	TCLP compliant (low mercury) lamps with barrier coat and high lumen phosphor (minimum 3,100 initial lumens). Premium long-life-rated lamps.
Fluorescent T-5 and T-5HO lamps F14T5, F21T5, and F28T5; F24T5HO, F39T5HO, and F54T5HO	Primary lighting systems in commercial, institutional, and low and high bay industrial spaces	Standard T-5 and T-5HO lamps.
Metal halide pulse start lamps Over 250 watts	Primary lighting systems in large spaces with very high ceilings and/or special lighting requirements.	Pulse-start lamps only. Be certain to specify pulse start ballasts. Use linear reactor ballasts on 277-volt systems.
Fluorescent T-8 lamps F17T8, F25T8	Secondary and specialized applications in commercial, institutional, and low bay industrial spaces	TCLP compliant (low mercury) lamps with barrier coat and 800 series phosphor. Premium long-life-rated lamps.
Compact fluorescent long lamps F40TT5, F50TT5, and F55TT5	Specialized applications in commercial, institutional, and low bay industrial spaces	Standard long twin tube lamps
Compact fluorescent 4-pin lamps CF13, CF18, CF26, CF32, CF42, CF57 and CF70	Downlighting, wallwashing, sconces, and other common space and secondary lighting systems in commercial, institutional, and low bay industrial spaces	Standard twin-, quad-, triple-tube and four-tube lamps.
Halogen MR16 lamps	Accent lighting for art and displays only – do not use for general lighting	Halogen IR 12-volt compact reflector lamps
Ceramic PAR and T HID Lamps PAR20, PAR30, PAR38, ED17, and T-6	Downlighting, accent lighting, and other special, limited applications in commercial, institutional, and low bay industrial spaces; retail display lighting	39-, 70-, 100-, and 150-watt ceramic lamps
Halogen infrared reflecting PAR30 and PAR38 lamps	Applications requiring full range dimming; retail display lighting	Halogen IR 50-, 60-, 80-, and 100-watt reflector lamps

Metal halide systems greater than 150 watts should use linear-reactor pulse-start type ballasts wherever 277-volt power is available; for other voltages, pulse-start lamps and ballasts shall be used.

Lamps. The lamps listed in Table 11-4 represent the best common lamp types to employ. Note that this list is not comprehensive, and a better choice for a particular project may not be listed. However, for the majority of applications, this list is a good guide.

The lamps recommended for primary lighting systems are both energy efficient and have long life, representing excellent cost benefit. Lamps for other applications generally are less efficient, have shorter life, or both. Also, designers should use the minimum number of different types of lamps on a project to reduce maintenance costs and improve stocking.

Lighting Power Density Criteria

A complete, hardwired lighting system, to be efficient, should be installed with the following lighting power density requirements:

- Private offices shall not exceed a connected power density of 0.9 watts per square foot.

- Open office areas shall not exceed a connected power density of 0.8 watts per square foot.

- Conference rooms and similar spaces shall not exceed a connected power density of 1.2 watts per square foot.

- Core areas, including lobbies, elevator lobbies, mailrooms, lunchrooms, restrooms, copy rooms, locker rooms, and similar spaces, shall not exceed a connected lighting power density of 0.8 watts per square foot.

- Hallways, corridors, storage rooms, mechanical and electrical rooms, and similar spaces shall not exceed a connected power density of 0.7 watts per square foot.

- Any other space not listed shall not exceed a connected power density of 0.6 watts per square foot.

Additional lighting, such as lighting within furniture systems, should not be installed in a space unless a more complete analysis and design are undertaken. These systems need to be carefully coordinated with the permanent lighting systems of the building. *Exception*: portable plug-in lamps and under-cabinet luminaires attached to the underside of modular furniture, overhead cabinets, bins, or shelves should be used where needed.

There are a few space types, such as video teleconferencing rooms, showrooms, retail space, and food service space, that usually require more lighting power than provided above. For these uncommon space types, an appropriate lighting power density requirement should be determined from ASHRAE/IESNA/ANSI 90.1-2001 (or the latest edition).

Application Notes

Open Offices. For general illumination in spaces with ceilings 9'-6" or higher, consider suspended linear fluorescent indirect, direct/indirect, or semi-indirect lighting systems, supplemented by task lights. General layouts should be between 0.6 and 0.8 W/ft^2 using high-performance luminaires and T-8, T-5, or T-5HO lamps. Task lights can be used where needed. If troffers are preferred, consider using T-8 lamps as specified with low-ballast-factor ballasts. This will ensure appropriate energy use while maintaining recommended light levels. Task lighting should be added underneath shelves and bins as required.

Private Offices. Suspended linear fluorescent lighting should be a first consideration for private offices, although recessed troffers can also be used. Luminaires should use T-8 or T-5 lamps. Lighting power density should be around 0.8-0.9 W/ft^2. Task lights can be used where needed.

Executive Offices, Board and Conference Rooms. Executive offices can be designed similarly to private offices (above). If desired, a premium approach using compact fluorescent downlights, wallwashers, and/or halogen accent lights can be used, but the overall design should not exceed 1.2 W/ft^2. If the number of executive offices is high, lighting power levels should be reduced to match the recommendations for private offices, above.

Classrooms. Classrooms should be lighted using direct/indirect classroom lighting systems, with about 0.9 W/ft^2 of connected power using T-8 "super" lamps and efficient electronic ballasts.

Corridors. In general, corridors should be lighted using compact fluorescent sconces, downlights, ceiling-mounted or close-to-ceiling decorative diffuse fixtures, or similar equipment. Power density should be about 0.5-0.6 W/ft^2 overall. Note that these luminaires may be equipped with emergency battery backup when needed as an alternative to less attractive "bug eye" type emergency lighting.

High Bay Spaces. Industrial, grocery, and retail space without ceilings or with very high ceilings (usually 15 ft and above) need special lighting fixtures. For mounting heights up to 20-25 feet, first try to use fluorescent industrial luminaires employing T-8 lamps, keeping in mind that two "super" 4-ft T-8 lamps and a high light output "overdrive" ballast at 77 watts produce as much light (mean lumens) as a 100-watt metal halide lamp that, with ballast, consumes 120 watts. And four "super" T-8 lamps with overdrive ballasts at 154 watts produce as much light as a 175-watt pulse start metal halide (195-205 watts) or a standard 250-watt metal halide lamp (286-295 watts with ballast).

For mounting heights above 25 feet, consider T5HO high-bay luminaires. Similar savings relative to metal halide are possible. High-wattage metal halide should be reserved for very high mounting (above 50 ft) and for special applications such as sports lighting.

Other Applications. The following luminaire types are generally recommended for these areas:

- Artwork, bulletin/display surfaces, etc., use compact fluorescent wallwashers or low voltage monopoint lights.
- Utility spaces, including cable and equipment rooms, use two-lamp strip lights, industrials, or surface luminaires.
- Lobby spaces, cafeterias, and other public spaces as much as possible use appropriate selections from among these luminaires.

For commercial buildings, these recommendations assume standard acoustical tile ceilings. For industrial buildings, open bar joist construction is assumed. Ceiling heights are assumed to be standard as well.

Sources of Further Information

Illuminating Engineering Society of North America (IESNA), *Lighting Handbook*, http://www.iesna.org

California Energy Commission, Title 24 2005 Reports and Proceedings, *http://www.energy.ca.gov*

DAYLIGHTING

General Description

Most buildings have *some* type of daylighting. The majority of commercial, industrial, and institutional buildings have windows and in some cases skylights, clerestories, and more extensive daylighting systems. Currently, the qualities of daylight are secondary to the thermal performance of the building envelope; therefore, most fenestration in modern buildings introduces a combination of benefit and problem as far as lighting design is concerned.

From an energy perspective, the most obvious use of daylight is to permit the dimming or extinguishing of the electric lighting system. This process, called "daylighting," is discussed in this section because of its significant potential. However, the prediction of daylight savings is not easy. Because we often justify the added cost of daylighting elements, such as dimming ballasts and photoelectric controls, by these savings, being able to predict daylighting savings with some certainty could be a very important and powerful tool.

From a lighting design perspective, daylight can be treated as any other light source and used to compose lighting design solutions with illuminance, luminance, contrast, color, and other lighting design elements. However, the lighting designer is challenged to deal with the fact that the light source location is given and that, in most cases, the only means available to change its characteristics is through blinds, shades, or other mechanical forms of attenuation and shielding.

It is possible to simulate the performance of natural lighting to determine the amount and, to a certain extent, the quality of available daylight under varying conditions of season, time of day, and weather. However, this is exhaustive analytical work of a highly specialized nature, and it is recommended that appropriate experts perform such studies. In the meantime, some buildings can benefit tremendously from some *simple* daylighting considerations.

Basic Top Lighting

Basic toplighting involves using simple skylights in the roof. (This is not to say that other toplighting configurations, such as the clerestory, roof monitor, or sawtooth roof, are not workable; indeed, they often have advantages over horizontal skylights.) Needless to say, there are many architectural considerations including structure, waterproofing, and other details. However, when used in a manner similar to light fixtures, laid out to provide uniform illumination, top lights are an acceptable way to illuminate single-story, large spaces using daylight.

Toplighting is best when a number of smaller skylights are used, much the way lighting systems use many light fixtures rather than one big light source in the middle of the room. Skylights should be diffuse or prismatic, *not* clear. Skylights do not have to incorporate light control louvers, since the optimum size of the skylight is chosen for "passive" skylighting (i.e., no active or moving elements needed to regulate the amount of interior light).

To determine the optimum size of skylights, one can download a program called SkyCalc from *http://www.h-m-g.com/skylighting/skycalcreg.htm*. This program, which is optimized for California and the Northwest in the U.S., can be applied with some care anywhere in North America. It takes into account location, utility rates, and other basic data and yields recommended skylight area.

Note: The ideal amount of fenestrated roof is generally around 5%. Most architects design skylights that are too big. An HVAC&R designer's input here, especially when backed up by calculations, can save a lot of energy.

When/Where It's Applicable

Daylighting is most likely to be suitable for large volume, single-story or top-story space types with ordinary structures. These include:

- Gyms
- Industrial workspace
- "Big box" retail
- Grocery stores
- Exhibition halls
- Storage
- Warehousing

In each case, automatic lighting controls that dim or extinguish electric lights when there is adequate daylight are essential or the energy savings will not be realized. (See also subsequent section on "Lighting Controls.")

Pros/Cons of Daylighting

Pro

1. Daylighting offers significantly reduced energy costs (can be more than 60%) and reduced HVAC load (as long as solar gains don't outweigh electric lighting reductions)

2. It extends the electric lighting maintenance cycle (lamps last two to three times as long in calendar years)

3. It ensures low power use

4. There are improved human factors and enjoyment of space.

Con

1. Daylighting requires close architectural, structural, and lighting design coordination

2. There is no assurance that the design will meet exact project lighting requirements

3. There is increased building cost

4. There is a risk of poor design or installation workmanship, resulting in roof leaks

5. Daylighting may not be suitable for uncommon room shapes, sizes, and/or finishes

6. There is net decreased roof insulation.

Sources of Further Information

Advanced Lighting Guidelines: 2001 Edition, *http://www.newbuildings.org*

Heshong-Mahone Group, *http://www.h-m-g.com, http://www.h-m-g.com/skylighting/skycal-creg.htm*

THE LIGHT CONVEYOR

The light conveyor is a specialized technique whereby light from a source is transmitted some distance from the source to light spaces, either along its length or some distance away. The source can be either natural light or an artificial source. It is described in ASHRAE GreenTip #22.

LIGHTING CONTROLS

General

While all modern energy codes require automatic shutoff controls for commercial buildings, implementing automatic controls in all building projects is a sound money and energy-saving idea. There are two ways to reduce lighting energy use through controls:

- Turn lights off when not needed (reduce hours)
- Reduce lighting power to minimum need (reduce kilowatts)

By code, each interior space enclosed by ceiling high partitions must have separate local switching and some form of automated-off control (occupancy sensing, time-based scheduling, or other). In addition, wherever possible, provide separate switching for lights in daylighted zones. In order to comply with code requirements and ensure maximum energy savings, specify the most appropriate lighting control option(s) as described below and outlined in Table 11-1.

Control Options

1. Ceiling-mounted motion sensor with transformer/relay, auxiliary relay, and series switch.

The sensor should be located to look down upon the work area in order to detect small hand motion as well as major movements. The sensor may be mounted to the upper wall if a ceiling location is not workable. More than one sensor can be used for a large room or a room with obstructions, such as a library or server room. The main transformer relay should control the overhead lighting system (usually 277 -volt) and the auxiliary relay should control at least one-half of a receptacle to switch task lights and other applicably controlled plug loads. Note that the light switch is in series so that it can only turn lights off in an occupied room; it can not override the motion sensor's "Off" control.

2. Similar to above, but without auxiliary relay and connection to receptacle. Must control at least two luminaires or banks of lighting groups and be equipped with two manual override (Off) switches for either high-low light level switching or alternate fixture switching. May also be used to control multiple dimmers or a multi-channel preset dimming controller.

3. Ceiling-mounted motion sensors connected to programmable time controller. During programmed "On" times, the lights remain on. During programmed "Off" times, motion within the space initiates lights on for a time out period. Controller shall be programmable according to day of the week and shall have an electronic calendar to permit programming holidays.

4. Workstation motion sensor connected to a plug strip or task light with auxiliary receptacle.

5. One or more ceiling-mounted motion sensors with transformer/relay, minimum two luminaires controlled.

6. Switchbox motion sensor, one or more luminaires controlled.

7. Programmable time controller with manual override switch(es) located in a protected or concealed location. Separate zones for retail and similar applications where displays can be controlled separately from general lighting. May also control dimmers.

8. In addition to any of the above, an automatic daylighting sensor connected to dimming ballast(s) in each luminaire in the daylighted zone.

9. A motion sensor connected to a high-low lighting system.

When using controls such as motion sensors or

Table 11-5. Recommended and Optional Lighting Controls

Type of Space	Minimum Recommended Control	Optional Control(s)
Private office, exam room	1	2 2+4 1+8 2+4+8 2+8
Open office	3	3+4 3+8 3+4+8
Conference rooms, teleconference rooms, boardrooms, classrooms	2	1 2+8 1+8
Server rooms, computer rooms, and other clean work areas	5	
Toilet rooms, copy rooms, mail rooms, coffee rooms	5 or 6	
Individual toilets, janitor closets, electrical rooms, and other small spaces	6	
Corridors, hallways, lobbies (private spaces only)	3	3+8
Public corridors	3	
Public lobbies	7	7+8
Industrial work areas	7	7+8
Warehousing and storage	9 (HID systems) 3 or 5 (fluorescent systems)	3 or 5 +8 (fluorescent)
Stores, newsstands, food service	7	
Mechanical rooms	Manual Switching only	
Stairs	None	Motion sensors can be used to reduce light levels to minimum egress lighting levels only

daylight sensors, be very thorough and carefully read the manufacturer's literature. Different sensors work for different applications, and their sensing systems are optimized. For instance, avoid wallbox motion sensors except in spaces where their sensing field is appropriate. For spaces with small-motion work, a look-down sensor (from the ceiling) generally works much better than a look-out sensor (from a wallbox).

Applicability

The above controls are applicable to most commercial, institutional, and industrial buildings. Use common sense in special spaces, keeping in mind safety and security. Never switch path-of-egress lighting systems except with properly designed emergency transfer controls.

Pros/Cons

Pro
1. Low to moderate costs for most space types
2. Virtually no maintenance
3. Generally will lower energy use.

Con
1. If controls are not properly commissioned, unacceptable results may occur until they are fixed.

2. There is no assurance that the controls meet exact project lighting requirements.
3. Substitutions and value engineering can easily cause bad results.

COST CONSIDERATIONS

Lighting Systems

The systems described above are generally low-to-moderate-cost lighting systems. On the average, they also use low maintenance lamps and ballasts. The combination of low first cost, low maintenance, and low energy use leads to lighting choices that are among the most economical available.

Lamps and Ballasts

The costs of premium lamps and ballasts over conventional lamps and ballasts can be as much as 100% of the cost of the materials. This can increase the cost of a lighting system by 20-30%.

However, premium lamps, especially the T-8 4-ft lamps shown, offer the following specific benefits:

• Increased lamp life by as much as 50%. In a T-8 application, this can be 5,000 to 10,000 hours. The cost of replacing a lamp is about 75% labor and 25% material. Relamping cost savings alone pay the difference.

- Reduced lamp energy use when used with the correct ballast. In a typical T-8 application, this means achieving energy savings of around 6 watts per lamp. At 3000 annual hours and 8.5 cents per kWh, the combination saves over $1.50 per year in energy costs, per lamp. The premium for a two-lamp ballast and lamps is about $12.00. The energy savings pay for the added costs in about four years. (Costs are as of year 2003.)

Daylighting

Daylighting is a potentially complex undertaking in which the first cost of lighting remains the same, the cost of lighting controls increases, and the added cost of skylights and/or structural changes/complications are incurred as well. To be cost-effective, this needs to be offset by a combination of HVAC energy savings, lighting energy savings, HVAC system first-cost reduction, and perhaps savings from utility incentives or tax credits. Expect daylighting systems to yield a four-to-five-year simple payback *with* a utility incentive, six to eight years or more *without*.

Controls

The lighting control systems described above are generally low to moderate cost. However, using better quality sensors and separate transformer/relay packs with remote sensors costs much more than wallbox devices. Savings can range from modest to considerable, depending on the building and occupants.

SOURCES OF FURTHER INFORMATION

Illuminating Engineering Society—North America (IESNA), *Lighting Handbook*, http://www.iesna.org

Advanced Lighting Guidelines, http://www.newbuildings.org

California Energy Commission, Title 24 2005 Reports and Proceedings, http://www.energy.ca.gov

Rising Sun Enterprises, http://www.rselight.com

RealWinWin, http://www.realwin.com

Energy Trust of Oregon, http://www.energytrust.org

New Buildings Institute, The http://www.newbuildings.org

Heschong Mahone Group, http://www.h-m-g.com

California High Performance Schools, http://www.chps.net

Better Bricks, http://www.betterbricks.com

Eley Associates, http://www.eley.com

Savings by Design, http://www.savingsbydesign.com

ASHRAE GreenTip #22: Light Conveyor

GENERAL DESCRIPTION

A light conveyor is large pipe or duct with reflective sides that transmits artificial or natural light along its length.

There are two types of such light-directing devices. The first is a square duct or round pipe made of plastic. By means of how the inside of the duct or pipe is cut and configured, light entering one end of the pipe is both reflected off these configurations (just as does light through a prism) and transmitted through. That reflected light continues to travel down the pipe, but the relatively small amount of light transmitted through the pipe provides continuous lighting along the pipe. Because some light is absorbed and escapes along the length of the pipe (i.e., is "lost"), the maximum distance that light can be "piped" into a building is about 90 ft.

There are a few installations where sun-tracking mirrors concentrate and direct natural light into a light pipe. In most applications, however, a high-intensity electric light is used as the light source. Having the electric light separate from the space where the light is delivered isolates the heat, noise, and electromagnetic field of the light source from building occupants. In addition, the placement of the light source in a maintenance room separate from building occupants simplifies replacement of the light source.

A second light-directing device is a straight tube with a highly reflective interior coating. The device is mounted on a building roof and has a clear plastic dome at the top end of the tube and a translucent plastic diffusing dome at the bottom end. The tube is typically 12 to 16 inches in diameter. Natural light enters the top dome, is reflected down the tube, and is then diffused throughout the building interior. The light output is limited by the amount of daylight falling on the exterior dome.

WHEN/WHERE IT'S APPLICABLE

The first light conveyor system is best suited to building applications where there is a need to isolate electric lights from the interior space (for example, operating rooms or theaters) or where electric light replacement is difficult (for example, swimming pools or tunnels). For the reflective tube system,

The authors of this GreenTip are Stephen Carpenter and David Grumman.

each device can light only a small area (10 ft^2) and is best suited to small interior spaces with access to the roof, such as interior bathrooms and hallways.

PROS AND CONS

Pro

1. A light conveyor transports natural light into building interiors
2. The first type of light conveyor isolates the electric light source from the lighted space
3. The first type of light conveyor reduces lighting glare
4. It lowers lighting maintenance costs

Con

1. A light conveyor may have greater capital costs than traditional electric lighting
2. The tube type may increase roof heat loss
3. The tube type runs the risk of poor installation, resulting in leaks
4. The effectiveness may not be worth the additional cost

KEY ELEMENTS OF COST

Because of the specialized nature of these techniques, it is difficult to address specific cost elements. As an alternative to conventional electric lighting techniques, it could add to or reduce the overall cost of a lighting system—and the energy costs required—depending on specific project conditions. A designer should not incorporate any such system without thoroughly investigating its benefits and applicability and should preferably observe such a system in actual use.

SOURCES OF FURTHER INFORMATION

Preliminary Evaluation of Cylindrical Skylights
McKurdy, Harrison and Cooke
23rd Annual SESCI Conference
Solar Energy Society of Canada Inc.
116 Lisgar, Suite 702
Ottawa ON
Canada K2P 0C2
tel: 613-234-4151
fax: 613-234-2988
http://www.solarenergysociety.ca

Chapter 12
Plumbing and Fire Protection Systems

Plumbing and fire protection systems are normally not considered within the purview of the HVAC&R designer's expertise. Nevertheless, both subsets of designers, in practice, must work closely in putting together a functional building mechanical system. Indeed, frequently the designer of HVAC&R systems and plumbing systems is one and the same. (Fire protection, the main role of which is safety of building occupants, particularly in times of sudden emergencies, is not a main determinant of green building design, especially in the long-term sense, and is thus not addressed in this guide.)

It is important in green building design for the practitioners of each design discipline to be familiar with what the other disciplines may bring to an effective green design. This is especially so with plumbing design. The editors of this guide have thus chosen to include discussion of some key aspects of plumbing design that can have an impact on green design—including several significant ASHRAE GreenTips. Several of these GreenTips may have an impact in other areas as well. For instance, point-of-use hot water heaters would not only save heating energy and distribution energy, they could also result in the use of less water.

Authors contributing to this chapter are Kevin Dickens, David Grumman, Michael Haggans, and Stephen Carpenter.

WATER SUPPLY

This basic resource is obviously essential at every building site, but what has changed over the last several decades is the realization that it is fast becoming a *precious* resource. While the total amount of water in its various forms on the planet is finite, the amount of fresh water, of a quality suitable for the purposes for which it may be used, is not uniformly distributed (e.g., 20% of the world's freshwater is in the United States' Great Lakes); elsewhere it is often nonexistent or in very meager supply. Nevertheless, water must be allocated somehow to the world's populated lands, many of which are undergoing rapid development. In short, it is becoming more and more difficult to provide for the adequate and equitable distribution of the world's water supply to those users for whom it is essential.

This trend has implications for not only *how prudently we use the water* we have, but what we do to *avoid contaminating water* supplies. While many of the measures to protect and preserve the world's fresh water supplies are beyond ASHRAE's purview, there are a number of simple things relating to building sites that *can* be done as part of a green design effort.

While it is obvious that water purity must meet the health and safety standards prescribed by the authorities (see below), there are other techniques that can contribute not only to using lesser quantities of the highest quality water needed at a site but requiring less energy to "process" that water (i.e., distribute it, heat it, and dispose of it once used).

Some key techniques of this nature are covered below.

Regarding the quality of the water provided for a given building/building site, the design team should:

- Supply local or municipal water that exceeds the requirements of the Environmental Protection Agency (EPA) or more stringent local requirements for potable and heated water.
- Meet the EPA *National Primary Drinking Water Regulations* (NPDWR), including Maximum Contaminant Level (MCL), by testing or by installing appropriate treatment systems. The quality of the municipal water supply shall be evaluated at applicable points, including restrooms/showers, kitchen/pantry areas, drinking fountains, architectural fountains, and/or indoor water features.
- Exceed NPDWR Maximum Contaminant Level Goals (MCLG) and Secondary Standards by testing or by installing appropriate treatment systems. The quality of the municipal water supply shall be evaluated at applicable points, including restrooms/showers, kitchen/pantry areas, drinking fountains, architectural fountains, and/or indoor water features.

Some of the techniques for reducing the demand for domestic water in a building are well known and in fairly widespread use. These include in-pipe water restrictors (such as in shower heads) and spring-closing or timed lavatory faucets, especially in public or semi-public washrooms. ASHRAE GreenTip #23 addresses other water-conserving fixtures that can be used.

ASHRAE GreenTip #24 would also impact the amount of pure fresh water used on a site by making use of "used" water for purposes where potability is not a requirement.

DOMESTIC WATER HEATING

One of the earliest techniques used for lowering the energy required for domestic water heating, going back to the mid-1970s, was reducing the temperature of the water supplied. The pre-Arab-oil-crisis norm for domestic hot water was 140°F, and the energy-saving recommendation thereafter was 105°F to 110°F. While this can save heating energy, where hot/cold mixing valves are utilized (as with some shower controls), it may also cause more hot water to be used. In addition, the dangers of legionellosis, which thrives at the lower heated water ranges, have revised the prudent recommendation for the hot water supply temperature to 115°F-120°F. As a further protection against possible legionellosis, this can be achieved by generating 140°F centrally (in a well-insulated heater/storage tank) and then mixing to the lower temperature through a mixing valve.

Another energy-reducing technique, which can also reduce the water quantity used, is covered in GreenTip #25.

Another technique to reduce water-heating cost is combining the function of domestic and space water heating, where allowed by codes. See chapter 9, "Energy Conversion Systems," for a GreenTip on combination space and water heating systems.

Yet another water heating technique, with more limited and specialized application, is covered in GreenTip #26.

SANITARY WASTE

See ASHRAE GreenTip #24, which deals with sanitary waste water, but the purpose is to conserve potable water.

STORM DRAINAGE

A similar purpose stems from GreenTip #27, though the water "source" differs.

ASHRAE GreenTip #23: Water-Conserving Plumbing Fixtures

GENERAL DESCRIPTION

Water conservation strategies save building owners both consumption and demand charges.

Further, municipal water and wastewater treatment plants save operating and capital costs for new facilities. As a general rule, water conservation strategies are very cost-effective when properly applied.

The Energy Policy Act of 1992 set reasonable standards for the technologies then available. Now, there are plumbing fixtures and equipment capable of significant reduction in water usage. For example, a rest stop in Minnesota that was equipped with ultra-low-flow toilets and waterless urinals has recorded a 62% reduction in water usage.

The following tables list the maximum water usage standards established by the Energy Policy Act of 1992 for typical fixture types. Also listed are water usages for flush-type and flow-type fixtures. Listing of conventional fixture usages allows comparison to the low-flow and ultra-low-flow fixture usages.

Table 12-1. EPCA Maximum Flows

Fixture Type	Energy Policy Act of 1992 Maximum Water Usage
Water Closets (GPF)	1.6
Urinals (GPF)	1.0
Showerheads (GPM) *	2.5
Faucets (GPM) *	2.5
Replacement Aerators (GPM)*	2.5
Metering Facets (gal/cycle)	0.25

* At flowing water pressure of 80 pounds per square in. (psi)

Table 12-2. Flush-Fixture Flows

Flush-Fixture Type	Water Use (GPF)
Conventional Water Closet	1.6
Low-Flow Water Closet	1.1
Ultra-Low-Flow Water Closet	0.8
Composting Toilet	0.0
Conventional Urinal	1.0
Waterless Urinal	0.0

Table 12-3. Flow-Fixture Flows

Flow-Fixture Type	Water Use (GPM)
Conventional Lavatory	2.5
Low-Flow Lavatory	1.8
Kitchen Sink	2.5
Low-Flow Kitchen Sink	1.8
Shower	2.5
Low-Flow Shower	1.8
Janitor Sink	2.5

WHEN/WHERE IT'S APPLICABLE

Applicable state and local codes should be checked prior to design as some of them have "approved fixture" lists; some code officials have not approved the waterless urinal and low-flush toilet technologies. Waterless urinals and low-flow lavatory fixtures usually pay back immediately. Toilet technology continues to evolve rapidly, so be sure to obtain test data and references before specifying; some units work very well, while others perform marginally.

Options that should be considered in design of water-conserving systems include:

- Infrared faucet sensors
- Delayed action shutoff or automatic mechanical shutoff valves
- Low-flow or ultra-low-flow toilets
- Lavatory faucets with flow restrictors
- Metering faucets (at 0.25 gallons per cycle)
- Low-flow kitchen faucets
- Domestic dishwashers that use 10 gallons a cycle or less
- Commercial dishwashers (conveyor type) that use 120 gallons per hour
- Waterless urinals
- Closed cooling towers (to eliminate drift) and filters for cleaning the water.

PROS AND CONS

Pro

1. Water conservation reduces a building's potable water use, in turn reducing demand on municipal water supply and lowering costs and energy use associated with water.

2. It reduces a building's overall waste generation, thus putting fewer burdens on the existing sewage system.

The author of this GreenTip is James Keller.

ASHRAE GreenTip #23: Water-Conserving Plumbing Fixtures (continued)

3. It may save capital cost since some fixtures, such as waterless urinals and low-flow lavatories, are actually less expensive to install initially.

Con

1. Some states and municipalities have "approved fixture" lists that may not include certain newer and more efficient fixtures.
2. Maintenance of these fixtures is different and will require special training of staff.

KEY ELEMENTS OF COST

The following provides a possible breakdown of the various cost elements that might differentiate a building utilizing water-conservating plumbing fixtures from one that does not and an indication of whether the net cost is likely to be lower (L), higher (H), or the same (S). This assessment is only a perception of what might be likely, but it obviously may not be correct in all situations. **There is no substitute for a detailed cost analysis as part of the design process.** The listing below may also provide some assistance in identifying the cost elements involved.

First Cost

- Low-flow and ultra-low-flow flush toilets   S
- Waterless urinals   L
- Low-flow to ultra-low-flow faucets and shower heads   S/H
- Water conserving dishwashers   S/H

Recurring Cost

- Potable water   L
- Sewer discharge   L
- Maintenance   L/S
- Training of building operators   S/H
- Orientation of building occupants   S
- Commissioning   S

SOURCES OF FURTHER INFORMATION

Del Porto, D., and C. Steinfeld. 1999. *The Composting Toilet System Book*. The Center for Ecological Pollution Prevention.

Public Technology, Inc., U.S. Department of Energy and the U.S. Green Building Council. 1996. *Sustainable Building Technical Manual – Green Building Design, Construction and Operations*. Public Technology, Inc.
http://www.epa.gov/OW/you/chap3.html
http://www.usgbc.org

ASHRAE GreenTip #24: Graywater Systems

GENERAL DESCRIPTION

Graywater is generally wastewater from lavatories, showers, bathtubs, washing machines, and sinks that are not used for food preparation. Graywater is further distinguished from blackwater, which is wastewater from toilets and sinks that contain organic or toxic matter. Local health code departments have regulations that specifically define the two kinds of waste streams in their respective jurisdiction.

Where allowed by local code, separate blackwater and graywater waste collection systems can be installed. The blackwater system would be treated as a typical waste stream and piped to the water treatment system or local sewer district. However, the

The author of this GreenTip is Kevin Dickens.

graywater would be "recycled" by collecting, storing (optional), and then distributing it via a dedicated piping system to toilets, landscape irrigation, or any other function that does not require potable water.

A simple graywater irrigation system might be gravity fed and have no means of storage. In a commercial graywater system, such as for toilet flushing in a hotel, a means of short-term on-site storage, or more appropriately, a surge tank, is required. Graywater can only be held for a short period of time before it naturally becomes blackwater. The surge tank would be provided with an overflow to the blackwater waste system and a potable makeup line for when the end-use need exceeds stored capacity.

Distribution would be accomplished via a pressurized piping system requiring pumps and some low level of filtration.

ASHRAE GreenTip #24: Graywater Systems (continued)

WHEN/WHERE IT'S APPLICABLE

Careful consideration should be given before pursuing a graywater system. While a graywater system can be applied in any facility that has a nonpotable water demand and a usable waste stream, the additional piping and energy required to provide and operate such a system may outweigh any benefits. Such a system is best applied where the ratio of demand for nonpotable water to potable water is relatively high and consistent, as in restaurants, laundries, and hotels.

Some facilities have a more reliable graywater volume than others. For example, a school would have substantially less graywater in the summer months. This may not be a problem if the graywater was being used for flushing since it can be assumed that toilet use would vary with occupancy. However, it would be detrimental if graywater were being used for landscape irrigation.

PROS AND CONS

Pro

1. A gray water system reduces a building's potable water use, in turn reducing demand on the municipal water supply and lowering costs associated with water.

2. It reduces a building's overall wastewater generation, thus putting less tax on the existing sewage systems.

Con

1. There is an added first cost associated with the additional piping, pumping, and surge tank required.

2. There are additional materials and their associated embodied energy costs

3. There is negative public perception of graywater and health concerns regarding ingestion of nonpotable water.

4. Costs include maintenance of the system, including the pumps and surge tank.

5. Local health code authority has jurisdiction, potentially making a particular site infeasible due to that authority's definition of blackwater versus graywater.

KEY ELEMENTS OF COST

The following provides a possible breakdown of the various cost elements that might differentiate a building utilizing a graywater system from one that does not and an indication of whether the net incremental cost is likely to be lower (L), higher (H), or the same (S). This assessment is only a perception of what might be likely, but it obviously may not be correct in all situations. **There is no substitute for a detailed cost analysis as part of the design process.** The listings below may also provide some assistance in identifying the cost elements involved.

First Cost

• Collection systems	H
• Surge tank	H
• Water treatment	S/H
• Distribution system	H
• Design fees	H

Recurring Cost

• Cost of potable water	L
• Cost related to sewer discharge	L
• Maintenance of system	H
• Training of building operators	H
• Orientation of building occupants	S
• Commissioning cost	H

SOURCES OF FURTHER INFORMATION

Del Porto, D., and C. Steinfeld. 1999. *The Composting Toilet System Book.* The Center for Ecological Pollution Prevention.

Ludwig, Art. 1997. *Builder's Greywater Guide* and *Create an Oasis with Greywater.* Oasis Design.

Public Technology Inc., U.S. Department of Energy and the U.S. Green Building Council. 1996. *Sustainable Building Technical Manual—Green Building Design, Construction and Operations.* Public Technology, Inc.

U.S. Green Building Council. *LEED Reference Guide,* Version 2.0, June 2001.

http://www.advancedbuildings.org

ASHRAE GreenTip #25: Point-of-Use Domestic Hot Water Heaters

GENERAL DESCRIPTION

As implied by the title, point-of-use domestic hot water heaters provide small quantities of hot water at the point of use, without tie-in to a central hot water source. A cold water line from a central source must still be connected, as well as electricity, for heating the water.

There is some variation in types. Typically, such as for lavatories, the device may be truly instantaneous, or it may have a small amount of storage capacity. With the instantaneous type, the heating coil is sized such that it can heat a normal-use flow of water up to the desired hot water temperature (120°F, say). When a small tank (usually 3 to 10 gallons) is incorporated in the device, the electric heating coil is built into the tank and can be sized somewhat smaller because of the small amount of stored water available.

The device is usually installed under the counter of the sink or bank of sinks.

A similar type of device boosts the water supply (which is cold water) up to near boiling temperature (about 190°F). This is usually used for purposes of quickly making a cup of coffee or tea without having to brew it separately in a coffeepot or teapot.

WHEN/WHERE IT'S APPLICABLE

These devices are applicable wherever there is a need for a hot water supply that is low in quantity and relatively infrequently used *and* it is excessively inconvenient or costly to run a hot water line (with perhaps a recirculation line as well) from a central hot water source. Typically, these are installed in lavatories or washrooms that are isolated or remote, or both. However, they can be used in any situation where there is a hot water need, but where it would be too inconvenient and costly to tie in to a central source. (There must, of course, be available a source of incoming water as well as a source of electricity.)

PROS AND CONS

Pro

1. Point-of-use device is a simple and direct way to provide small amounts of domestic hot water per use.
2. Long pipe runs—and in some cases a central hot water heating source—can be avoided.

3. Energy is saved by avoiding heat loss from hot water pipes and, if not needed, from a central water heater.
4. In most cases where applicable, it has lower first cost.
5. It is convenient—especially as a source of 190-210°F water supply.
6. When installed in multiple location, central equipment failure doesn't knock out all user locations.
7. It may save floor space in the central equipment room if no central heater is required.

Con

1. This is a more expensive source of heating energy (though cost may be trivial if usage is low and may be exceeded by heat losses saved from central heating method).
2. Water impurities can cause caking and premature failure of electrical heating coil.
3. It cannot handle changed demand for large hot water quantities or too-frequent use.
4. Maintenance is less convenient (when required) since it is not centralized.
5. T & P (temperature and pressure) relief valve and floor drain may be required by some code jurisdictions.

KEY ELEMENTS OF COST

The following provides a possible breakdown of the various cost elements that might differentiate a point-of-use DHW heater from a conventional one and an indication of whether the net incremental cost for the system is likely to be lower (L), higher (H), or the same (S). This assessment is only a perception of what might be likely, but it obviously may not be correct in all situations. **There is no substitute for a detailed cost analysis as part of the design process.** The listings below may also provide some assistance in identifying the cost elements involved.

First Cost

- Point-of-use water heater equipment — H
- Domestic HW piping to central source (including insulation thereof) — L
- Central water heater (if not required) and associated fuel and flue gas connections — L

The author of this GreenTip is David Grumman.

ASHRAE GreenTip #25: Point-of-Use Domestic Hot Water Heaters (continued)

- Electrical connection   H
- T & P relief valve and floor drain
  (when required by code jurisdiction)   H

Recurring Cost

- Energy to heat water proper   H
- Energy lost from piping not installed
  (and perhaps central heater)   L
- Maintenance/repairs, including replacement H

SOURCES OF FURTHER INFORMATION

Domestic Water Heating Design Manual. 1998. American Society of Plumbing Engineers, Chicago, IL.

Fagan, D. 2001. A comparison of storage-type and instantaneous heaters for commercial use. *Heating/Piping/Air Conditioning Engineering,* April.

ASHRAE GreenTip #26: Direct-Contact Water Heaters

GENERAL DESCRIPTION

A direct-contact water heater consists of a heat exchanger in which flue gases are in direct contact with the water. It can heat large quantities of water for washing and/or industrial process purposes. Cold supply water enters the top of a heat exchanger column and flows down through stainless steel rings or other devices. Natural gas is burned in a combustion chamber, and the flue gases are directed up the heat exchanger column. As the gases move upwards through the column, they transfer their sensible and latent heat to the water. A heat exchanger or water jacket on the combustion chamber captures any heat loss from the chamber. The gases exit only a few degrees warmer than the inlet water temperature. The heated water may be stored in a storage tank for "on-demand" use. Direct-contact water heaters can be 99% efficient when the inlet water temperature is below 59°F.

The low-temperature combustion process results in low emissions of NO_x and CO; thus, the system is in effect a low-NO_x burner. It is also a low-pressure process since heat transfer occurs at atmospheric pressure.

Although there is direct contact between the flue gases and the water, there is very little contamination of the water. Direct-contact systems are suitable for all water heating applications including food processing and dairy applications; the water used in

The authors of this GreenTip are Stephen Carpenter and David Grumman.

these systems is considered bacteriologically safe for human consumption.

WHEN/WHERE IT'S APPLICABLE

The high cost of direct-contact water heaters (due to stainless steel construction) restricts their use to where there is a large, almost continuous, demand for hot water. Appropriate applications include laundries, food processing, washing and industrial processes. The system can also be used for closed-loop (or recirculating) applications such as space heating. However, efficiency—the primary benefit of direct contact water heating—will be reduced because of the higher inlet water temperature resulting from recirculation.

PROS AND CONS

Pro

1. Increases part-load and instantaneous efficiency
2. Reduces NO_x and CO emissions
3. Increases safety
4. Increases system response time.

Con

1. High cost
2. Less effective in higher pressure or closed-loop applications or where inlet water temperatures must be relatively high.
3. Results in considerable water usage beyond that required for the process itself due to high evaporation rate.

ASHRAE GreenTip #26: Direct-Contact Water Heaters (continued)

KEY ELEMENTS OF COST

The following provides a possible breakdown of the various cost elements that might differentiate a direct-contact water heater from a conventional one and an indication of whether the net cost for the alternative option is likely to be lower (L), higher (H), or the same (S). This assessment is only a perception of what might be likely, but it obviously may not be correct in all situations. **There is no substitute for a detailed cost analysis as part of the design process.** The listings below may also provide some assistance in identifying the cost elements involved.

First Cost

- Water heater   H
- Operator training (unfamiliarity)   H

Recurring Cost

- Water heating energy   L

Direct-contact boilers are two to three times the price of indirect or conventional boilers, primarily because of the stainless steel construction. In high and continuous water use applications, however, the payback period can be under two years.

SOURCES OF FURTHER INFORMATION

National Sanitation Foundation and American National Standards Institute. 2000. *NSF/ANSI 5-2000e: Water Heaters, Hot Water Supply Boilers, and Heat Recovery Equipment.* Ann Arbor, MI: NSF.

http://www.quikwater.com/qw_services_home.htm

ASHRAE GreenTip #27: Rainwater Harvesting

GENERAL DESCRIPTION

Rainwater harvesting has been around for thousands of years. Rainwater harvesting is a simple technology that can stand alone or augment other water sources. Systems can be as basic as a rain barrel under a downspout or as complex as a pumped and filtered graywater system providing landscape irrigation, cooling tower makeup, and/or building waste conveyance.

Systems are generally composed of five or less basic components: (1) a catchment area, (2) a means of conveyance from the catchment, (3) storage (optional), (4) water treatment (optional), and (5) a conveyance system to the end use.

The catchment area can be any impermeable area from which water can be harvested. Typically this is the roof, but paved areas such as patios, entries, and parking lots may also be considered. Roofing materials such as metal, clay, or concrete based are preferable to asphalt or roofs with lead-containing materials. Similarly, care should be given when considering a parking lot for catchment due to oils and residues that can be present.

Conveyance to the storage will be gravity fed like any stormwater piping system. The only difference is that now the rainwater is being diverted for useful purposes instead of literally going down the drain.

Commercial systems will require a means of storage. Cisterns can be located outside the building (above grade or buried) or placed on the lower levels of the building. The storage tank should have an overflow device piped to the storm system and a potable water makeup if the end-use need is ever greater than the harvested volume.

Depending on the catchment source and the end use, the level of treatment will vary. For simple site irrigation, filtration can be achieved through a series of graded screens and paper filters. If the water is to be used for waste conveyance, then an additional sand filter may be appropriate. Parking lot catchments may require an oil separator. The local code authority will likely decide acceptable water standards, and, in turn, filtration and chemical polishing will be a dictated parameter, not a design choice.

Distribution can be via gravity or pump depending on the proximity of the storage tank and the end use.

The author of this GreenTip is Kevin Dickens.

ASHRAE GreenTip #27: Rainwater Harvesting (continued)

WHEN/WHERE IT'S APPLICABLE

If the building design is to include a graywater system or landscape irrigation—and space for storage can be found—rainwater harvesting is a simple addition to those systems.

When a desire exists to limit potable water demand and use, depending on the end-use requirement and the anticipated annual rainfall in a region, harvesting can be provided as a stand-alone system or to augment a conventional makeup water system.

Sites with significant precipitation volumes may determine that reuse of these volumes is more cost-effective than creating stormwater systems or on-site treatment facilities.

Rainwater harvesting is most attractive where municipal water supply is either nonexistent or unreliable, hence its popularity in rural regions and developing countries.

PROS AND CONS

Pro

1. Rainwater harvesting reduces a building's potable water use, in turn reducing demand on the municipal water supply and lowering costs associated with water.
2. Rainwater is soft and does not cause scale buildup in piping, equipment, and appliances. It could extend life of systems.
3. It can reduce or eliminate the need for storm water treatment or conveyance systems.

Con

1. There is added first cost associated with the cisterns and the treatment system.
2. Additional materials and their associated embodied energy costs.
3. The storage vessels must be accommodated. Small sites or projects with limited space allocated for utilities would be bad candidates.
4. Costs include maintenance of the system, including the catchments, conveyance, cisterns, and treatment systems.
5. There is no U.S. guideline on rainwater harvesting. The local health code authority has jurisdiction, potentially making a particular site infeasible due to backflow prevention require-

ments, special separators, or additional treatment.

KEY ELEMENTS OF COST

The following provides a possible breakdown of the various cost elements that might differentiate a building utilizing rainwater harvesting from one that does not and an indication of whether the net cost is likely to be lower (L), higher (H), or the same (S). This assessment is only a perception of what might be likely, but it obviously may not be correct in all situations. **There is no substitute for a detailed cost analysis as part of the design process.** The listings below may also provide some assistance in identifying the cost elements involved.

First Cost

• Catchment area	S
• Conveyance systems	S
• Storage tank	H
• Water treatment	S/H
• Distribution system	S
• Design fees	H

Recurring Cost

• Cost of potable water	L
• Maintenance of system	H
• Training of building operators	H
• Orientation of building occupants	S
• Commissioning cost	H

SOURCES OF FURTHER INFORMATION

Gerston, J. Rainwater Harvesting: A New Water Source. *http://twri.tamu.edu*

Public Technology Inc., U.S. Department of Energy and the U.S. Green Building Council. 1996. *Sustainable Building Technical Manual – Green Building Design, Construction and Operations.* Public Technology, Inc.

U.S. Green Building Council. 2001. *LEED Reference Guide*, Version 2.0.

Waterfall, Patricia H. *Harvesting Rainwater for Landscape Use. http://ag/arizona.edu/pubs/water/az1052/harvest.html*

Water Efficiency Clearinghouse, The *http://www.waterwiser.org*

Irrigation Association, The *http://www.irrigation.org*

Chapter 13
Controls

Controls may be thought of as the "nervous system" of a building's mechanical and electrical infrastructure. As such, controls can wield a lot of leverage in affecting how efficiently a building operates, often with little incremental upfront effort or cost. Below are some effective control guidelines and techniques to consider in a green building design endeavor.

INDIVIDUAL (OCCUPANT)

A high level of individual occupant control for thermal, ventilation, and lighting systems in buildings will support optimum health, productivity, and comfort conditions.

Thermal

Provide a minimum of one operable window per 200 square feet for all regularly occupied areas.

Provide a minimum of one airflow and temperature control each for 50% of occupants in all regularly occupied areas, or implement a program similar to the Environmental Protection Agency's *IEQ Tools for Schools* that empowers occupants in the building operation process.

Daylighting/Electric Lighting

Provide a minimum of one lighting control zone per 200 square feet for all regularly occupied areas.

Provide a minimum of one lighting control for

Authors contributing to this chapter are Michael Haggans and Mick Schwedler.

each 50% of occupants in all regularly occupied areas, or implement a program similar to the EPA's IEQ *Tools for Schools* that empowers occupants in the building operation process.

(See also chapters 6 and 11, which cover lighting in more detail.)

SYSTEMS AND EQUIPMENT

It is possible to design, install, and operate truly integrated systems today. These systems require unit-level and system-level control points as well as control methods. Some methods of using controls to reduce building energy consumption include the following.

Fan Setpoint Optimization (Required by 90.1-2001 on DDC/VAV Systems)

This is a method to reduce operating pressure within an air-handling system. At each point in time, the fan pressure setpoint is changed to ensure that the critical zone's damper is 90-95% open. Significant energy can be saved by using this method.

Ventilation Reset

Ventilation reset satisfies ventilation requirements while dynamically reducing the amount of ventilation air that needs to be conditioned.

Temperature Reset

Temperature reset is one of the most used, yet least understood, control methods, and it should only be used in certain conditions. Raising chilled water or chilled supply air temperatures often reduces energy consumption of the chiller compressor. Since this motor is often the largest in the system, at first glance this seems to make sense. However, raising air or water temperatures may require more airflow or waterflow. This would, in turn, significantly increase the energy used by fans and pumps at part-load conditions, especially those used in variable flow systems. Thus, the following guidelines should be followed:

- With variable flow systems, do NOT use a temperature reset sequence until conditions are such that the fan or pump "load" is low.
- With constant flow systems, temperature reset may be beneficial.

Pump Pressure Optimization

This is a method to reduce operating pressure in a pumped hydronic system. At each point in time, pump pressure setpoint is changed to ensure that the *critical* zone's valve is 90-95% open. Care must be taken to identify the critical zone correctly and then, of course, data on valve position, however remote, must be transmitted to the device controlling system pressure Significant energy can be saved using this method.

Chiller-Tower Optimization

As condenser water temperature leaving a cooling tower is reduced, the tower must expend more energy, but the corresponding chiller uses less. Conversely, as the water temperature leaving a cooling tower rises, tower energy consumption goes down, but chiller consumption goes up. The point of minimum energy consumption is a function of tower efficiency and the impact reset has on chiller efficiency. Dynamically calculating the optimal temperature at each load and ambient condition can yield an optimal operating condition. Such a control protocol is available from a number of control system providers.

DISTRIBUTED AND CENTRAL MONITORING/CONTROL

Control of building systems can be performed either on-site or remotely. There are advantages and disadvantages to each.

On-site control allows operators familiar with a specific system or building to retain and increase their expertise on that system or building. Optimally, on-site operators receive fundamental system and equipment training and use this knowledge to improve plant operation. System familiarity allows the operator to understand the unique aspects of a plant. A major drawback is that an operator rarely works with a plant for a period of 10 or more years. Therefore, the advantage of familiarity becomes moot.

Remote monitoring allows experts familiar with various operating strategies to apply them to many buildings. However, familiarity with a specific building may not be as high as when site monitoring is used. This results in general, rather than specific, operating decisions. Thus, the plant may run fairly well, though it is unlikely to be optimal.

ASHRAE GreenTip #28: Mixed Air Temperature Reset

GENERAL DESCRIPTION

Mixed air temperature (MAT), in this case, refers to the temperature of the mix of outside and return (recirculated) air that exists on an operating supply air-handling unit prior to any "new" thermal energy being added to the airstream. In the days when constant air volume (CAV) systems were prevalent, it was customary to set the MAT controls to maintain a constant 55°F nominally. (The controls would adjust the relative positions of outside and return air dampers to apportion the relative quantities of each airstream to satisfy the MAT setpoint, but never allowing less than the code-required minimum outside air.) In the "wintertime"—or heating season—when the outside air temperature was generally below 55°F, the MAT would be the "cooling" airstream or cold deck—the lowest temperature air available for zones that needed cooling in this season. As heating was required, heat would be added at some point, either through a "hot deck" airstream within the air-handling unit, or through reheat by downstream coils.

The reset technique is based on the premise that the MAT from a supply air-handling system is colder than any one zone requires to maintain the set conditions of that zone. To the extent that this condition prevails, it means that the mixed (or cold) airstream must be mixed with some warm (hot deck) air to yield the proper supply air temperature to satisfy even the zone requiring the *lowest* temperature air supply. Since warmer air would need to be mixed in to do this, that would require "new" energy and is thus somewhat wasteful of heating energy (a form of simultaneous heating and cooling). In the heating season, cooling – being derived from outside air – is free.

The idea is to reset the MAT to a temperature that just satisfies the space with the lowest cold air demand. Reset controls involve raising the setpoint of the MAT controls based on input that indicates the demand of that zone needing the coldest air – limited still by the need to main the *minimum* quantity of outside air. This, in turn, requires sensors that can monitor that and other zone demands continuously; this input could come from hot deck/cold deck mixing dampers, mixing box damper positions, or thermostat output signals that indicate zone temperature demands. The goal would be to raise the MAT just enough so that the zone with the lowest supply air temperature demand was satisfied on a continuing basis. (As conditions change over time, that zone may change.)

The author of this GreenTip is David Grumman.

WHEN/WHERE IT'S APPLICABLE

As stated above, this technique, in most cases, *should only be used on CAV systems*. If it is used with variable air volume (VAV) systems, it can often backfire since other energy variables (such as fan energy, in the case of air systems) may change in the opposite direction from heating energy saved, possibly resulting in a net increase in energy use or cost. Thus, if it *is* applied to VAV systems, it should come into play when any other affected variable is already at its minimum (e.g., fan already at its minimum turndown rate).

As the season becomes warmer and outside temperature rises, this technique may become less and less effective, especially since the served zones may require more cooling and ever lower supply air temperatures.

Although there may not be a lot of constant volume (CAV) air systems being installed in new designs, there are still plenty operating in existing buildings (though it shouldn't be applied to CAV systems converted to variable volume). This technique does lend itself well to retrofit, and since the controls are basically the same for large or small sized air-handling systems, the savings can be large for a relatively capital cost.

PROS AND CONS

Pro

1. MAT reset saves heating energy and associated operating cost.

2. It can yield a low payback, especially on larger air-handling systems.

3. It is relatively low in capital cost in the full spectrum of energy retrofits.

Con

1. MAT reset may require greater attention to periodic controls calibration.

2. To be effective, there must be evidence that worst zone demands will allow sufficient upward reset of temperature to realize appreciable savings.

3. Sampling of zone demands may be difficult to do in remote or scattered locations.

4. It is relatively easy to do as a retrofit on existing systems.

ASHRAE GreenTip #28: Mixed Air Temperature Reset (continued)

KEY ELEMENTS OF COST

The following provides a possible breakdown of the various cost elements that might differentiate an MAT reset system from a conventional one and an indication of whether the net cost for the alternative is likely to be lower (L), higher (H), or the same (S). This assessment is only a perception of what might be likely, but it obviously may not be correct in all situations. **There is no substitute for a detailed cost analysis as part of the design process.** The listings below may also provide some assistance in identifying the cost elements involved.

First Cost

- Reset controls and installation   H
- Zone input sensors and connection to reset controls   H

Recurring Cost

- Heating energy (heating coil)   L
- Maintenance   H
- Operator training   H

SOURCES OF FURTHER INFORMATION

ASHRAE. 1999. *1999 ASHRAE Handbook—HVAC Applications.*

ASHRAE GreenTip #29: Cold Deck Temperature Reset with Humidity Override

GENERAL DESCRIPTION

Cold deck temperature (CDT) reset is very similar to MAT reset, but it applies to the air temperature leaving a cooling coil—or CDT of a constant air volume (CAV) air-handling unit during "summertime," or the season when mechanical cooling is required. In this situation, the object is to save cooling energy supplied at the cooling coil by allowing the set CDT to "ride up" above a nominal design level (55°F, say) as long as all zone cooling needs are met.

The control needs and techniques are similar to MAT reset (reviewing the GreenTip for which is a prerequisite to considering this one) with one addition: a humidity override. When in the mechanical cooling mode in moderate to humid climates, mechanically cooled air serves the function of dehumidification (latent cooling) as well as sensible cooling. The degree of humidification achieved in the occupied zones served depends largely on the CDT being maintained. Thus, if CDT is allowed to ride up for cooling purposes, it should not be allowed to rise beyond the temperature needed to maintain comfort humidity conditions. Thus, the occupied zone humidity parameter sets an upper limit for the reset function.

Zone humidity input can be sensed from a sampling of served zones themselves, or one could sense the return airstream at the air-handling unit. The latter would yield an *average* humidity of all spaces served rather than the highest humidity of any one space. However, given that return air humidity would probably be a lot easier and less expensive to sense than that of several remote zones, it may be "good enough" to serve the purpose.

The upper limit of humidity chosen as the limiting factor for this reset technique would depend on what the building operator feels is within the comfort tolerance of the occupants. While a nominal relative humidity level of 50% is often the goal for cooling season comfort, higher levels can be tolerated, and sometimes an upper limit of 55% to 60% may be selected. Whatever is chosen, however, is easily adjustable. High-quality humidity sensing equipment is recommended.

Reducing the CDT off the cooling coil can also result in savings at other "upstream" components of the building's cooling system, such as not-as-cold temperatures off a central chiller or reduced chilled water flow in a variable flow pumping system. (In fact, this is where the cost savings would actually be realized.) If considering this technique, the designer should ensure that the piping, valving, and control configurations are such that "up-the-line" energy and cost savings are indeed achievable.

The author of this GreenTip is David Grumman.

ASHRAE GreenTip #29: Cold Deck Temperature Reset with Humidity Override (continued)

WHEN/WHERE IT'S APPLICABLE

The same constraints apply here as with MAT reset. Again, before doing this, the designer should be sure that there are likely to be opportunities for significant upward reset to take place. If it is found that there is just one space that is likely to always need the design cold deck temperature during the cooling season, regardless of weather or other changing conditions, then this technique is probably not a good bet.

PROS AND CONS

Pro

1. CDT reset saves cooling energy and associated operating cost.
2. It can yield a good payback when the situation is right, although not as low as MAT reset.
3. Capital cost is still relatively low (though more controls are required than with MAT reset).

Con

1. There are the same drawbacks as with MAT reset, plus.
2. There could be added problems with excessive space humidity if the humidity sensing is not accurate.

KEY ELEMENTS OF COST

The following provides a possible breakdown of the various cost elements that might differentiate a CDT reset system from a conventional one and an indication of whether the net incremental cost for the alternative option is likely to be lower (L), higher (H), or the same (S). This assessment is only a perception of what might be likely, but it obviously may not be correct in all situations. **There is no substitute for a detailed cost analysis as part of the design process.** The listings below may also provide some assistance in identifying the cost elements involved.

First Cost

• Same elements as for MAT reset, plus	H
• Humidity sensor(s) and connection reset controls	H

Recurring Cost

• Cooling energy	L
• Maintenance	H
• Operator Training	L

SOURCES OF FURTHER INFORMATION

ASHRAE. 2003. *2003 ASHRAE Handbook—HVAC Applications.*

Chapter 14
Expressing and Testing Concepts

Expressing concepts is very important in green design because that is the way ideas and intentions are communicated to the owner and others on the design team. This is especially true since green design requires the close and active participation of many different parties.

There are three ways of expressing concepts in the design of buildings; two of these are the traditional *verbal* means and the other is the *diagrammatic or pictorial* means. The third has come of age more recently along with computers: modeling.

VERBAL

Both the written and the spoken word play an especially important part in green design. Because there are many meetings or charettes where ideas are explored and intentions voiced, getting across what is expressed accurately assumes significance. Putting what has been expressed, then, down on paper succinctly and clearly (memorializing it) also is critical to the various team members as they each go about filling their respective roles. To illustrate, one need only read chapter 18, "Commissioning," for it to become apparent how important a written record of "what happened" during design (i.e., design intent, assumptions, etc.) is to a successful follow-through of a well-executed green design.

Authors contributing to this chapter are David Grumman and Mick Schwedler.

DIAGRAMMATIC/PICTORIAL

The use of diagrams, sketches, photos, renderings, etc., a tried and true method of communicating a lot of information, continues to be an essential part of green design. The old adage "one picture is worth a thousand words" most certainly applies here. But there is now available a relatively new way of "creating a picture" of a building, an energy system, a year of operations—that is modeling.

MODELING

This computer-age technique plays such an important part in green design because of its speed, its accuracy, and its comprehensiveness.

Everyone is familiar with how speedy computers are, once the input data is entered. The "slow" part in this process is the human analyst, the one who converts intentions and ideas into computer modeling program input, which it is why it is *so* important for that analyst to be very conversant with the modeling process. This is especially true for load and energy calculations that impact HVAC&R systems. The team has an idea, and they want an answer *fast* as to how well that idea works!

Most would also acknowledge that computers are accurate: they don't make "careless" mistakes. Again, if there are inaccuracies, they usually come from the human side, which is why the analyst must be an expert at avoiding "garbage in."

Modeling programs have another advantage, especially the more sophisticated ones: they are comprehensive in what they can analyze simultaneously. The human mind can only accommodate so many ideas or concepts at once without getting confused and bogged down; a properly conceived model will not get confused and can provide answers that may be counterintuitive. As an example, a good modeling program can track heat gain from lights, plug loads, and solar energy along with heat loss from the building envelope and infiltration, do it for every hour or every day of the year in whatever weather conditions are assumed, take into account mass effects of the structure, and still yield an accurate answer. It would be impossible for the human mind to do this in a reasonable time, unless it was very good at guessing!

Evaluating Alternative Designs

Modeling of alternative designs is made easier by the plethora of modeling tools available today. The chosen model should meet specific requirements depending on the level of accuracy needed. Large error can be introduced into modeling if users forget the "garbage in/garbage out" rule. To reduce the chance of inappropriate or misunderstood input, modeling programs can employ input and output formats that allow the user quick "reality checks."

Various stages of design, requirements, and associated tools are shown in Table 14-1.

Parametric Analysis

See the discussion of this subject in chapter 6, "Conceptual Engineering Design."

Table 14-1. Summary of Available Analysis/Modeling Tools

Stage	Requirements	Tools	Reality Checks
Scoping	- Quick analysis - Comparative results - Reduce alternatives to consider - Control strategy modeling	- System Analyzer™ - Modified bin analysis (where load is not entirely dependent on ambient conditions)	- Operation cost per ft^2 - Payback or other financial measure
System Design	- Accurate output - Industry-accepted methods	- HAP - TRACE 700 - Elite Design	- cfm/ft^2 - cfm/ton
Energy/Cost Analysis	- Accurate - Industry-accepted methods - Flexible - Allows modeling of complex control strategies - Complies with ECB method requirements of ASHRAE 90.1-2001 - Works for existing building and systems	- EnergyPlus - DOE - HAP - TRACE 700 - SUNREL	- Btu/h-ft^2 per year - Operation cost per ft^2 - Payback or other financial measure
Monitoring	- Simplicity - Intuitive interface - Systemwide - Interoperable	- BacNET—compatible automation systems	- Trended operating characteristics - Benchmark comparisons (such as system kW/ton)

Chapter 15
Completing Design and Documentation for Construction

DRAWINGS/DOCUMENTS STAGE

Once the project has reached the working drawing/construction document stage, the green design concepts and resulting configurations should be well set, and the task of incorporating them into the documents that contractors will use to build the project should be relatively routine. However, quality control at this stage is especially important in green design projects.

Many firms have a routine procedure to review the documents for quality before they are released to contractors, ensuring concepts are adequately depicted and described and catching errors and omissions. This process should also include a green design concept review, preferably by one or more design team members that were in on the early stages of the project. This is particularly true if those preparing the construction documents were not part of that process. This is not the time to allow an excellent green design to become diluted or slip away.

SPECIFYING MATERIALS/EQUIPMENT

Green Building Materials

A source for guidance on selecting and specifying materials for a green project is:

http://www.athenasmi.ca

Authors contributing to this chapter are David Grumman, Jay Enck, Michael Haggans, Blair McCarry, and Steve Turner.

Further, as a guide that could prove helpful to some, refer to "One Design Firm's Materials Specification Checklist," on page 130.

Controlling Construction Quality

It is far easier to control construction quality in the design and specification stage of a project than during its construction. During preparation of the final construction drawings and specifications is not the time to be sloppy or careless in spelling out the quality expected in the field to carry through the green design concepts developed so diligently in the early design stages. Some further thoughts on this subject, many applicable to the design phase, are covered in chapter 17, "Construction."

COSTING

Design Costs

While professional design fees are not normally a subject discussed in the ASHRAE world of standards and guidelines, it is one of the really big potential impediments to green design. Now why would any consulting engineer, in business do competent work and to stay afloat, agree to be paid to reduce the cost of the mechanical system based on mechanical system construction cost? If a good job were done, that engineer's fee would be reduced! It would be more in the engineer's interest to get high-efficiency chillers, additional controls, or whatever installed at

ONE DESIGN FIRM'S MATERIALS SPECIFICATION CHECKLIST

❑ Choose at least a portion of materials/products that are:
- Local and/or indigenous, reducing the environmental impacts resulting from transportation and supporting the local economy.
- Extracted, harvested, recovered, manufactured regionally within a radius of 500 miles.
- Have low embodied energy.
- Reused, recycled, and/or recyclable, reducing the impacts resulting from extraction of new resources.
- Salvaged building materials (lumber, millwork, plumbing fixtures, hardware, etc.)
- Post-consumer recycled content material and/or post-industrial recycled content (recovered) material.
- Nonhazardous to recycle, compost, or dispose of.
- Renewable and sustainably harvested (no old growth timber), preferably with minimal associated environmental burdens, reducing the use and depletion of finite raw and long-cycle renewable materials.
- Rapidly renewable building materials, including any non-wood materials that are typically harvested within a ten-year or shorter cycle.
- Nontoxic/nonpolluting in manufacture, use, and disposal.

❑ Use finished materials, products, and furnishings that are free of known, probable, and suspected carcinogens, mutagens, teratogens, persistent toxic organic pollutants, and toxic heavy metals pursuant to EPA's *Toxicity Characteristic Leaching Procedure (TCLP) Test*, 40 CFR Part 260. (Based on EPA's *Universal Waste Rule* and Part 260, building owners and their contractors must use the TCLP to determine if they are generators of hazardous waste and thus subject to EPA and state hazardous waste regulations when disposing of mercury lamps and other waste products.)

❑ Specify lead-free solder for copper water supply tubing; do not use plastic for supply water.

❑ Avoid plastic foam insulation.

❑ Specify natural, nontoxic, low VOC-emitting, non-solvent-based finishes, paints, stains, and adhesives.

❑ When specifying painting:
- Consider surfaces that don't require painting.
- Choose paints that have been independently certified (such as Green Seal).
- Choose latex over oil-based paint.
- Increase direct-to-outdoors ventilation when painting.
- Dispose of oil-based paints like hazardous waste.
- Recycle latex paint or save for touch-ups.

❑ Avoid the use of materials containing or produced with ozone-depleting CFCs or HCFCs (often embedded in foam insulation and refrigeration/cooling systems).

❑ Avoid CFC-based refrigerants in new base-building HVAC&R systems. When reusing existing base-building HVAC equipment, complete a comprehensive CFC phaseout conversion.

❑ Commit to working with manufacturing teams who provide performance/service contracts of integrated systems for service delivery, product longevity, adaptability, and/or recycling.

❑ Favor suppliers who will minimize packaging and will take back excess packaging such as pallets, crates, cardboard, and excess building materials.

❑ Maximize the use of materials that retain a high value in future life cycles.

❑ Specify products or systems that extend manufacturer responsibility through a lease or take-back program that ensures future reuse or recycling into a product of similar or higher value.

❑ To guide material selection choices during the design process, educate designers and elicit life-cycle information from manufacturers to encourage selection of building materials and furnishings with favorable life-cycle performance.

❑ Select materials from manufacturers that are committed to improving their overall environmental performance at their manufacturing facilities and their suppliers' facilities.

an additional cost; these components might have a short payback that could be justified, and some owners might accept them. So the engineer gets a bit more fee, and project energy usage is reduced a bit. Life is good!

But....the energy usage of the building did not really change that much!

What if the fee structure were changed so that innovative design with significantly reduced energy usage was encouraged? Some alternative approaches that can be tried follow.

Fixed Fees. If professional fees were fixed at the "normal" level, the fees would not be reduced if the cost of the mechanical work were reduced. While this is not a really positive incentive for green design work, it at least removes the disincentive. The designer actually has to work harder to do less (smaller mechanical system).

Premium Fees. If an engineering designer is actually doing more and contributing to a project beyond normal service, such as working in the "reduce the load" area, he or she is providing a higher and more valuable level of service. When a client goes into a "scary" area such as green design, engineers that can provide an added "value" service not only will be more likely to get the project but will get paid for it, too.

This is stepping beyond the world of "commodity service," where anyone can do the project, so the market goes for the lowest cost. The new model is the value-added world that will pay more for better engineering input. Just look at the range of cars on the road. Many of them are not the least expensive models available.

In the end, there has to be better value for the client if that client is going to go for a different structure. If capital costs are the same or similar and the operating costs are significantly reduced, there is a big return for the client for some amount of additional fees.

Modeling Costs. There are opportunities for additional fees in the area of energy performance computer modeling. This might be done at the initial "reduce the load" stage or later to evaluate design options, or in the code compliance submission stage (because you did not use the prescriptive route), or to demonstrate LEED compliance. The modeling could be done in house if capabilities are available, or they could be contracted out.

Further, some form of modeling is usually required to demonstrate projected results when a design outside the standard design for the region is used.

Performance Fees. An opportunity for increased fees with some risk is performance-based fees. With this approach, a basic fee is paid for design and construction work. Should the project meet the reduced energy performance goals (adjusted for common hours of operation, weather, etc.), an agreed premium fee is paid. It further could be staged, depending upon actual performance.

Programs. Sometimes there are government or industry programs to support using innovative or energy-saving technologies or creating lower-energy-use building designs. The design team should become familiar with the programs available in their region and utilize them when appropriate. These programs often provide design cost incentives, capital cost incentives, or tax incentives, resulting in a better financial performance by the project and increased acceptance of the lower-energy-use approaches

Capital Costs

System/Equipment Reductions Due to Green Design. The common perception is that green buildings will cost more. Most people's ingrained experience is that if you want something better, you have to pay more for it. When one goes to the store to buy something such as a car, stereo, or computer, the better performing models generally cost more.

For green buildings to become commonplace and eventually be the norm, they must be built without significant, if any, additional cost. To maintain traditional project cost levels (factoring out normal escalation over time) many practitioners have found that there is usually a cost transfer required from the mechanical system to other building elements (such as high-performance glass, say). A number of built examples of this phenomenon exist.

The key to proper cost analysis of sustainable buildings is broadening the scope of the cost analysis. As a further example, a radiant floor/displacement ventilation HVAC system may cost more to install by itself than a conventional system, but the elimination of dropped ceiling space and the resulting savings in slab-to-slab height required may translate into overall project savings.

As in this case, the economic advantage of green engineering is often found through the "no-build" offset. Since sustainably designed buildings are often life-cycle costed over longer time horizons, engineers (and owners) must similarly shift their focus.

Recurring Costs/Benefits

Operating/Maintenance. Reduced on-site energy use and the attendant reduction in energy costs are obviously a key benefit of successful green

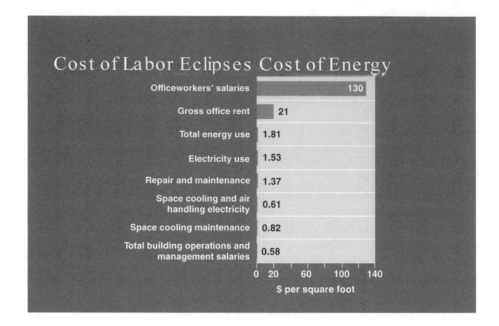

Figure 15-1 People cost vs. other costs in business operation.

design. This is accompanied by lowered use of the building's share of energy resources and other natural resources, which is one of the rationales for green design.

Maintenance costs may or may not be lowered on balance. While reduced maintenance would be expected to accompany smaller-sized equipment and systems where such result from green design, the fact that some green systems or features must be kept in proper operating order to continue to be effective over the long term would tend to drive the cost of maintenance somewhat higher than it would be otherwise. Thus, it is difficult to generalize about such costs, and projections of maintenance cost benefits are best made on a project-by-project basis.

The impacts on operating and maintenance costs have been covered extensively throughout this document. A more elusive benefit of green design is its impact on human productivity.

Human Productivity. While difficult to measure, the benefits of improving the workplace environment (*all* aspects of indoor environmental quality) and workers' felling of well-being can yield big gains in human productivity. Figure 15-1 shows the typical relationship among the various categories of cost of operating a business, with human costs outstripping all other costs several times over.

Some case study results of improved productivity are summarized below.

- Lockheed
  - 15% rise in production
  - 15% drop in absenteeism
- West Bend Mutual Insurance
  - 16% increase in claims processes
- ING Bank
  - 15% drop in absenteeism
- Verifone
  - 5% increase in productivity
  - 40% drop in absenteeism

Sources for further information:

- Greening the Building and the Bottom Line, Rocky Mountain Institute, *http://www.rmi.org*
- Better Bricks, *http://www.betterbricks.com*

Intangibles

Worth of Green Design. Reviewing green design work done by others allows engineers to see how built projects have created new opportunities and can guide efforts to sell and provide green engineering services. Performing sustainable design can yield important benefits to design engineers individually and to their firms. Improved client service, more repeat work, improved market position, enhanced public relations, and better employee satisfaction and retention are among the many benefits that numerous architectural firms and several pioneering engineering firms have derived from informing their practices with sustainable design expertise.

On the other hand, failure to address client concerns about green design can harm reputation. Disproportionate start-up costs, risk, or other perceived obstacles (such as the educational investment and commitment required to change engineering thinking and culture) may be perceived as being associated with undertaking sustainable design. Managing each of these issues, communicating frankly, and crafting creative solutions as required can reduce exposure to these potentially negative issues.

Section 3:
Post-Design—
Construction to Demolition

Chapter 16
Builder/Contractor Selection

Successful projects depend upon the entire team of players involved: architect, engineers, and contractors. As for the architect and engineer, it is imperative that the builder or contractor associated with the project be ethical, reliable, and experienced. Two basic approaches in the construction of a project include the design/build approach and the design/bid-build (D/B-B) approach.

DESIGN/BUILD

Design/build (D/B) construction typically is a response to a Request-for-Proposal (RFP) developed by an owner. The RFP is usually a document that defines the general scope of the project and then solicits price proposals to accomplish this work. The work effort to prepare the specific design of the project is to be included in the D/B offering. The D/B team usually consists of an architect, engineers for the various disciplines involved, a general contractor, and the trade subcontractors. This entire team should be in place until the project is turned over to the owner.

The D/B team may or may not have previous experience in producing this type of construction. As the D/B team develops the design, it must respond to the premises defined in the original scope of work. The qualifications, integrity, and capability of the D/B

The author of this chapter is Charles Wilkin.

team are assumed to meet the expectations of the owner. However, the owner must first define the project requirements and expectations before soliciting proposals. In addition, the owner should pre-qualify the D/B team prior to accepting price proposals. It is not appropriate to reject proposals after the D/B team has expended significant effort to develop pricing. Furthermore, to reject the proposal based on a decision that the D/B team is not qualified to perform the project could lead to legal recourse by that entity.

DESIGN/BID-BUILD

Design/bid-build construction is the traditional process undertaken by public and private owners. The initial design process often includes a project definition stage, or programming, in which the owner works with the design professionals to define the specific scope of the project. The design professional utilizes this information to prepare a set of bidding documents. The bid documents are then available for qualified contractors to prepare pricing. The lowest responsible price is usually selected and the contractor then constructs the projected.

FACTORS IN CHOOSING AN APPROACH

In both of the above scenarios, the team or contractors should be pre-qualified to perform the work prior to a request for pricing. Pre-qualification involves certain information that allows selection of potential constructors:

- Experience in similar work
- Record of past performance by responsible references
- Financial capability
- Workload.

Experience, past performance, and financial stability are all important factors. A record of exemplary performance and fiscal capability may be more important than experience in similar work. In any case it valuable to pre-select the teams or contractors from whom you request pricing. Successful projects occur due to careful planning and implementation.

Chapter 17
Construction

"There is many a slip 'twixt the cup and the lip" is an old proverb that may be applicable to the design/construction process. To minimize gaps between design intent and what is actually built, the green-conscious engineer should provide a level of construction administration above the norm. That engineer (or an independent agent) may also provide mechanical/electrical system commissioning. (See chapter 18, "Commissioning," and a related section in chapter 4 as well.)

CONSTRUCTION PRACTICES AND METHODS

In design, the specifications should prescribe that certain construction methods and procedures must be followed to ensure a fully realized green project. This would include topics such as reduced site disturbance, handling of construction waste, control of rainwater runoff, and IAQ management during construction. Some items for consideration, which may or may not be applicable to the mechanical/electrical contractors on site, are listed on page 140.

Finally, and of considerable interest to the HVAC&R engineer, it is recommended that there be developed a Construction IAQ Management Plan that the contractor would be required to follow.

Authors contributing to this chapter are David Grumman, Michael Haggans, and Wayne Robertson.

SMACNA's *IAQ Guideline for Occupied Buildings under Construction* is cited by the U.S. Green Building Council as a source document. The contractor should particularly protect installed or stored absorptive materials, such as insulation or sheetrock, from water damage or other contamination. Water damage is especially insidious if materials get wet, are installed wet, and are then covered up. If air-handling units run during construction, the contractor should replace any filters before occupancy. (ASHRAE Standard 52.2 deals with this subject.)

THE ENGINEER'S ROLE IN CONSTRUCTION QUALITY

In construction, the engineer's key role encompasses shop drawing review, equipment substitutions, handling of change order and value engineering requests, and site visits and inspections.

Shop Drawing Review

There should be a thorough review, not a hasty one, of shop drawing submittals. The specifications should require their timely submission so that there is time for proper review and so that the shop drawing review process does not delay the project. The purpose of the review is to ensure that the contractor is correctly interpreting the specs and drawings and is not missing any important details. Areas for emphasis include checking motor horsepower and efficiency ratings, checking air filter details, checking for proper clearances around equipment for servicing, and checking anything else relevant on the project concerning green design elements. (This is all in addition to the normal elements of review, of course).

Alternative Makes, Substitutions, and "Or Equivalent"

Specifications may be written with several named manufacturers (often three) of a given product, or it may name one and say "or equivalent." In both cases, the system designed is based usually on a single make. If others are named, it usually means they are acceptable if they meet the specified conditions and if they fit. The shop drawing reviewer must determine whether any alternative makes fill the bill, including meeting the green design aspects.

If "or equivalent" language is used to specify equipment, the job is harder. It is advisable to be certain that what the contractor proposes is truly equivalent if not superior to the specified components or systems. Contractors may have legitimate reasons for proposing alternative products, such as better delivery times or negative experiences with the products specified. Such "equivalent," or outright substitution, proposals from the contractor should be treated seriously but examined carefully to ascertain that they will not adversely impact the project goals. If they don't meet the requirements, the objections should first be discussed with the contractor; only if no satisfactory alternative can be agreed on should they then be rejected. (And the best time to spell out these ground rules is when specifying the equipment in the first place during design.)

Change Order Requests

Some change orders are legitimate, such as an owner changing the scope, unforeseen conditions, expansion or reduction of project scope, or a contractor encountering unforeseen conditions. However, any change order that only cheapens the project or lowers the project's green design standards without counteracting benefits, should be regarded with skepticism. Likewise any "value engineering" (VE) offers should be carefully studied for their impact on

---

CONSTRUCTION FACTORS TO CONSIDER IN A GREEN DESIGN

- Determine locations for construction vehicle parking, temporary piling of topsoil, and building material storage to minimize soil compaction and other site impacts.
- Control erosion to reduce negative impacts on water and air quality.
- Design to a site sediment and erosion control plan that conforms to best management practices in the EPA's *Storm Water Management for Construction Activities*, EPA Document No. EPA-832-R-92-005, or local erosion and sedimentation control standards and codes, whichever is more stringent.
- Conserve existing natural areas and restore damaged areas to provide habitat and promote biodiversity.
- Schedule construction carefully to minimize impacts.
- Avoid leaving disturbed soil exposed for extended periods.
- Fill trenches quickly to minimize damage to severed tree roots.
- Avoid building when the ground is saturated and easily damaged.
- Carefully estimate the amount of material needed to avoid excess.

- Design to accommodate standard lumber and drywall sizes.
- Assess construction site waste stream to determine which materials can be reduced, reused, and recycled.
- Conduct a waste audit, quantifying material diversion by weight.
- Recycle and/or salvage construction and demolition debris.
- Specify materials that minimize waste and reduce shipping impacts through bulk packaging, dry-mix shipping, reused bulk packaging, recycled-content packaging, or elimination of packaging.
- Develop and implement a waste management plan, quantifying material diversion by weight.
- Research markets in area for salvaged materials.
- Establish on-site construction material recycling areas and recycle and/or salvage construction, demolition, and land clearing waste.
- Contract with licensed haulers and processors of recyclables.
- Require subcontractors to be responsible for their waste (including lunch wastes); create incentives for minimizing waste.
- Educate employees and subcontractors.
- Monitor and evaluate waste/recycling program.

the project's green design goals. (VE is often offered under the assumption that first cost savings are paramount to the owner and project team.) The need for careful study remains true even in the case of genuine value engineering done by trained professionals who perform real trade-off analyses to arrive at the "best value" for a project. Before beginning such a VE exercise, the VE facilitator should be apprised of the green design objectives so that his/her suggestions and recommendations are consistent with the project goals and the priority those goals have with respect to first cost or life-cycle cost.

Site Visits/Observations

Site visits should be planned for key times and involve the engineer's best personnel. HVAC work should be viewed before it is covered up. Check that equipment nameplates are correct. For example, consider fan motors: If high-efficiency was specified, check in the field to be certain that is what is being installed. Look up the manufacturer's data on motor efficiency and see that it matches the specification. Check that absorptive construction materials (e.g., insulation) are being stored in accord with the IAQ Construction Management Plan and that no contamination has occurred. Check for air filters in any operating air-handling units.

Final punch list preparation, followup, and the final "sign-off" observation are particularly important. If the earlier site visits and observations were done thoroughly and at appropriate intervals and if the contractor has been "part of the team" and in accord with the green design goals, the final punch list should be minimal and the final observation should go smoothly.

Chapter 18
Commissioning

Commissioning is not only an accepted part of good design generally but an essential, and in some cases required, part of green building design and construction. *ASHRAE Guideline 1, The HVAC Commissioning Process* (latest approved version), should be followed as minimum practice. The U.S. Green Building Council's LEED manual also provides commissioning guidance. There is also a brief section on commissioning in chapter 4 of this guide.

An important part of green design is verification that the goals defined by the owner and integrated by the design and construction team are actually achieved as intended, from the first day of occupancy. This verification involves all stakeholders, from designers, to construction contractors, to operating staff, to occupants. Commissioning is not an exercise in blame; it is rather a collaborative effort to identify and reduce potential design, construction, and operational problems by resolving them early in the process at the least cost to everyone.

The 1993 National Conference on Building Commissioning provided the definition: "*Commissioning is a systematic process of assuring that a building performs in accordance with the design intent and the owner's operational needs.*" This process provides many benefits to the owner, the design

Authors contributing to this chapter are Jay Enck, David Grumman, Michael Haggans, and Wayne Robertson.

and construction teams, building occupants, and building operators. What owner—particularly a long-term owner—doesn't want reduced risk, fewer change orders (and the resulting cost avoidance), improved energy efficiency, lower operating costs, satisfied tenants, and a building that operates as intended from day one of occupancy? What contractor or designer doesn't dream of a project with few or no problems or callbacks and their resulting additional costs? Although numerous commissioning service models exist, it is this author's opinion that commissioning must be performed by a third-party provider or the owner's own commissioning team in order to receive maximum benefit from discovering problems when corrective action is still the responsibility of the consultants and contractors.

Commissioning can be broken down into five phases: pre-design, design, construction, acceptance, warranty, and continuous commissioning (or recommissioning). Distinct commissioning activities occur during each of the five phases. How and to what extent an owner incorporates commissioning generally depends on how long the owner holds the property, the owner's staff capabilities, and time constraints. Other factors include the funding methodology for design, construction, and operation; project schedule; and ownership experience. This chapter will cover the selection and role of the commissioning provider, a discussion of various commissioning models, the choice of building systems for commissioning, and the long-term benefits provided by verification of project goals.

One of the most beneficial attributes of sustainable development principles contained in the U.S. Green Building Council's (USGBC) Leadership in Environmental and Energy Design (LEED™) rating system is the inclusion of commissioning. If a building's green features do not perform, there is little benefit in having incorporated them in the design. Commissioning provides verification that the building systems operate as intended.

CA'S ROLE AND OWNER'S PROJECT REQUIREMENTS

It is the commissioning authority's (CA) role to lead the collaborative team effort required to balance competing interests in the owner's favor. To accomplish this task, a benchmark is needed. This benchmark is a document called the Owner's Project Requirements (OPR).

The OPR is a written document that details the functional requirements of a project and the expectations of how it will be used and operated. This includes project and design goals, measurable performance criteria, budgets, schedules, success criteria, and supporting information.

In the pre-design phase of a project, an owner may express orally (or in a formal written document) the basic requirements of the project. This is called *pre-design programming data*. This information typically may include justification for the project, program analysis/requirements, intended building use, basic construction materials and methods, proposed systems, project schedule, and general information (such as attaining LEED™ certification).

A key element of a CA's role, in the preferred pre-design phase model, is to develop the OPR. Much of the pre-design programming data could be part of the OPR. However, since there is such a large amount of information generated in the programming phase of a project, only the concepts most important to the owner—to be tracked through design and construction—should be included. Information extraneous to the actual design, such as justification for the facility, permitting details, history or policy issues, etc., should not become part of the OPR.

The OPR forms the basis from which the commissioning provider verifies that the developed project meets the needs and requirements of the owner. An effective commissioning process depends on a clear, concise, and comprehensive OPR document. This written document details the functional requirements of the facility and the expectations of how it will be used and operated. The OPR document includes project and design goals, measurable performance criteria, budgets, owner directives, schedules, and supporting information. It also includes information necessary for all disciplines to properly plan, design, construct, operate, and maintain systems and assemblies.

If no formal program exists, the OPR can be used to assist with identifying the criteria the design team is tasked with meeting. However, the main purpose of the OPR is to document the owner's needs and requirements and the assumptions made by the designers in meeting the OPR and to provide a summary of this information to the operators of the project after the design and construction team have long left the project. As such, the OPR provides the benchmark against which the design, construction, and project operating performance can be measured.

The OPR is a living document that is updated by the commissioning provider throughout the life of the project, recording the concepts, calculations, decisions, and product selections used to meet the OPR as well as to satisfy applicable regulatory requirements, standards, and guidelines.

Further discussion of the CA's role during specific phases is included in the next section.

COMMISSIONING PHASES

The role of the commissioning authority (CA) varies according to the phase of the project when commissioning starts. Because of the nature of construction, the further along construction is, the more difficult and expensive changes become. Historically, owners and contractors set up a contingency fund to meet the unpredictable cost of later changes to a project. If the design does not meet the owner's needs, that owner may be forced to accept the project as is because changes to meet what an owner may really need would be too costly at that point. If the CA is engaged as late as the construction phase, there is some—but very limited—opportunity to address potential design problems. The longer an owner waits to engage a CA, the less influence the CA has on resolving problems cost-effectively. Using a comprehensive commissioning process that starts during design is the best approach, and the role the CA plays during construction (as outlined in this chapter) is based on the assumption of utilizing a best-practices approach.

Pre-Design

The contrast between the quality and quantity of information provided by owners is often related to their development experience. Institutional owners who have developed many buildings and who have held those properties for extended periods of time have often developed over the years the information that design teams need in order to understand an owner's basic needs. As previously stated, the greatest value of involving a CA in the pre-design phase is to develop a comprehensive OPR that serves as the project benchmark, guiding all project team members.

Design Phase

During the design phase of a project, the CA develops specifications that incorporate commissioning into the project. The specifications identify the roles and responsibilities of the project team, the systems that will be commissioned, and the criteria for acceptance of the commissioned systems. In addition to development of specifications, the CA conducts design reviews.

There are two different schools of thought about what the CA should focus on during a design review. The first is to look only for commissionability of the systems, that is, to only identify design elements that prevent functional testing. An example would be ductwork design that would not allow accurate flow measurements because its configuration causes turbulence. Design reviews that only assess commissionability provide valuable information and address how a system would be tested to verify commissioned system performance.

The second type of design-phase commissioning, practiced by this author, is more comprehensive; it combines peer review to assess the design, a constructability review to minimize potential change orders, a quality control review that identifies possibly confusing or conflicting information in the contract documents, a value engineering review that does not compromise the serviceability or performance of a facility, and possible alternatives the design team should consider beyond commissionability. Third-party comprehensive design-phase commissioning provides the greatest benefits. (See further discussion in the "Commissioning Models" section later in this chapter.)

The CA's comprehensive design reviews assess the design against the OPR and evaluate whether the design meets the intent. This review provides a "second pair of eyes" for the owner and designers; it reduces project risk, helps identify and resolve confusing information, evaluates constructability, identifies value engineering opportunities, and evaluates the commissionability of systems. Design-phase commissioning promotes communication, identifies disconnects, questions design elements that appear incorrect, and shares experience to produce a better set of contract documents.

Engineering News Record, several long-term owners, and insurance companies who provide errors and omissions (E&O) coverage to the design community—all have voiced their concerns about the quality of construction documents and have charted how E&O premiums are affected as a result of judgments or settlements. Design-phase commissioning reduces the risks of change orders, accompanying construction delays, and E&O claims, and it helps clarify construction documents. Design-phase commissioning, if correctly implemented, is a seamless process that provides benefits to the entire project team.

The role of the CA during design is to assemble a review team experienced in the type of facility being reviewed. Generally, the CA has a team of reviewers with specific background and experience to review the disciplines selected for design phase commissioning. This process often requires the most senior individuals as part of the design-phase commissioning provider team. (See also "Selection of a Commissioning Provider" section later in this chapter.) The process this author has developed over the years is as follows:

- Written comments from the reviewers are provided to the design team and owner.
- Comments are reviewed, and the design team responds back to the commissioning review team with written comments.
- Meetings are scheduled between the review team and the designers to adjudicate comments as necessary and for the owner to provide direction as needed.
- Design concerns, comments, and actions taken are recorded in the design review document. These are verified by the commissioning review team.

Using a best-practices approach, the design-phase commissioning process should occur four different times during the project, related to phase completion: at 100% of schematic design, 100% of design development, 95% complete construction documents, and 100% of construction documents. (Combining the review of the first two phases could be done on smaller projects.) An advantage of four reviews, however, is that the design is evaluated based on the OPR goals *before* the design development phase starts.

Changes to optimize building performance, daylighting considerations, and stacking/massing synergies can best be addressed during schematic design review. Review during design development allows the team to identify potential problems and constructability perspectives early enough to resolve any issues before the construction documents phase starts.

The quantity of design concerns typically increases most in the 95% construction document phase because more detail is provided about each building system and components. The concerns identified at that point typically revolve around details, finishes, coordination conflicts, etc., and resolving these concerns provides clearer direction to the contractors, resulting in better cost and schedule predictions.

Depending on the schedule of the project, it is not uncommon that concerns identified at the 95% construction documents phase often go unaddressed by a design team. This is especially true in fast track projects when designers, responding to owner and contractor demands for documents, struggle to finish and deliver their work product. This is why the 100% review is so important.

The financial benefits of design-phase commissioning are immense. On a project for the State of Louisiana, design phase commissioning was responsible for $3.4 million in first-cost savings and $5 million in contingency savings on a $100 million project.

Construction Phase

The CA's role during the construction phase is to review the 100% complete construction documents and submittals; develop and/or accept/integrate contractor prefunctional checklists; identify and track issues to resolution; develop, direct, and verify functional performance tests; observe construction of commissioned systems; review the O&M manuals provided under the contract; and provide a recommissioning manual. The purpose of these activities is to verify that the owner's project requirements have been met, commissioned systems are serviceable, commissioned systems perform as intended from the beginning, and operational personnel receive the training and documentation necessary for maintaining building performance.

The CA's review of 100% construction documents is to verify that the concerns addressed during design have been resolved. Sometimes agreement between the designers and the commissioning design review team is not reached during the design phase. An example of this would be a disagreement over building pressurization control: the designer may feel that the design provides adequate control, and the CA may disagree. The CA must verify whether or not the building is correctly pressurized through

performance tests. If the designer is correct, the CA closes the issue after verification. If the CA is correct, then the concern is raised again after the system fails to meet the required performance test, and the project team works to resolve the issue while the designers and contractors are still engaged in the project.

The CA reviews submittals to look for potential performance problems. An example of this would be a contractor's ductwork shop drawings showing high pressure loss fittings that would increase energy consumption. The CA review activity does not, nor is it meant to, take the place of the designer's review, which should reveal whether the contractors are following the designer's intent. Several purposes can be combined by the CA in his or her review of the submittals, depending on the role the owner defines for the CA. For instance, if the CA is also assisting the team with LEED^{TM} certification, the CA can verify that the sustainable development goals identified in the OPR are being meet.

At the start of construction, a CA may choose to be part of pre-bid conferences between the general contractor or construction manager to provide an oral description of commissioning activities, to describe the general roles and responsibilities the contractor will be asked to fulfill in the commissioning process, and to answer questions. Clear communication with the contractors during pre-bid has been proved important in preventing high bids due to a "fear factor" from contractors unfamiliar with the commissioning process.

In the early stages of construction, the CA develops a commissioning plan that defines the commissioning process, the roles and responsibilities of the project team, lines of communication, systems being commissioned, and a schedule of commissioning activities. The CA conducts an initial commissioning scoping meeting where the commissioning plan is reviewed by the project team and, based on this information, a final commissioning plan is developed and implemented.

Throughout construction the CA observes the work to identify conditions that would impair preventive maintenance or repair, hinder operation of the system as intended, and compromise useful service life and to verify other sustainability goals such as indoor air quality management during construction. The CA develops activities to help perfect installation procedures at the start of the specific construction activity, coordinate activities to help ensure design intent is met through pre-functional checklists, start-up procedures, and testing and balancing. When contractors indicate that they have completed their pre-functional checklist and feel that their systems will perform as intended, the CA verifies this by witnessing functional testing.

Acceptance Phase

The functional testing phase of the commissioning process is often referred to as the acceptance phase. With designer and contractor input, the CA develops system tests (functional tests) to ensure that the systems perform as intended under a variety of conditions. The tests should verify performance at the component level through inter- and intra-system levels. It is this author's practice to test the systems in failure mode also. Problems identified are resolved while contractors and materials are still on site and the designers engaged.

Warranty Phase

The first year of a project is critical to finding and resolving issues that arise, and the CA plays an important role in helping ensure that a facility performs at its optimum. The warranty period is also the period when the contractors and manufacturers are responsible for the materials and systems installed and the only time the owner has to identify warranty repairs. As such, the CA has specific responsibilities during this critical period to assist the owner and operational staff in identifying problems and assisting them with resolution at the lowest cost to the owner.

During the first couple of months, the CA verifies that systems are performing as intended through monitoring of system operation. Many systems can not be fully tested until the building is occupied. There might be a small percentage of system components that pass functional testing but, under actual load, fail to perform as intended. These components must be identified in the warranty period and replaced or repaired as necessary. The CA's role in conjunction with the operational staff is to search out problems that only become evident under actual load. To accomplish this, the commissioning provider performs several specific tasks.

The commissioning provider identifies system points to trend, verifying efficient system operation; installs independent data loggers to measure parameters beyond the capabilities of the building automation system (BAS); and monitors utility consumption. Using the trend system data from the selected BAS input points, the CA analyzes the information, looking for operational sequences that consume natural resources unnecessarily and conditions that could compromise occupant satisfaction with the working environment. In addition, the CA also looks for conditions that could result in building failure, such as high humidity in interstitial spaces in the building's interior, hot spots in the electrical distribution system, or analysis of electrical system harmonics where power quality is essential to the owner. These functions can only be tested after occupancy.

Additionally, some systems, such as the heating and cooling equipment, can only be fully tested when the season allows testing under design load conditions. The CA works closely with the operational staff to identify and help resolve issues that become apparent in the warranty period and verifies that the operational staff fully understands and meets their warranty responsibilities. In addition, the CA should provide to the operational staff the specific functional test procedures developed for their use in maintaining building performance for the life of the facility. By having the CA work with the operational staff during the warranty period, the operators gain valuable insight into how the building should operate and what to look for to ensure continued performance. This helps to overcome a typical industry problem owners experience: the bypassing of system components and controls because of the operational staff's lack of understanding.

Continuous Commissioning Phase

The warranty period is only one year in the life of a building that may remain in service for 50 to 100 years or more. Most of the time, remodeling and change of building use are the main reasons for change in building system operation and component performance. For owners to get maximum performance from their facilities, they must know when systems fall outside of allowable performance tolerances. This is best done through a measurement and verification (M&V) process where operating parameters are tracked and compared to a benchmark. (Where the term "M&V" is used subsequently, it means that actual measurement and verification is to be done as part of the performance evaluation process being discussed.)

The *International Performance Measurement and Performance Protocol (IPMPP)*, published by the U.S. Department of Energy through its Office of Energy Efficiency and Renewable Energy, provide several methods to establish operational benchmarks for energy consumption. With a green design, there are other parameters that must also be measured, including water consumption, waste generation, recycling, pesticide use, etc. The operational tracking of these parameters reduces total cost of ownership, impact on the environment, and quality of life.

An owner can obtain guidance on integrating sustainable operation practices by adopting the USGBC LEED EB program at this stage of the building's life.

See also chapter 19, "Operation/Maintenance/ Performance Evaluation."

SELECTION OF A COMMISSIONING PROVIDER

Currently there is no standard for selection of a CA. There is movement in the industry to provide certification. As with finding a doctor, lawyer, contractor, or design professional, the key element is that the commissioning provider should have experience in the types of systems an owner wants commissioned. In other words, an owner must match the experience with the job. A good CA generally has a broad range of knowledge: hands-on experience in operations and maintenance, design, construction, and investigation of building/system failures. CAs must also be detail-oriented, good communicators, and able to provide a collaborative approach that engages the project team.

SELECTION OF SYSTEMS TO COMMISSION

Commissioning of all systems using the whole-building approach has proven to be beneficial. However, due to budget constraints, owners may want to look at commissioning systems that will yield the greatest benefit to them. Long-term owners have an advantage and can apply their experience of where they have encountered problems historically and elect to commission only those systems. Others who do not have that depth of experience may wish to talk with long-term owners or insurance providers to gain perspective.

Commissioning was originally developed on the West Coast where energy efficiency was the prime driver. The commissioning process has expanded beyond the original commissioning of HVAC systems to include building envelope, electrical, plumbing, security, etc., in addition to the HVAC systems. This expansion from HVAC is often referred to as *whole building commissioning*.

There are many factors that define which building systems should be commissioned, but there are no published standards yet to help guide owners through such selection. It often depends on the associated risk of *not* commissioning. E&O insurance providers publish graphs of claims against design professionals by discipline. Interestingly enough, 80% of the claims against architects are for moisture intrusion. A 1984 World Health Organization Committee report suggested that up to 30% of new and remodeled buildings worldwide may be the subject of excessive complaints related to indoor air quality (IAQ). The reasons for sick buildings include inadequate ventilation, chemical pollutants from both indoor and outdoor sources, and biological contaminates. The problem of mold and mildew is being called the asbestos of the 2000s.

Commissioning provides several benefits, two of which are risk reduction and lower total cost of ownership. Based on a specific climate such as Phoenix, Arizona, the risk of *not* commissioning the building envelope is much less than in Atlanta, Georgia. Based on functional requirements, not commissioning the security systems in a conventional office building may have minimum risk compared to a federal courthouse. So what should be commissioned?

An owner generally needs help in determining what should be commissioned, and the best time for determining this is during the development of the OPR. Generally, there are three main system categories that should be commissioned: building envelope, mechanical systems, and electrical systems. Subsystems that could also be included are irrigation and/or process water systems. Depending on the functional requirements of a facility, additional typical systems that are commissioned include security, voice/data, selected elements of fire and life safety, and daylighting controls.

The U.S. Green Building Council's LEED™ rating system recognizes the benefits of commissioning and its importance to green building design, construction, and operation. While the LEED™ reference guide does not specifically identify which building systems must be commissioned, it does point out that energy efficient use of natural resources, indoor environmental quality, and productivity are important goals of sustainable development. As such, the LEED™ reference guide does imply that building systems that affect energy consumption, water usage, and indoor environmental quality should be commissioned.

Each element of green design needs verification to ensure that the design, construction, and operation of the green, high-performance facility meet the expectations of the team and realize the financial return envisioned by the owner.

COMMISSIONING MODELS

Independent third party commissioning is the preferred commissioning approach because it significantly reduces the potential for conflict of interest. It also allows for integration of commissioning professionals specialized to meet a project's specific needs, such as building envelope, security, mechanical conveyances, labs, etc.

Commissioning as part of the project design professional's responsibility does not typically result in an unbiased presentation of issues. Design teams don't intentionally provide bad designs; they are working with schedules, budgets, and multiple players in the process. Even if the CP is a different individual from any design team member but still within an organization or sister company with the same upper leadership, it is common practice not to bring attention to negative issues. Commissioning conducted under this model has a high probability of minimizing design issues during design and passing responsibility on to the construction team during construction, resulting in "after-the-fact" solutions and corresponding costs and delays. The earlier an issue is identified and resolved, the least cost there is to the project.

Commissioning as part of the general contractor's responsibility has many of the same problems as the model using the design professional. Contractors, by the very nature of the construction business, are focused on schedule and budget. This focus is not always in favor of the owner. Most contractors are quality-minded and do their best to identify problems and assist with resolutions (though often to their detriment because they inadvertently take responsibility for the design in doing so). If a constructability issue arises that will adversely affect the schedule or budget, the contractor may choose to "fix" the issue and hope that it doesn't create a warranty callback. The main problem is that many of the issues are discovered too late in the process, again resulting in change orders, construction delays, and additional costs.

Mechanical contractors have the same problems as general contractors in providing commissioning services. They work with a schedule and budget and review their own work or that of a supervisor or co-worker. The mechanical contractor's knowledge and experience are usually limited to the mechanical field; thus, they lack the background to commission other systems.

To truly be an owner's advocate, the CA must owe allegiance to no one but the owner. A third party CA will verify that the goals defined by the owner and integrated by the design and construction team are actually achieved as intended, from the first day of occupancy. If the CA is separate from the design professional or contractor, he/she will provide unbiased reporting of issues to the owner and guide the team toward timely solutions without having finger pointing, delays, and liability.

A COMMISSIONING CHECKLIST

Finally, from a somewhat different perspective and as a guide, following is a checklist on commissioning used by one design firm (not that of the author of the foregoing portions of this chapter.)

One Design Firm's Commissioning Checklist

- [ ] Begin commissioning process during the design phase; carry out full commissioning process from lighting to energy systems to occupancy sensors, etc.
- [ ] Verify and ensure that fundamental building elements and systems are designed, installed, and calibrated to operate as intended.
- [ ] Engage a commissioning authority (CA) that is independent of both the design and construction team.
- [ ] Develop owner's project requirements OPR) and review designers' basis of design to verify requirements have been met.
- [ ] Incorporate commissioning requirements into project contract documents.
- [ ] Develop and utilize a commissioning plan.
- [ ] Verify installation, functional performance, training, and operation and maintenance documentation.
- [ ] Complete a commissioning report.
- [ ] Additional commissioning:
  - Conduct a focused review of the design prior to the construction documents phase.
  - Conduct a focused review of the construction documents near completion of the construction document development effort that is prior to the issuing of documents for construction.
  - Conduct reviews of contractor submittals that are relative to systems being commissioned.
  - Provide information required for recommissioning systems in a single document to the owner.
- Have a contract in place to review with operational staff current building operation and condition of outstanding issues relative to original or seasonal commissioning and to provide assistance resolving issues within the one-year warranty period.
- [ ] Encourage long-term energy management strategies.
  - Provide for the ongoing accountability and optimization of building energy and water consumption performance over time.
  - Design and specify equipment to be installed in base building systems to allow for comparison, management, and optimization of actual vs. estimated energy and water performance.
  - Employ measurement and verification (M&V) functions where applicable.
  - Tie contractor final payments to documented M&V system performance and include in the commissioning report.
  - Provide for an ongoing M&V system maintenance and operating plan in building operations and maintenance manuals.
- [ ] Provide for the ongoing accountability and optimization of building energy and water consumption performance over time.
- [ ] Operate the building ventilation system at maximum fresh air for at least several days (and ideally several weeks) after final finish materials have been installed before occupancy.
- [ ] Provide for the ongoing accountability of waste streams, including hazardous pollutants.
- [ ] Use environmentally safe cleaning materials.
- [ ] Train operation and maintenance workers.

Chapter 19
Operation/Maintenance/ Performance Evaluation

Though the HVAC&R designer will not be the building operator, he or she can greatly facilitate its proper operation and maintenance by doing a good job of turning over the building to those who will operate it. This is an essential part of ensuring that a building designed green actually operates green. A proper commissioning process (covered in the previous chapter) is the first step. Great value can also be provided by the designer during seasonal commissioning or annual recommissioning, if provided for. At this time the designer can interact with operations and maintenance personnel and assist with operational issues that may have arisen since the original commissioning.

Vitally important as well is a competent and well-trained operating/maintenance staff, which of course is largely beyond the control of the designer. Building personnel can do much good—or inadvertent great harm—depending on whether they understand the impact of their actions on building operating efficiency. If the owner will allow (and pay for) the designer to play a significant role in *staff training*, it will provide even greater assurance that a

Authors contributing to this chapter are David Grumman, Michael Haggans, Blair McCarry, and Wayne Robertson.

building designed green will realize its full green potential over the long term.

The next step is following up on how the building actually performed. While this is beyond the scope of normal professional fees and is usually not done, the building industry needs this kind of follow-up data to verify that new design techniques are working and that change is occurring in how buildings are designed, in short, that green design is working. It is certainly worth an effort by the designer to convince the owner that this could be a worthwhile extra service.

Again as a guide, following is a continuation of the same design firm's checklist (parts of which appeared in earlier chapters) covering operations, maintenance, and performance evaluation.

DISPOSAL/RECYCLING

This is an area on which the design engineer normally has little impact. During design, however, he or she could anticipate eventual maintenance, demolition, and removal requirements of the materials, equipment, and systems for which he or she responsible.

The U.S. Green Building Council's LEED *Green Building Rating System* provides a good general guide on this topic.

ONE DESIGN FIRM'S OPERATIONS, MAINTENANCE, AND PERFORMANCE EVALUATION CHECKLIST

❑ Provide for the ongoing accountability and optimization of building energy and water consumption performance over time.

❑ Design and specify equipment to be installed in base building systems to allow for comparison, management, and optimization of actual vs. estimated energy and water performance.

❑ Provide for the ongoing accountability and optimization of building energy and water consumption performance over time.

❑ Comply with the installed equipment requirements for continuous metering as stated in *Option B: Methods by Technology* of the U.S. Department of Energy's *International Performance Measurement and Verification Protocol* (IPMVP) for the following:

  - Lighting systems and controls.
  - Constant and variable motor loads.
  - Variable frequency drive (VFD) operation.
  - Chiller efficiency at variable loads (kW/ton).
  - Cooling load.
  - Air and water economizer and heat recovery cycles.
  - Air distribution static pressures and ventilation air volumes.
  - Boiler efficiencies.
  - Building specific process energy efficiency systems and equipment.
  - Indoor water risers and outdoor irrigation systems.

❑ Allocate an appropriate percentage of building funds for ongoing monitoring of environmental performance, product purchasing, maintenance, and improvements.

❑ Provide for the ongoing accountability of waste streams, including hazardous pollutants.

❑ Use environmentally safe cleaning materials.

❑ Educate operation and maintenance workers.

❑ Facilitate the reduction of waste generated by building occupants.

  - Provide an easily accessible dedicated area, serving the project, for the collection and storage of materials for recycling including paper, glass, plastics, metals, and hazardous substances.

❑ After six months, evaluate existing ecosystems to determine if they have remained undisturbed.

❑ Assess building energy use to ensure it is at predicted levels.

❑ Determine if indoor air quality (IAQ) levels are at predicted levels (particularly CO_2 and airborne particulates).

❑ Measure water consumption and evaluate against target usage in original plan.

❑ Monitor water levels and determine if recycling and reuse of materials meet expectations.

❑ Monitor and evaluate additional sustainability goals for project.

  - Building specific process, energy-efficient systems and equipment.
  - Indoor water risers and outdoor irrigation systems.

Bibliography

These listings do not necessarily imply endorsement or agreement by ASHRAE or the authors with the information contained in the documents.

BOOKS AND SOFTWARE PROGRAMS

ACGIH. 1999. *Bioaerosols: Assessment and Control*, J. Nacher, ed. American Conference of Governmental Industrial Hygienists. *http://www.acgih.org.*

AIA. 1996. *Environmental Resource Guide.* J. Demkin, ed. New York: John Wiley & Sons.

Advanced Lighting Guidelines, 2001 edition. *http://www.newbuildings.org*

ASPE. 1998. *Domestic Water Heating Design Manual.* Chicago: American Society of Plumbing Engineers.

American Gas Association Cooling Center. January1994. *Manual for Direct-Fired Absorption.*

Arthus-Bertrand, Y. 2001. *Earth from Above: 365 Days.* Harry N. Abrams.

ASHRAE. 2003. *2003 ASHRAE Handbook—HVAC Applications.* Atlanta: American Society of Heating, Refrigerating and Air-Conditioning Engineers, Inc.

ASHRAE. 2001. *2001 ASHRAE Handbook—Fundamentals.* Atlanta: American Society of Heating, Refrigerating and Air-Conditioning Engineers, Inc.

ASHRAE. 2001. *ANSI/ASHRAE Standard 62-2001, Ventilation for Acceptable Indoor Air Quality* plus interpretations. Atlanta: American Society of Heating, Refrigerating and Air-Conditioning Engineers, Inc.

ASHRAE. 2001. *ANSI/ASHRAE/IESNA Standard 90.1-2001, Energy Standard for Buildings Except Low-Rise Residential Buildings*, Section 11. Atlanta: American Society of Heating, Refrigerating and Air-Conditioning Engineers, Inc.

ASHRAE. 2001. ANSI/*ASHRAE/IESNA Standard 90.1-2001, Energy Standard for Buildings Except Low-Rise Residential Buildings*, Informative Appendix G. Atlanta: American Society of Heating, Refrigerating and Air-Conditioning Engineers, Inc.

ASHRAE. 1996. *ASHRAE Guideline 1-1996, The HVAC Commissioning Process.* Atlanta: American Society of Heating, Refrigerating and Air-Conditioning Engineers, Inc.

ASHRAE. 1995. *Commercial/Institutional Ground-Source Heat Pump Engineering Manual.* Atlanta: American Society of Heating, Refrigerating and Air-Conditioning Engineers, Inc.

ASHRAE. 1992. *ASHRAE Standard 55-1992, Thermal Environmental Conditions for Human Occupancy.* Atlanta: American Society of Heating, Refrigerating and Air-Conditioning Engineers, Inc.

ASHRAE Learning Institute. Professional Development Seminar (PDS) on Optimizing the Design and Control of Chilled Water Plants.

ASTM. 1998. *ASTM D 6245-1998: Standard Guide for Using Indoor Carbon Dioxide Concentrations to Evaluate Indoor Air Quality and Ventilation.* American Society for Testing and Materials.

Brand, S. 1995. *How Buildings Learn: What Happens After They're Built.* New York: Viking Penguin USA.

Caneta Research Inc. CAN L5N 6J7, GS-2000TM (a computer program for designing and sizing ground heat exchangers). Mississauga, Ontario, Canada: Caneta.

CEC. 2002. *Part II: Measure Analysis and Life-Cycle Cost 2005, California Building Energy Standards*, P400-02-012. Sacramento: California Energy Commission.

CEC. 2001. *Nonresidential Alternative Calculations Methods Manual.* Sacramento: California Energy Commission.

Del Porto, D., and C. Steinfeld. 1999. *The Composting Toilet System Book.* The Center for Ecological Pollution Prevention.

Domestic Water Heating Design Manual. 1998. Chicago: American Society of Plumbing Engineers.

Dorgan, C., and J.S. Elleson. 1993. *Design Guide for Cool Thermal Storage.* Atlanta: American Society of Heating, Refrigerating and Air-Conditioning Engineers, Inc.

Elleson, J.S. 1996. *Successful Cool Storage Projects: from Planning to Operation.* Atlanta: American Society of Heating, Refrigerating and Air-Conditioning Engineers, Inc.

Evans, Benjamin. 1997. *Time-Saver Standards for Architectural Design Data.* McGraw-Hill, Inc.

Gerston, Jan. *Rainwater Harvesting: A New Water Source. http://twri.tamu.edu*

Gottfried, D. (Continuous updating). *Sustainable Building Technical Manual, Green Building Design, Construction, and Operations.* U.S. Green Building Council. *http://www.usgbc.org*

Hawkin, P., A. Lovins, and L.H. Lovins. 1999. *Natural Capitalism.* Little Brown.

Illuminating Engineering Society of North America, Energy Management Committee, proposed revisions to ASHRAE/IESNA Standard 90.1-2001, January 2002.

Illuminating Engineering Society of North America, RP-33-99, Lighting for Exterior Environments; RP-20-98, Lighting for Parking Facilities. New York: IESNA. *http://www.iesna.org*

Illuminating Engineering Society of North America (IESNA). *Lighting Handbook. http://www.iesna.org*

International Energy Conservation Code, 2000 edition. *http://www.iecc.org*

Kavanaugh, Stephen P., and Kevin Rafferty. 1997. *Ground-Source Heat Pumps: Design of Geothermal Systems for Commercial and Institutional Buildings.* Atlanta: Amercian Society of Heating, Refrigerating and Air-Conditioning Engineers, Inc.

Kinsley, M. 1997. *Economic Renwal Guide.* Rocky Mountain Institute.

Kreith, Frank, and Jan Kreider. 1989. *Principles of Solar Engineering*, 2d ed. Hemisphere Pub.

LEED Reference Package. *http://www.usgbc.org*

Ludwig, Art. 1997. *Builder's Greywater Guide and Create an Oasis with Greywater.* Oasis Design.

Massachusetts State Building code, Construction Details.

Mendler, S.F., and Odell, W. 2000. *HOK Guidebook to Sustainable Design.* New York: John Wiley & Sons, Inc. *http://www.wiley.com*

National Sanitation Foundation and the American National Standards Institute (NSF/ANSI 5-2000e). 2000. *Water Heaters, Hot Water Supply Boilers, and Heat Recovery Equipment.* Ann Arbor, MI: NSF.

Nattrass, B., and M. Altomare. [DoP]. *The Natural Step for Business; Wealth, Ecology and the Evolutionary Corporation.* Gabriola Island, British Columbia: New Society Publishers. *http://www.newsociety.com*

Natural Capitalism, see Hawkin et al.

Natural Resources Canada, Energy Diversification Research Laboratory, Varennes PQ CAN J3X 1S6, Telephone 1-450-652-4621. "RETScreen" (Renewable Energy Analysis Software).

Natural Resources Canada, Office of Coordination and Technical Information, Ottawa, Ontario, Canada K1A 0E4. *Photovoltaic Systems Design Manual.*

Outdoor Lighting Research, California Outdoor Lighting Standards, June 6, 2002. *http://www.cec.org*

Pacific Gas and Electric. *CASE Initiative: High-Albedo Roofs. http://www.newbuidings.org/architecture.htm*

Photovoltaic Systems Design Manual. Natural Resources Canada, Office of Coordination and Technical Information, Ottawa ON CAN K1A 0E4.

Portland, Oregon, Office of Sustainable Development. *http://www.coolroofs.org* and *http://www.greenroofs.com*

Public Technology Inc., U.S. Department of Energy

and U.S. Green Building Council. 1996. *Sustainable Building Technical Manual – Green Building Design, Construction and Operations. Public Technology, Inc.* http://www.epa.gov/OW/you/chap3.htm and http://www.usgbc.org

RETSCREEN (Renewable Energy Analysis Software), telephone 1 450 652 4621 *http://www.retscreen.gc.ca*

SMACNA. *Indoor Air Quality Guideline for Occupied Buildings Under Construction.* Chantilly, Va.: Sheet Metal and Air Conditioning National Association, Inc.

Trane. 1999. *Absorption Chiller System Design.* Trane Applications Engineering Manual, SYS-AM-13. LaCrosse, Wisc.: Trane Company.

Trane. 1994. *Water-Source Heat Pump System Design.* Trane Applications Engineering Manual, SYS-AM-7. Lacrosse, Wisc.: Trane Company.

U.S. Department of Energy, Office of Energy Efficiency and Renewable Energy. *The International Performance Measurement and Performance Protocol (IPMPP).*

U.S. Environmental Protection Agency. *Universal Waste Rule, 40 CFR Part 260.*

U.S. Environmental Protection Agency. *Toxicity Characteristic Leaching Procedure (TCLP) Test, 40 CFR Part 260.*

U.S. Green Building Council. 2001. *LEED Reference Guide*, Version 2.0.

Waterfall, P.H. *Harvesting Rainwater for Landscape Use.* http://ag.arizona.edu/pubs/water/az1052/

Watston, R.D., and K.S. Chapman. 2002. *Radiant Heating and Cooling Handbook.* McGraw-Hill.

WATSUN-PV (simulation software). University of Waterloo, Waterloo, Ontario, Canada.

PERIODICALS AND REPORTS

Andersson, L.O., K.G. Bernander, E. Isfält, and A.H. Rosenfeld. 1979. Storage of heat and coolth in hollow-core concrete slabs. Swedish experience and application to large, American style buildings. Second International Conference on Energy Use and Management, Lawrence Berkeley National Laboratory, LBL-8913.

Balaras, C.A. 1995. The role of thermal mass on the cooling load of buildings. An overview of computational methods. *Energy and Buildings* 24(1): 1-10.

Bahnfleth, W.P., and W.S. Joyce. 1994. Energy use in a district cooling system with stratified chilled water storage. *ASHRAE Transactions* 100(1): 1767-1778.

Bauman, F., and T. Webster. 2001. Outlook for underfloor air distribution. *ASHRAE Journal* 43(6).

Braun, J.E. 1990. Reducing energy costs and peak electrical demand through optimal control of building thermal storage. *ASHRAE Transactions* 96(2): 876-888.

California Building Energy Standards. P400-02-012, May 16, 2002.

California Energy Commission, Title 24 2005 Reports and Proceedings, *http://www.energy.ca.gov*

California Energy Commission. 1996. Source Energy and Environmental Impacts of Thermal Energy Storage. Tabors, Caramanis & Assoc.

Chapman, K.S. ASHRAE RP-907, Final Report, Development of Design Factors for the Combination of Radiant and Convective In-Space Heating and Cooling Systems. Atlanta: American Society of Heating, Refrigerating and Air-Conditioning Engineers, Inc.

Chapman, K.S. 2002. Development of radiation transfer equation that encompasses shading and obstacles. *ASHRAE Transactions* 108(2): 997-1004.

Chapman, K.S., J. Rutler, and R.D. Watson. 2000. Impact of heating systems and wall surface temperatures on room operative temperature fields. *ASHRAE Transactions* 106(1): 506-514.

Chapman, K.S., J.M. DeGreef, and R.D. Watson. 1997. Thermal comfort analysis using BCAP for retrofitting a radiantly heated residence. *ASHRAE Transactions* 103(1): 959-965.

Chapman, K.S., J.E. Howell, and R.D. Watson. 2001. Radiant panel surface temperature over a range of ambient temperatures. *ASHRAE Transactions* 107(1): 383-389.

Coad, W.J. 1999. Conditioning ventilation air for improved performance and air quality. *Heating/Piping/Air Conditioning,* September.

DeGreef, J.M., and K.S. Chapman. 1998. Simplified thermal comfort evaluation of MRT gradients and power consumption predicted with the BCAP methodology. *ASHRAE Transactions* 104(1).

Duffy, G. 1992. Thermal storage shifts to saving energy. *Engineering Systems.*

Del Porto, D., and C.Steinfeld. 1999. *The Composting Toilet System Book.* Center for Ecological Pollution Prevention.

Fagan, D. 2001. A comparison of storage-type and instantaneous heaters for commercial use. *Heating/Piping/Air Conditioning*, April.

Fiorino, D.P. 1994. Energy conservation with stratified chilled water storage. *ASHRAE Transac-*

tions 100(1): 1754-1766.

Fiorino, D.P. 2000. Six conservation and efficiency measures reducing steam costs. *ASHRAE Journal* 42(2).

Galuska, E. 1994. Thermal storage system reduces costs of manufacturing facility. *ASHRAE Journal*, March.

Gansler, R.A., D.T. Teindil, and T.B. Jekel. 2001. Simulation of source energy utilization and emissions for HVAC systems. *ASHRAE Transactions* 107(1): 39-51.

Gerston, J. Rainwater Harvesting: A New Water Source. *http://twri.tamu.edu*

Goss, J.O., L. Hyman, and J. Corgett. 1996. Integrated heating, cooling and thermal energy storage with heat pump provides economic and environmental solutions at California State University, Fullerton. *EPRI International Conference on Sustainable Thermal Energy Storage*, pp.163-167.

Green Builder Magazine. http://www.greenbuilder.com/sourcebook/GasWaterHeat.html

Grondzik, W.T. 2001. Indoor environmental quality issues in sustainable design. *Seminar presntation at 2001 ASHRAE Annual Meeting, Cincinnati, Ohio. http://www.polaris.net/~gzik/ieq/ieq.htm*

Hayter, S., P. Torcellini, R. Judkoff. 1999. Optimizing building and HVAC systems. *ASHRAE Journal* 41(12): 46-49.

Jones, B., and K.S. Chapman. ASHRAE RP-657, Final Report, Simplified Method to Factor Mean Radiant Temperature (MRT) into Building and HVAC System Design. Atlanta: American Society of Heating, Refrigerating and Air-Conditioning Engineers, Inc.

Keeney, K.R., and J.E. Braun. 1997. Application of building precooling to reduce peak cooling requirements. *ASHRAE Transactions* 103(1):463-469.

Kintner-Meyer, M., and A.F. Emery. 1995. Optimal control of an HVAC system using cold storage and building thermal capacitance. *Energy and Buildings* 23:19-31.

Kosik, W.J. 2001. Design strategies for hybrid ventilation. *ASHRAE Journal* 43(10): 18-19, 22-24.

Lawson. 1988. Computer facility keeps cool with ice storage. *HPAC*, August.

Mathaudhu, S.S. 1999. Energy conservation showcase. *ASHRAE Journal* 41(4): 44-46.

McDonough, W. 1992. The Hannover Principles: Design for Sustainability. Presentation, Earth Summit, Brazil.

McKurdy, G., S.J. Harrison, and R. Cooke. Prelimi-

nary evaluation of cylindrical skylights. 23rd Annual Conference of the Solar Energy Society of Canada Inc., Vancouver, British Columbia. *http://www.solarenergysociety.ca*

Morris, W. 2003. The ABCs of DOAS. *ASHRAE Journal* 45(5).

Mumma, S.A. 2001. Designing dedicated outdoor air systems. *ASHRAE Journal* 43(5).

National Air Duct Cleaners Association (NADCA). *General Specifications for the Cleaning of Commercial Heating, Ventilating and Air Conditioning Systems. http://www.nadca.com.*

Office of Industrial Technologies, Energy Efficiency, and Renewable Energy, U.S. Department of Energy. *Energy Tip Sheet #1*, May 2002.

O'Neal, E.J. 1996. Thermal storage system achieves operating and first-cost savings. *ASHRAE Journal*, April.

Optimizing the Design and Control of Chilled Water Plants. Professional Development Seminar (PDS), ASHRAE Learning Institute.

Palmer, J.M., and K.S. Chapman. 2000. Direct calculation of mean radiant temperature using radiant intensities. *ASHRAE Transactions* 106(1): 477-486.

Public Technology Inc., U.S. Department of Energy and U.S. Green Building Council. 1996. *Sustainable Building Technical Manual—Green Building Design, Construction and Operations.* Public Technology, Inc. U.S. Department of Energy and U.S. Green Building Council.

Reindl, D.T., D.E. Knebel, and R.A. Gansler. 1995. Characterizing the marginal basis source energy and emissions associated with comfort cooling systems. *ASHRAE Transactions* 101(1): 1353-1363.

Ruud, M.D., J.W. Mitchell, and S.A. Klein. 1990. Use of building thermal mass to offset cooling loads. *ASHRAE Transactions* 96(2):820-829.

Scheatzle, David. ASHRAE RP-1140 Final Report, Establishing a Base-Line Data Set for the Evaluation of Hybrid HVAC Systems. Atlanta: American Society of Heating, Refrigerating and Air-Conditioning Engineers, Inc.

Schell, M., and D. Int-Hout. February 2001. Demand control ventilation using CO_2. *ASHRAE Journal* 43(2).

Tabors, Caramanis and Associates. 1996. Source energy and environmental impacts of thermal energy storage. California Energy Commission, February.

Taylor, S., P. Dupont, M. Hydeman, B. Jones, and T. Hartman. 1999. *The CoolTools Chilled Water Plant Design and Performance Specification*

Guide. San Francisco, Calif.: PG&E Pacific Energy Center.

Taylor, S. 2002. Primary-only vs. primary-secondary variable flow chilled water systems. *ASHRAE Journal* 44(2): 25-29.

Taylor, S., and Stein, J. 2002. Balancing variable flow hydronic systems. *ASHRAE Journal* 44(10): 17-24.

Trane Company. 2002. *A Guide to Understanding ASHRAE Standard 62-2001.* Publication IAQ-TS-1, July.

Trane Company. 2000. Energy conscious design ideas—Air-to-sir rnergy tecovery. *Engineers Newsletter*, Vol. 29, No. 5.

Torcellini, P., S. Hayter, and R. Judkoff. 2002. *Zion National Park Visitor Center; Significant Energy Savings Achieved Through a Whole Building Design Process.* National Renewable Energy Laboratory. *http://www.nrel.gov*

U.S. Department of Energy, Office of Industrial Technologies. 2002. Energy efficiency and renewable energy. *Energy Tip Sheet #1*, May.

U.S. Environmental Protection Agency. *Storm Water Management for Construction Activities.* EPA document No. EPA-8320R-92-005

Waterfall, P.H. Harvesting rainwater for landscape use. *http://ag.arizona.edu/pubs/water/az1052/*

Watson, R.D., K.S. Chapman, and L. Wiggington. 2001. Impact of dual utility selection on 305 m^2 (1000 ft^2) residences. *ASHRAE Transactions* 107(1): 365-370.

Watson, R.D., K.S. Chapman, and J.M. DeGreef. 1998. Case study: Seven-system analysis of thermal comfort and energy use for a fast-acting radiant heating system. *ASHRAE Transactions* 104(1).

WEB SITES

Advanced Buildings
  http://www.advancedbuildings.org
Advanced Lighting Guidelines
  http://www.newbuildings.org
Air-Conditioning and Refrigeration Institute
  http://www.ari.org
Alliance to Save Energy
  http://www.ase.org
American Council for an Energy Efficient Economy
  http://www.aceee.org
American Gas Association, Washington DC 20001
  http://www.aga.org
American Gas Cooling Center
  http://www.gascooling.org
American Institute of Architects
  http://www.aia.org

Athena™ Sustainable Materials Institute
  http://www.athenasmi.ca
Better Bricks
  http://www.betterbricks.com
BREEAM® Canada
  http://www.breeamcanada.ca
California Energy Commission, Part II: Measure Analysis and Life-Cycle Cost 2005, California Buliding Energy Efficiency Standards, Part IV
  http://www.energy.ca.gov/2005_standards/documents/2002-08-27_workshop/2002-08-14_4th_GROUP_ELEY.pdf
California Energy Commission, Title 24 2005 Reports and Proceedings
  http://www.energy.ca.gov
California Collaborative for High Performance Schools
  http://www.chps.net
Canadian Earth Energy Association, Ottawa, Ontario, Canada K1P 6E2
  http://www.earthenergy.org
Canadian Renewable Energy Network
  http://www.canren.gc.ca/
Carpenter, S. and Kokko, J. Advanced Buildings Web Site (Canada)
  http://www.advancedbuildings.org
Center of Excellence for Sustainable Development (CESD)
  www.sustainable.doe.gov
Centex (link to Centex, the most energy-efficient building in the U.S. in 1999)
  http://www.energystar.gov/index.cfm?fuseaction=labeled_buildings.showProfile&profile_id=1306
Centre for Photovoltaic Engineering UNSW
  http://www.pv.unsw.edu.au/solpages.html
Combo Heating Systems: A Design Guide, Union Gas, Chatham ON, CAN N7M 5M1
  http://www.uniongas.com
Commercial Building Incentives Program (CBIP)
  http://oee.nrcan.gc.ca/newbuildings/cbip.cfm
Commercial Energy Systems, Closed Water Loop Water-Source Heat Pump Systems
  http://cipco.apogee.net/ces/hucw.asp
CoolTools Chilled Water Plant Design, Pacific Gas and Electric (PG&E)
  http://www.hvacexchange.com/cooltools/
DOE Building Technologies Program: Building Commissioning
  http://www.eere.energy.gov/buildings/operate/buildingcommissioning.cfm
Eley Associates
  http://www.eley.com
Energy Efficiency and Renewable Energy Network

(EREN)
http://www.eren.doe.gov

Energy Efficiency and Renewable Energy Network (EREN), Commercial Buildings Energy Consumption Tool
http://eere.energy.gov/buildings/energydata.cfm

Energy Efficiency and Renewable Energy Network (EREN), Energy Outlet, The
http://www.energyoutlet.com

Energy Outlet, The
http://www.energyoutlet.com

Energy Trust of Oregon
http://www.energytrust.org

Environmental Protection Agency, see *USEPA*

eQUEST, Building Energy Analysis Tool
http://www.energydesignresources.com

EZ-Conserve
http://www.ezconserve.com

Geothermal Heat Pump Consortium
http://www.geoexchange.org

Green Building Advisor, The
http://www.greenbuildingadvisor.com

Green Building Challenge
www.greenbuilding.ca

Green Builder Source Books
http://bookstore.greenbuilder.com/index.books

GreenSpec
http://www.buildinggreen.com/menus/index.cfm

Hannover Principles, The
http://www.mindfully.org/Sustainability/Hannover-Principles.htm

Heerwagen, Judith. 2001. PNNL Scientist Studies Worker Productivity in Energy-Efficient Buildings.
http://www.eere.energy.gov/femp/newsevents/femp_focus/sept01_pnnlscientist_studies.html

Heshong-Mahone Group, Sky lighting
http://www.h-m-g.com/skylighting/skycal-creg.htm

Heshong-Mahone Group Study for PG&E, Daylighting impacts on retail sales
http://www.h-m-g.com

Heshong-Mahone Group study for PG&E, Daylighting impacts on school performance
http://www.h-m-g.com.

Hewlett Foundation, Link to LEED Gold Building
http://www.usgbc.org/Docs/Certified_Projects/Cert_Reg67.pdf

High Performance Buildings Research Initiative
http://www.highperformancebuildings.gov

Illuminating Engineering Society of North America
http://www.iesna.org/

IEA Heat Pump Program, Heat Pumps in Residential and Commercial Buildings

http://www.heatpumpcentre.org/tutorial/building.htm

IEA Heat Pump Centre (HPC), the International Energy Agency's Information Centre for Heat Pumping Technologies, Applications and Markets.
http://www.heatpumpcentre.org/tutorial/building.htm

Irrigation Association, The
http://www.irrigation.org

Lawrence Berkeley National Laboratories
http://www.arch.ced.berkeley.edu/vitalsigns

Lawrence Berkeley National Laboratory, Radiance Home Web Site.
http://radsite.lbl.gov/radiance/HOME.html

LEED^R (*see U.S. Green Building Council*)

McQuay's Chilled Water System Manual
http://www.mcquay.com

Minnesota Sustainable Design Guide
http://www.sustainabledesignguide.umn.edu

National Oceanic and Atmospheric Administration (NOAA))
http://www.noaa.gov

National Renewable Energy Laboratory
http://www.nrel.gov

Natural Resources Canada, Energy Diversification Research Laboratory

NAVFAC, Design of Sustainable Facilities and Infrastructure
http://www.navfac.navy.mil/safety/

New Buildings Institute
http://www.newbuildings.org

New Buildings Institute Version 1.0 release, Energy Benchmark for High Performance Buildings
http://www.newbuildings.org/ebenchmark/index.htm

New York City High Performance Guidelines
http://home.nyc.gov/html/ddc/html/ddcgreen/

New York's Batter Park City Authority
http://www.batteryparkcity.org/guidelines.htm

Oikos: Green Building Source
http://www.oikos.com

Pacific Gas and Electric (PG&E), CoolTools Chilled Water Plant Design
http://www.hvacexchange.com/cooltools/ctsoft_frm.htm

Pacific Gas and Electric (PG&E), *CoolTools*
http://www.hvacexchange.com/cooltools/

Photovoltaic Resource Site
http://www.pvpower.com

Public Technology, Inc., U.S. Green Building Council, U.S. Department of Energy. Sustainable Building Technical Manual – Green Building Design, Construction and Operations. Public

Technology, Inc. 1996 Rating System
http://www.epa.gov/OW/you/chap3.htm
and
http://www.usgbc.org

RealWinWin, Inc.
http://www.realwinwin.com

Renewable Energy Deployment Initiative (REDI) (a Canadian federal program that supports the deployment of renewable technologies; some technologies qualify for incentives)
http://www.nrcan.gc.ca/redi

Rising Sun Enterprises
http://www.rselight.com

Rocky Mountain Institute
http://www.rmi.org

Savings by Design
http://www.savingsbydesign.com

Solstice/Center for Renewable Energy and Sustainable (CREST)
http://solstice.crest.org

Sustainable Building Guidelines
http://www.ciwmb.ca.gov/GreenBuilding/Design/Guidelines.htm

Sustainable Building Sourcebook, Green Building Program
http://www.greenbuilder.com/sourcebook

Sustainable Buildings Industry Council
http://www.sbicouncil.org

Sustainable Communities Network (SCN)
http://www.sustainable.org

Sustainable Sources
http://www.greenbuilder.com/sourcebook/Photovoltaic.html

Tips for Daylighting with Windows
http://windows.lbl.gov/pub/designguide/dlg.pdf

Trane Company, *Multiple-Chiller-System Design and Control Manual*
http://www.trane.com

Tristate Apogee

http://tristate.apogee.net/cool/cchc.asp

Tri-State Generation and Transmission Association Inc., Closed Water-Loop Heat Pump
http://tristate.apogee.net/cool/cchc.asp

Union Gas, Chatham, Ontario, Canda N7M5M1, Combo Heating Systems: A Design Guide
http://www.uniongas.com

U.S. Department of Energy
http://www.eere.energy.gov/pv/

U.S. Department of Energy
http://www.eere.energy.gov/consumerinfo/rebriefs/ad6.html

U.S. Department of Energy, Consumer Information Program
http://www.eere.energy.gov/

U.S. Department of Energy, Federal Energy Management Program
http://www.eere.energy.gov/femp/

U.S. Environmental Protection Agency, Energy Star Program
http://www.energystar.gov

U.S. Environmental Protection Agency, Energy Star Web site
http://www.energystar.gov/powermanagement/index.asp

U.S. Environmental Protection Agency, Target Finder and PIER Construction Specifications
http://www.newbuildings.org

U.S. Environmental Protection Agency, Ground Water and Drinking Water, Regulations and Guidance (NPDWR)
http://www.epa.gov/safewater/regs.html

U.S. Green Building Council, LEED[R] Green Building Rating System
http://www.usgbc.org

Water Efficiency Clearinghouse, The
http://www.waterwiser.org

Whole Building Design Guide, The
http://www.wbdg.org

Terms, Definitions, and Acronyms

<	=	is less than
>	=	is greater than
Δ	=	change or change in
AC	=	alternating current
A/C	=	air-conditioning
AFF	=	above finished floor
ANSI	=	American National Standards Institute
ASHRAE	=	American Society of Heating, Refrigerating and Air-Conditioning Engineers
BAS	=	building automation system
BF	=	ballast factor
BIE	=	buildings' impact on the environment
BREEAM®	=	Building Research Establishment Environmental Assessment Method
brownfield	=	real estate property that is, or potentially is, contaminated
Btu	=	British thermal unit
C	=	centigrade (temperature scale)
C-2000	=	Canadian Integrated Design Process program (see p. 34)
CA	=	commissioning authority
CAN	=	Canada
CAV	=	constant air volume
CBIP	=	Commercial Buildings Incentive Program
CDT	=	cold deck temperature
CETC	=	Canmet Energy Technology Centre, a division of Natural Resources Canada, Canadian Energy Ministry
CEO	=	chief executive officer
CFD	=	computational fluid dynamics
cfm	=	cubic feet per minute
charette	=	intense effort to solve a design problem within a limited time
CLF	=	cooling load factor
CLTD	=	cooling load temperature difference
CO	=	carbon monoxide
CO_2	=	carbon dioxide
condenser	=	device to dissipate (get rid of) excess energy in A/C systems
COP	=	coefficient of performance
CPU	=	central processing unit
Cx	=	commissioning
daylighting	=	lighting (of a building) using daylight directly or indirectly from the sun
DC	=	direct current
DDC	=	direct digital controls
delta-T or t	=	change or change in
DOAS	=	dedicated outside air system
DoE or DOE	=	Department of Energy
DX	=	direct expansion
E	=	ventilation effectiveness

EDC = environmental design consultant

EDG = engine-driven generator

Energy Star = a government-backed program/rating system that helps consumers achieve superior energy efficiency

enthalpy = the thermodynamic property of a system resulting from the combination of observable properties (per unit mass) thereof: namely, the sum of internal energy and flow work; flow work is the product of volume and specific mass (i.e., energy transmitted into or out of a system or transmitted across a system boundary

entropy = a measure of the molecular disorder of a system, such that the more mixed a system is, the greater its entropy, and the more orderly or unmixed a system is, the lower its entropy

energy source = on-site energy in the form in which it arrives at or occurs on a site (e.g., electricty, gas, oil, or coal)

energy resource = raw energy that (1) is extracted from the earth (wellhead or mine mouth), (2) is used in the generation of the energy source delivered to a building site (e.g., coal used to generate electricty), or (3) occurs naturally and is available at a site (e.g., solar, wind, or geothermal energy)

EPA = Environmental Protection Agency

ETS = environmental tobacco smoke

F = fahrenheit (temperature scale)

f-chart = method of calculating solar fraction

fenestration = window treatment

GBC = Green Building Challenge

gpm = gallons per minute

Green = see p. 3

greenfield = real estate property that is pristine (is not contaminated, either potentially or in fact)

GreenTip = see p. xi

Guideline = an ASHRAE publication similar to a standard but less strict on consensus

HID = high intensity discharge

HVAC&R = heating, ventilating, air-conditioning and refrigerating

hybrid ventilation = combination of natural and mechanical outside air ventilation

hydronic = pertaining to liquid flow

IAQ = indoor air quality

IDP = integrated design process

IEQ = indoor environmental quality

IESNA = Illuminating Engineering Society of North America

insolation = entry into a building of solar energy

K = Kelvin or absolute (temperature scale)

kW = kilowatt

kWh = kilowatt-hour

latent load = thermal load due strictly to effects of moisture

LEED^{TM} = Leadership in Energy and Environmental Design

leeward = the downwind side—or side the wind blows away from

low-E = low emissivity

MAT = mixed air temperature

media = energy forms distributed within a building, usually air, water, or electricity

MNEBC = Model National Energy Code for Buildings

MTG = micro-turbine generator

nonrenewables = energy resources that can generally be freely used without net depletion or that have the potential to renew in a reasonable period of time

NO_x = oxides of nitrogen

NRC = Natural Resources Canada

NREL = National Renewable Energy Laboratory

OC = on centers

OPR = owner's project requirements

P.E. = professional engineer

PV = photovoltaic

parametric analysis = in situations where multiple parameters affect an outcome, an analysis that determines the magnitude of one or more parameter's impact alone on that outcome

plug loads	=	loads (electrical or thermal) from equipment plugged into electrical outlets
precooling	=	cooling done prior to the time major cooling loads are anticipated
Px	=	performance
R (as in R-100)	=	resistivity to thermal heat transfer
RAIC	=	Royal Architectural Institute of Canada
renewables	=	energy resources that have definite, although sometimes unknown, quantity limitations
RMI	=	Rocky Mountain Institute
SCL	=	solar cooling load
ft²	=	square foot or square feet
sensible load	=	thermal load due to temperature but not moisture effects
skin	=	building envelope
stack effect	=	tendency of relatively warm air in a tall column (such as a building) to rise
Standard	=	in ASHRAE, a document that defines properties, processes, dimensions, materials, relationships, concepts, nomenclature, or test methods for rating purposes
sustainability	=	providing for the needs of the present without detracting from the ability to fulfill the needs of the future
TC	=	Technical Committee (an ASHRAE group with a common interest in a particular technical subject)
TCLP	=	toxicity characteristic leaching procedure
TG	=	Technical Group (a preliminary technical committee)
Title 24	=	slang for California's Building Energy Efficiency Standards (Title 24, Part 6 of the California State Building Code)
ton	=	cooling capacity, equal to 12,000 Btu/h
TTF	=	thermal test facility
USGBC	=	United States Green Building Council
VAV	=	variable air volume
windward	=	the upwind side, or side the wind blows toward
zonation	=	how areas in a building are zoned (for A/C purposes)

Index